ALSO BY MATT LEE AND TED LEE

The Lee Bros. Charleston Kitchen

The Lee Bros. Simple Fresh Southern

The Lee Bros. Southern Cookbook

HOTBOX

Inside Catering,
the Food World's
Riskiest Business

HOTBOX

Matt Lee
and
Ted Lee

Henry Holt and Company   New York

Henry Holt and Company
Publishers since 1866
175 Fifth Avenue
New York, New York 10010
www.henryholt.com

Henry Holt® and 🄷® are registered trademarks of
Macmillan Publishing Group, LLC.

Library of Congress Cataloging-in-Publication Data

Names: Lee, Matt (Cookbook author), author. | Lee, Ted, author.
Title: Hotbox : inside catering, the food world's riskiest business /
Matt Lee and Ted Lee.
Description: First edition. | New York : Henry Holt and Company, 2019.
Identifiers: LCCN 2018035756 | ISBN 9781627792615 (hardcover)
Subjects: LCSH: Caterers and catering—Management.
Classification: LCC TX921 .L44 2019 | DDC 642/.4—dc23
LC record available at https://lccn.loc.gov/2018035756

Our books may be purchased in bulk for promotional, educational, or business
use. Please contact your local bookseller or the Macmillan Corporate and
Premium Sales Department at (800) 221-7945, extension 5442, or by e-mail at
MacmillanSpecialMarkets@macmillan.com.

First Edition 2019

Illustrations by Lauren Nassef
Designed by Meryl Sussman Levavi

Printed in the United States of America

1 3 5 7 9 10 8 6 4 2

Hotbox *is dedicated to everyone who labors*
so others might celebrate.

"You're only as good as your last soufflé."

—Sean Driscoll

Contents

Contents

HOTBOX

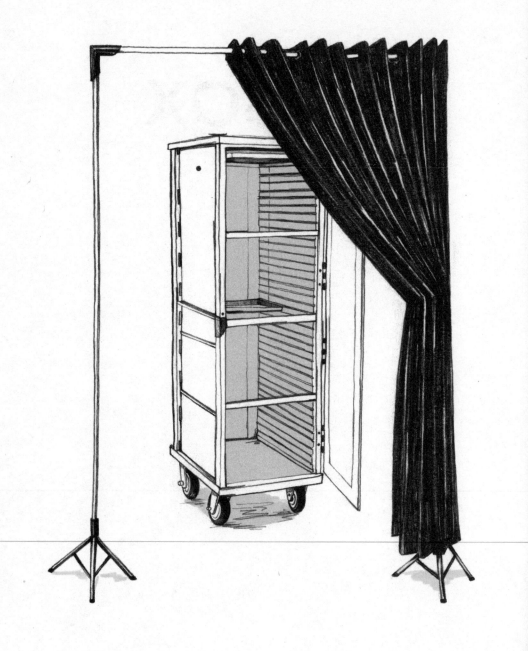

Introduction

We Know What You're Thinking . . . Catering? Like, rubber-chicken dinners?

We know you're thinking this because we were once like you. Not so long ago, we considered catering the elevator music of the culinary arts: when a chef scales up the numbers of plates into the hundreds and thousands, how could the quality of food not suffer?

So just hear us out. And come along with us, to narrow, tree-lined West Twelfth Street in Manhattan's Greenwich Village. Step inside the tall brick town house—as it happens, a landmark of American gastronomy—where a chance encounter with a trio of catering chefs lured us into their largely hidden world and utterly upended our thinking about rubber chicken and dry salmon.

We'd been invited by two friends, restaurant chefs from

Atlanta's acclaimed Miller Union, to observe a special dinner they were cooking at the James Beard House, the former residence of food journalist, cookbook author, and pope of American food, James Beard. Almost every night of the year, the James Beard House hosts guest chefs from restaurants all around the country, invited by the James Beard Foundation (the food world's Academy, whose annual awards show is the restaurant community's Oscars) to prepare their most impressive dishes for a crowd of eighty food-obsessed New Yorkers and members of the food press. Cooking at the Beard House is a great honor, but no single chef who's worked its kitchen there would say it's a pleasure: the scale of the space is residential, but with hulking commercial ovens and dishwashers the ground floor heats up rapidly. That night was a ridiculously warm one in June.

Knowing well the challenges of the house, our Atlanta friends had recruited a buddy of theirs, Patrick Phelan, executive chef for a top New York caterer, Sonnier & Castle, to help them. And Patrick brought along his coworkers Juan and Jorge Soto. When the three caterers—all in their thirties—arrived in the kitchen, they had a wholly different mien from the Atlanta guys, Steven Satterfield and Justin Burdett. You've probably seen your share of restaurant chefs in real life or on TV, and know they roll with a certain flair, with brio, tattoos and piercings, statement hair (or facial hair), rare Japanese knives, their names embroidered on their chef coats. By contrast, the caterers' affect revealed almost nothing: Patrick, Juan, and Jorge's chefs' jackets bore no names and they wore black polyester pillbox-style beanies. They pulled generic knives wrapped in dish towels from fraying, lumpy backpacks. None of the three had seen this kitchen before the evening they arrived, nor had they ever cooked the recipes they were about to produce. They blended into the wallpaper, anonymous to almost everyone dining at and even working this event, but something about the way they sized up this unfamiliar kitchen nevertheless conveyed gravitas. These were Special Ops culinary mercenaries, poised for a battle.

Since there was barely room enough for the five chefs, we spent the evening observing the plating up of dishes from the kitchen doorway and ferrying deli containers of ice water into the inferno. Things started to really accelerate when it came time to fire the third and fourth courses, eighty servings each of a sautéed quail and a braised oxtail crepinette (a crispy little puck), both of which needed to be burnished brown and cooked just right—not overdone—and in an instant. For the next half hour the three caterers were everywhere at once, slammed as any restaurant line at 8:45 p.m., but entirely in control. (Satterfield moved to the other side of the serving counter, to expedite and apply finishing touches, and to otherwise stay out of the way.) Without a wasted gesture or motion, the catering chefs worked sheet pans in ovens and sauté pans on every burner—at times sheet pans *on* raging burners, a makeshift griddle!—as gracefully and agilely as modern dancers. Their clipped dialogue was inscrutable to us, the vocabulary unfamiliar, issued at low volume amid the clatter. Hand, elbow, and head gestures were sufficient for most of what they needed to say to each other.

The dinner was a huge success, due in no small part to Patrick, Juan, and Jorge, and the food that evening was everything the restaurant chefs could have hoped for: exquisitely delicious, perfectly executed, on a par with the food Miller Union serves every day back home in Atlanta. (Satterfield has since won a James Beard Award.)

Afterward we followed the Sonnier & Castle crew to a bar nearby. When we marveled at their virtuosity with an unfamiliar menu in suboptimal circumstances, both Sotos smiled and shrugged.

"*De nada*," Juan said, laughing.

Jorge turned serious. "You gotta understand. For us . . . ? This is fun."

"We did—what?—eighty covers tonight?" Patrick added. "These guys can do lamb chops for fourteen hundred. I tell them I need three hundred well-done, three hundred rare, eight hundred medium-rare. I tell them what time to serve-out. And I can walk away."

"It's not too hard," Juan said. "You have to know the proofer."

Patrick explained: the proofer is another word for the hotbox—an upright aluminum cabinet on wheels, lifeblood for caterers—that conveys the partially cooked food from the refrigerator at the caterer's prep kitchen to the site of the party. So those lamb chops for fourteen hundred would have been seared in advance at the caterer's prep kitchen, just enough to get perfect coloring on the outside, but more or less raw inside. Then they slide on sheet pans into the proofer. The proofer rolls into a fridge to chill until it's time to move them onto the truck for the ride to the venue. Once on-site, the hotboxes are emptied and transformed into working ovens, with each sheet pan of lamb placed over other sheet pans that hold only lit cans of Sterno.

"*Sterno?*" we protested. "Isn't that for keeping chafing pans of rubber chicken warm on a hotel buffet?"

Not in catering at this level, he explained. All hot event food consumed in New York City gets heated and finished in this way. "The side dishes for that lamb, the quinoa, roasted parsnips, whatever. Even the bread and the plates. All of it comes out of a hotbox."

"You have to watch," Juan added, pointing to his eye. "Feel," he said, rubbing his thumb between his forefingers. "And listen." He tugged an earlobe. "And organize. Always organize. But if you do, you can get it right."

We were certain we could *not* get it right—neither of us has the sensory knowledge, the mettle, or the wits. But the more we listened to these catering pros, the more captivated we were by their strange world of food-crafting-in-the-field, unlike anything we'd ever seen go down in a home or restaurant.

Patrick prodded Juan to tell us a horror story, about the time a hot proofer got too close to a sprinkler head at the New York Public Library and the plating line—food, chef, kitchen assistants—got soaked in a rust-water rain and still managed to serve dinner to three hundred people oblivious to the back-of-house disaster. You had to be cool, calm, and, especially, resourceful, whatever situation you were dealt, whether it was being conscripted from the kitchen to translate Venezuelan president Hugo Chávez's Spanish into English for Oliver Stone, or discovering, only at the moment when she stepped into the yacht's kitchen afterward, that you'd cooked an intimate thirtieth birthday dinner for Kim Kardashian.

Juan and Jorge Soto gathered their bags, said they had to get back to the Bronx. They were facing a 5:00 a.m. call time the next day. Patrick signaled for the check—he was headed back to the prep kitchen to get ahead of two events the following evening.

Walking to the subway, we peppered Patrick with questions, spooling out hypothetical nightmares at a giant party.

5

"What if all the hotboxes won't fit on one truck?"

"We rent another."

"What if two—or ten—chefs don't show up the night of the party?"

"Won't happen."

"What if the truck breaks down on a hot day? Is there ice in the proofer to keep the lamb chops chilled until it's time to heat them back up?"

"Good question."

Anyone who cooks professionally knows the first principle of food safety is the danger zone, between 40 degrees and 140 degrees Fahrenheit, within which bacteria such as *Clostridium perfringens* are happiest and able to multiply exponentially. It's why you want to keep raw food below 40 degrees until the moment you cook it and cooked food above 140 degrees until it's time to serve. A common cause of food poisoning is from leftovers that lingered too long at room temperature before they went back in the fridge. This hotbox rigmarole the Sonnier crew had described seemed to add an extra cycle of heating and cooling to the lamb chops, but also another calculus of time and temperature in transporting the food to the venue.

"Look, we're monitoring our temps every step of the way," Patrick said. "But I'll be honest: if you work in catering, you're gonna spend a lot of time in the danger zone. If you can't get comfortable in the zone, you won't survive a day on the job. Next question."

We had so many more questions for Patrick, and that's how we ended up in his prep kitchen.

* * *

Even if you've never been a guest at Kim's birthday party or a charity gala for fourteen hundred New York swells, likelier than not you've attended a catered event: a wedding, a holiday party, a *quinceañera*, a reception. Maybe you wondered how it all came together: *What's happening behind that black curtain?* The thought might have been sparked by a moment as fleeting as seeing a server strain to lift a chafing dish (and may have disappeared just as quickly, your mind drifting back to your grandmother shuffling around the dance floor). You measure a party's success, ultimately, by how much it focuses attention on the enjoyment of celebrants and guests, by its apparent effortlessness. Obscuring all toil, and *especially* the stories of the people who made the occasion happen, is the caterer's ultimate goal.

But not ours.

In *Hotbox*, we're taking you with us behind the pipe and drape—trade lingo for that black curtain—into a world engineered never to be seen, populated by individuals you're never meant to hear from, performing deeds you can't help being curious about (even if you kinda don't want to know). In truth, our early analogy—the Special Ops team—was underdeveloped since that night at the James Beard House our Atlanta restaurant pals had made things easier: they brought the prepped rabbit and oxtail, and their kitchen was a fully equipped location with its own refrigerators and natural gas–powered ovens. Hot and cold running water! Event caterers aren't just chefs, they're haulers and builders, too, since they're not only transporting the food to a remote spot, but also fashioning a kitchen out of thin air (oftentimes on sites as blank as a grass field or a cement loading dock), and there's rarely ever running water. As such, they have more in common with MASH, a mobile army surgical hospital, than Special Operations—or a restaurant, for that matter. The tent campaign of loading and unloading the kitchen infrastructure and the delicate, squishy food involves so much travel, a factor that rarely disturbs the tight calculations of a restaurant chef, comfortable in her own familiar kitchen. In "off-premise" catering (as distinguished from banquet-hall catering or corporate cafeterias), there's the expanse of actual miles—over minutes—the food must traverse: packed from the prep kitchen into rolling hotboxes, coolers, milk crates, and plastic bins, and onto the box truck for the journey to the venue; then unloaded from the truck onto elevators or carried up staircases to whatever hall or back room is designated the "kitchen." Just as important, there is also the cognitive distance separating the minds of the kitchen prep crew that par-cooked and packed the food from those on the team receiving it in their makeshift party kitchen, unwrapping and setting up everything, finding every item—or not, forcing the dreaded (and inevitable) re-run.* And lastly, there are the servers, the cater waiters, those warm bodies from staffing agencies, typically freelancers who may work for a handful of competing firms from one night to the next, entrusted with moving and handling the food once it's left the kitchen, to be presented to the guest. With rare exceptions, a catering chef hands his food to a total stranger.

All this discontinuity and travel geometrically multiplies the hazards standing in the way of a catering chef aiming to

---

* Ordered by the executive chef, a return trip of the truck to the prep kitchen to pick up something that's been either left behind or hopelessly lost at the site.

serve what was originally intended, that perfect plate, whose stunning flavors and stylish presentation clinched the deal at the client tasting many months prior. And in this context, time becomes a presence as tangible, fungible, and daunting as the weather—more so when the scale of the event is factored into the equation. While an epic fail at a restaurant table might cost the house a few customers, when there are eight hundred hungry guests on the event floor waiting for dinner to be served, havoc-wreaking scenarios—an electrical brownout blows power to the fryers and the stage lights; the host's toast runs twenty minutes too long, condemning the lamb to overcooked toughness; a server faints and takes down with him a jack stand* of 120 plated desserts—may become apparent only at the moment they happen, and have greater consequences.

True, the stakes for the caterer are not nearly as high as for the army surgeon, but the vast majority of events that top New York firms cater to are pretty significant—charity galas, weddings, product launches, milestone birthdays, annual board meetings, political debuts, and movie premieres in one of the biggest, richest, most competitive cities in the world. As the minutes tick down to the serve-out of the first hors d'oeuvre, there's more at risk than just the hundreds of thousands of dollars a client may have spent on the evening's food, booze, and labor; there are the emotions of a bride and groom on their big day, the reputation of a top movie studio, or the longevity of an esteemed, hundred-year-old nonprofit. There are the memories of people celebrating some of the most momentous nights of their lives.

---

* A tall but compact four-sided metal stand on casters, for holding and moving large numbers of completed plates.

Considering all that these catering chefs are up against, and regularly conquer—their nerve-rattling tightrope sprints through A-list celebrity territory, the exquisite food torture, a season's worth of MacGyver-y kitchen rescues that throw propriety, food safety, and convention out the door because "we have to make this work *right now!*"—the fact that they don't get the attention or respect afforded restaurant chefs is astonishing. There's no James Beard Award for them, yet the food that catering chefs create is often every bit as succulent and dazzling as what's served at the gastronomic temples of the nation. And they're cooking with handicaps a restaurant chef couldn't fathom.

This book is our report from having steeped in the culture of catering and special events for four years, getting to know the business from the inside out, what makes it work, and what kinds of people choose to dwell in it. While reporting and writing this book, we worked as kitchen assistants, prep and party chefs for catering firms in New York City and in Charleston, South Carolina. We researched the business and its history extensively, and interviewed everyone we could: the denizens of catering kitchens, the chefs, and the kitchen assistants, or "K.A.s," but also workers and leaders in every corner of special events, from the founders of influential catering firms, to salespeople who sell the menus, to the supporting industries, like lighting and rentals, to the party planners and event directors for whom catering is just one of a constellation of services they're buying that adds up to a special event. It's a realm where you find remarkable, often downright eccentric characters, working in extreme conditions, under insane stress, with the highest of expectations, mostly in lamentable spaces.

Their goal is to make tonight appear special and intimate, unique and ephemeral. And then they do it again the very next day.

When we were working as catering kitchen assistants, most of our colleagues were aware we were studying the industry, taking mental notes. It didn't seem to raise suspicions or matter much to the boots on the ground—except insofar as we were slow working and green: how you perform is everything to your character in catering. As for the people in the executive suite upstairs, they were a bit more circumspect, but ultimately cool with us working there as well. The catering business depends upon eager, nimble workers, and especially embraces ones inquisitive about the best way to get the job done. And when you're comfortable employing a kitchen brimming with mercenaries, who flow almost seamlessly from firm to firm, you're necessarily less concerned with revealing institutional secrets. Our usual journalistic strategy always has the two of us collaborating and doubling up on any interview or experience, but for this project we mostly worked different days in the prep kitchen and in the evenings, as our assigning chefs dictated. Sometimes we worked the same gig on different parts of the job; other times, we were across the prep table from each other. We shared our field notes, photographs, and thoughts with each other on a daily basis and we worked so many hours on so many similar assignments, for the same firms, that our observations and discoveries overlapped and became interchangeable.

To avoid shifting points of view, we adopt a first-person singular perspective—you could call it the royal "I"— throughout the book, calling out which brother is narrating at the head of each chapter, even if the other brother's experiences may have informed it. And while that might seem odd, it's actually quite natural: most people we encountered in catering thought we were the same person due to our similar age, build, baldness, and skill level. (We're brothers, but not twins.) And in fact our kitchen nicknames, conferred by a lead chef in that absurdist way sobriquets typically are, were the same: "Virginia." (He knew we were from the South, and he'd cooked there once, at a wedding near Richmond.) When it's appropriate to do so, we snap back to the plural "we."

Regarding naming: in cases where we worked alongside people in the trenches, we will introduce a person's full name initially if we knew it in the course of the working relationship, but otherwise we use only the first name, or nickname, which in the collaborative working environment was the only moniker that mattered. For historical figures and subjects we interviewed with pad and pen or laptop, we refer to them by their surname after the first instance.

We begin by dropping you directly into hors d'oeuvres preparation at one of the largest parties on New York's fall social calendar, the Park Avenue Armory Gala, about two years into our time in catering, and about forty-five minutes before the call for first hors d'oeuvres platters. From there, we gently rewind, taking you back to our first work days, getting acclimated to the prep kitchen. You'll learn along with us the stresses and strains on body—and especially mind—as we adapt to the *cooking interruptus* of catering. We'll take excursions at two junctures in our narrative into the history of moveable feasts, witnessing the rise of the industry over three generations in the modern era. There are some brief interludes sprinkled throughout, including a catering-style recipe for pasta salad for six hundred, tables of surprising statistics, and a test-drive of a hotbox at home. And as the parties we work become more and more elaborate—the weddings!—the menus increasingly customized, as allergies begin to occupy a greater and greater presence in the culinary world overall, we'll circle back to our initial question: why is catering such a shrouded world? We'll try to answer the corollary questions: who benefits from its invisibility? And what does that say about the way we celebrate occasions today?

We've thrown out a few key terms in this introduction—"hotbox," "jack stand," "re-run." These are just the first words in a whole new lexicon we're about to introduce you to, along with a set of bizarre but effective cooking concepts, and a subculture you may have crossed paths with, that was right under your nose if you'd only known where to look. Our hope is that you'll never attend a party—or even entertain on your own—in quite the same way after reading this account.

1

Manchego Mayhem

Matt Struggles in the Trenches

I have one job—building the Pepper-Crusted Beef on Brioche with Celery Root Salad, an elegant little bite to be passed during cocktail hour at the Park Avenue Armory Gala, a black-tie dinner for 760 people. In theory, it's an easy hors d'oeuvre, a thin coin of rosy beef on bread with a tuft of salad on top. It's 4:50 now and the doors open at 6:30, so I've got some time to assemble this thing. The ingredients can be served at room temperature—*any* temperature, really—and they were prepared earlier today by a separate team of cooks at the caterer's kitchen on the far West Side of town, then packaged on sheet pans and in plastic deli containers for a truck ride to the venue. All I have to do is locate the ingredients in the boxes and coolers, find some space to work—my "station"—and begin marshaling a small army of beef-on-toasts so I've got enough of a quorum, 240 pieces or so, that when serve-out begins I'll be able to keep pace with replenishment demand through a forty-five-minute cocktail hour.

Jhovany León Salazar, the kitchen assistant leading the hors d'oeuvre ("H.D.") kitchen, shows me the photo the executive chef supplied that reveals the precise architecture of this bite: a slice of seared beef tenderloin, rare in the center and the size of a Kennedy half-dollar, resting on a slightly larger round of toasted brioche.* On top of the beef is a tangle of rich celeriac slaw—superfine threads of shredded celery root slicked with mayo, with a sprinkling of fresh chives showered over the whole. This is New York–caliber catering intelligence at work: take a throwback classic—the beef tenderloin carving station—to a higher, more knowing plane in a single bite. Here, the colors are lively, the scale is humane, the meat perfectly rosy-rare and tender, its edge seared black with ground pepper and char, the celeriac bringing novelty, though its flavor is familiar enough. It's a pro design that satisfies the meat-'n'-potatoes crowd without talking down to the epicures.

The kitchen tonight—like every night, no matter the venue—is as makeshift as a school bake sale, a series of folding tables covered with white tablecloths and fashioned into a fort-like U. Since there are two warm hors d'oeuvres on the menu, our crew has a hotbox standing by—the tall, aluminum cabinet on wheels that both serves as transport vehicle for food and, once it's on-site and loaded with a few flaming cans of jel-

---

* "Brioche" is the kindest word for this favored delivery platform—a thin toast-cracker.

lied fuel (the odor-free version of Sterno is favored), becomes the oven. Imagine the most flame-averse venues—the New York Public Library, City Hall, the Metropolitan Museum of Art—even there, the ghostly blue flames in the hotbox pass muster with the fire marshal. In fact, this one fudge, this unspoken exception to the no-open-flames rule, is the secret to restaurant-quality catering in New York City.

Our hors d'oeuvre kitchen is at the far end of a vast hall-way, partitioned into a series of open rooms stretching the crosstown length of the fifty-five-thousand-square-foot Armory, a former soldiers' drill hall, now a coveted New York venue for seated dinners where attendance runs into the high hundreds or low thousands. You could say we're in one of the *wings*, in theater parlance, and it's as dark and dank as a bomb shelter. We share this bunker with a sanitation team* (one of three scattered throughout the venue), which at this point in the evening is furiously ripping open a mountain of plastic-wrapped pink crates and unpacking, in clinks and clatters, the rented glasses, cutlery, plates, and linens and shuttling them to the waiters. The servers are directed by their captain, a flesh-ier George Clooney type in a gray suit, talking intermittently into a mic on his lapel, to ferry their matériel either to the bars (if highball glasses or flutes), to the tables in the dining room (if wineglasses, cutlery, or linens), or to the kitchens (if plates). Clad in black pants and black oxford shirts, the servers shuttle briskly back and forth, quiet, looking like well-dressed movers;

17

---

* The caterer's on-site crew in charge of miscellaneous tasks including rentals distribution at the beginning of the night, setting up the coffee percolators, and handling all refuse removal at the end of the evening.

when it's time to drop the main course on this party, they'll resemble stressed-out mimes.

I had arrived at the front entrance of the Armory for my 3:30 p.m. call time and found Bethany Morey, the executive chef's assistant, standing in a band of sunshine breaking through the chilly afternoon. She was a six-foot oracle, guarding an enormous, coffered wood door.

She tapped a pen down her clipboard, scanning the page. "You're in the H.D. kitchen, with Jhovany," and she pulled open the massive door. "Into the drill hall, then a hard right and keep going, behind the black curtain."

I was nervous, as always, and somewhat disoriented, but relieved to be assigned to the hors d'oeuvres kitchen. I'd learned over the last few years there's something comforting in the tight focus on small bites at the start of the evening, when there's freshness and motion, and noise and chaos building in the air—this thing is *on*! Make no mistake, an H.D. kitchen can go to shit readily: canapés are typically twelve pieces to a platter, and if you're behind in assembly from the start, you'll never catch up. A service captain and the head chef will berate you for the duration while you flail and sputter like Lucy and Ethel at the chocolate factory conveyor belt. But despite being much younger than I am, Jhovany is a seasoned pro—a guy who tells you exactly what he needs in very few words, and never fails to flash a smile or a thumbs-up and a *bueno!* when he sees that you've understood and can get the job done. I know enough after these two years in catering not to do the math, but I've done it since and I'll tell you now: feeding one beef-on-toast to each of the 760 mouths at this party would require sixty-three platters' worth of effort. Fortunately for me, a group that large will typically consume less than half that amount with several other hors d'oeuvres available.

When I strode into Jhovany's kitchen, everything was dialed in: white cloths on the prep tables pulled taut, dry packs and coolers laid in neat rows underneath. I was the last of his kitchen crew to arrive and all the other kitchen assistants were already on task. Wilmer ferried sheet pans of food—the brioche toasts; tiny, boat-shaped pastry shells; blistered cherry tomatoes; shrimp on skewers—from the hotbox to the open shelving unit called a "speed rack," emptying the hotbox cabinet so he could fire it up with Sternos. Roxana minced long bunches of chives. Dutch pulled half-pint containers of flaky Maldon salt and coarsely ground black pepper from a red plastic tote called a "dry pack," meaning there's nothing perishable or wet in it. Gustavo unwrapped two chef's knives from the layers of plastic they wore for safe shipping to the site—even a bundle of dish towels gets cocooned in plastic wrap in this way, to keep them together, compact and clean.* Manuel dressed each station with boxes of purple food-service gloves and rolls of paper towels. Saori unwrapped cutting boards and distributed them.

In that first hour, before Jhovany doled out the station assignments, he delegated tasks rapid fire. Soon as I'd finished one, he'd have another instantly. Heading to the venue on the subway, I'd read through the menu Bethany emailed me the day before, but with six hors d'oeuvres, each with four or five com-

---

* By the end of your first few parties, after ripping open a hundred triple-wrapped bundles, you get a precise feel for the tolerances and breaking points of industrial-strength plastic wrap.

ponents to assemble, the big picture was still a total blur. I got paired with Saori to pick the smallest, brightest-green tarragon leaves from a half-dozen gnarly bunches, maybe 20 percent good stuff. We set up next to Roxana, who was now mincing flat-leaf parsley. At another table, Manuel and Wilmer sliced asparagus into thin coins. Once we'd finished picking tarragon, Jhovany told me to locate and unwrap the pans of brioche toasts, which had been packed with small envelopes of a silica gel desiccant to keep them crisp. The air in the kitchen seemed dry enough and I was thinking serve-out would be soon enough that the brioche wouldn't go soggy, but I'd been wrong about details like this before.

"Jhovany," I said, holding up one of the tiny silica packets. "*Basura?*"*

He checked the time on his phone. "*Si, señor.*"

Jhovany assigned each kitchen assistant a station, and things began to come into focus. He posted at the entry to the floor† an 11 × 17–inch sheet of paper listing in all-caps English all six hors d'oeuvres (more for the servers' benefit than our own), but I was grateful for the executive chef's salesmanship, his bon mots adding some gloss of culinary idealism to what was beginning to feel like a kitchenful of well-manipulated slop.

So, to the left of me, Saori corrals the elements for Poached Gulf Shrimp with Chili Dust and Squid Ink Aioli. To my right, Roxana snips the tip off a ricotta-filled plastic bag and sets it tip-side down in a quart container for her Heirloom Tomato Crostini with Lemon Ricotta and Fresh Basil. Dutch is on

---

* "Trash?"

† The dining room, in cater-speak.

Tandoori Chicken Skewer with Red Curry, Orange, Achiote, and Crispy Phyllo, and Manuel lays out ranks of pastry boats on a sheet pan for his Smoked Salmon Crisp with Caviar, Lemon, and Chive. Behind me, Howard, Wilmer, and Gustavo collaborate on Sunny-side Quail Egg with Tomato and Asparagus on Brioche because it requires the most finesse, skill, and hands: Wilmer will run the hotbox, calibrating the flickering Sternos to ensure that the raw quail eggs on their sheet pan—each egg cracked into its own tiny individual foil cup sprayed with oil—bake just enough that the yolk is thickly runny and warm but not hard-cooked. Gustavo will invert each perfectly cooked egg onto the blistered cherry tomato that Howard's gently flattened on the brioche and then top it with two slivers of asparagus.

Jhovany hovers around the kitchen, watching as I assemble my station. He pulls a piece of beef from my aluminum pan, tastes it, then pulls another. *"Necesitas Maldon,"* he says. I'll need to shower the beef with flakes of crispy Maldon salt before the celery-root slaw goes down.

I pull a pan of brioche toasts out of the speed rack and line an empty sheet pan with paper towels. I take handfuls of the toasts, stack them like poker chips halfway up my left forearm, then lay them down on the pan with my right hand in neat rows—*boom, boom, boom*—reaching for more when the stack is gone. I fill the sheet pan readily (and note that the piece count is 140) before moving on to the beef layer. Each tenderloin fits perfectly in my left palm and I peel off the thin slices and lay the beef on top of the brioche, dead center. When the sheet pan's full, I remember the Maldon, sprinkle it gingerly over the top. I look to Jhovany. *"Esta bien?"*

"Poquito mas," he says, and reaches into the container for a

small handful. He showers a few more pinches, lightning quick. "Like that," he says.

I pull the top off the container of celery-root slaw—still chilly and stiff—and pick up what I think is just the right amount of slaw on the end of the spoon, guiding it onto the beef with a fingertip. But it flops over the dark edge of the beef and slumps over the side of the toast. For the next, I try pinching a smaller amount with just thumb and index finger. The slaw sticks to my rubber-gloved fingertip, and when I try to shake it off it lands entirely out of range of the target. Next attempt, instead of using the bowl of the plastic spoon, I use the tip of the spoon handle. This is more promising, but now the blob of celery is not enough. So I dip again, drop again. Now it is too much. I look at my watch and I feel my pulse quickening, my face flushing with color.

Jhovany appears. *"Mi amigo. Menos grande,"* he says, and picks up the plastic spoon to demonstrate. "Like this," he says, dipping the tip of the handle in the slaw and teasing with his index finger a fingernail-sized dollop into the center of the beef, so a ring of the beef's pink center is just visible around the edge of the slaw. It's perfect, exactly as in the photo. He picks up one of my pathetic examples and eats it, then hands the other sloppy one to me. "Flavor is good."

It *is* good. But the flavor has nothing to do with anything I did to these ingredients, and I still have yet to assemble a single Pepper-Crusted Beef on Brioche with Celery Root Salad that looks the way it should. I have Jhovany's live sample to go by, so I try again with the tip of the spoon handle, and . . . *close*! But then the next is a disaster—too much slaw again, slumping over the side of the beef. And the next one is too little, so I dip again, which means that getting one of these looking correct is taking me half a minute. At this rate, I'll be lucky if I have one hundred pieces by show time, and I need at least two hundred. I look at my watch again. My mouth is parched.

I step away for a quick second to get some water from a table near the sanitation area, where there are gallon jugs of water and plastic cups for staff. I have to pee already, but there's no time for that; the venue's so big that the restrooms in either direction are nearly a ten-minute round-trip. Through the entrance into the next bunker, I can see one of the three dinner kitchens dispersed among the wings of the Armory tonight. Each is staffed with ten kitchen assistants and a head chef, and each will serve 255 guests tonight, divide-and-conquer being the only sane strategy for serving 760 people warm and tasty food that should remind no one of the cold, overcooked, and damp meat-plates-under-domes, skins forming on the sauces, that once defined a catered event.

I see a few familiar faces in the far kitchen—Jorge Soto, Marilu, Geronimo—a hive of white coats and black beanies. I know from the menu that they're plating up the first course, a tapas assortment, a preset.* At 7:15, once cocktail hour's over, Jhovany will leave two of us behind to shut down the H.D. kitchen and distribute the rest of the team among the three dinner kitchens to help plate up the main course. But here, drinking this water in my state of stress, that moment seems impossibly far away.

Back at my station, I get to work. In ten minutes, I've got

23

---

* A plated dish that's already waiting at each guest's place when they sit down to dinner. This is a pro move, merciful to guest and staff alike, shaving at least a half hour off the event. But the food must be designed to survive an hour or more at room temperature with texture and flavor intact.

six examples of this beef—half a platter—worthy of being sent to the floor, and I'm sweating through the T-shirt under my chef's coat. Saori's experimenting with swooshes of squid-ink aioli on her plate. She sees me struggling with the spoon and offers up a fine pair of stainless culinary tongs—like an oversized set of tweezers, from the pocket of her chef's jacket. For a split second tears well in my eyes, I'm so grateful to her. The tweezers give me much more control over the amount of slaw I pick and, the more I make, I learn to fold the pinch of slaw onto itself as I drop it, to circumscribe the nest, make the threads less scattered, more mounded. I find I'm still double-dipping, but I've brought the execution time down to about twenty seconds, and I've brought down my failure rate, too, to nearly none. I've got eighteen now. Twenty-seven. I get a nod from Jhovany. Thirty-two.

I'm thinking about the miracle of repetitive gesture and cognition, the coordination of hand and eye, and how the mind remembers the weight of the pinch of slaw, the feel of the tongs' resistance, when Jhovany's voice cuts through the trance.

"*Mira!*" he says. "I need three guys on the floor, *rapido!*" He points to me, Gustavo, and Howard in turn. Something's happened. "Go find Chef. Now!"

I look at Jhovany. "*Plàstico?*" I ask, thinking I should cover my station with plastic wrap if I don't know how long I'll be gone. He shakes his head firmly. So I just lay Saori's tweezers down next to the incomplete sheet pan of peppered beef and I go.

Two years in and I know this moment well—it's the instant when whatever critical task you're performing, on deadline, is superseded by a demand for labor so much more pressing that you have to drop everything and run to where you're needed now. This culinary triage, re-prioritizing ever-escalating emergencies on the fly, is a state of being for successful caterers, for whom every night is a different venue and a custom menu tailored to a new client. And for all the attention, all the preparation brought to bear in the previous ten months on every detail of that night's party—the minute-by-minute run of show, the mapped-out site plan, and the cook time of the potato-crusted halibut—none of that envisions the crazy contingencies that arise when the resources are summoned to prepare and serve a three-course dinner simultaneously to 760 people in a space that was empty at 2:00 p.m. and must be empty again and swept clean by midnight.

Called to the unknown emergency, I leave Jhovany's kitchen and pass through a dark, curtained-off concourse of the Armory packed with enormous black crates of lighting and sound equipment, electric cables snaking along the floor. I jog under a thirty-foot-tall wooden archway and into the vaulted drill hall, washed in streams of majestic light from high above. Waiters and service captains scurry like a colony of ants between two rows of long tables—arranged parallel to each other and angled in a chevron pattern facing a stage, where a technician performs a mic check: "One TWO! One TWO! *TWO!*"

I spot Chef at the center of the commotion, standing next to a speed rack, and a dozen or so K.A.s like me streaming toward him in their white jackets and black beanies. The tables are glittering with all the cutlery and glasses, and the presets—square china plates of what look to be an assortment of small bites—are down. Fitting with the gilded theme, the curtains defining the perimeter of the room seem strafed with gold leaf. The nature of the crisis still isn't evident.

"All right, listen up!" Chef shouts, pulling one of the white

25

plates from a speed rack. "You see this beautiful tapas plate? Look carefully how it's arranged." The group closes in around him, murmuring. He talks us through the geography. The square plate is divided into three rows. Bottom row, left to right: a Smoked Whitefish Toast with Beet Relish, a Grilled Shrimp Toast with Lemon Aioli, then four bias-cut grilled crostini* in a compact pile. Second row, left to right: two thin rods of Manchego cheese, one resting on the other, forming an "X"; two pitted dates stuffed with herbed chèvre, one leaning against the other. The top row of the plate is empty, because the servers would soon be placing three shot glasses filled with more menu items across the top: Smoked Duck Rillettes with Pickled Cippolini; Black Olive Tapenade with Toasted Fennel, Chili, and Orange Oil; and Five-Spice Roasted Almonds with Cayenne and Sea Salt.

"But," Chef says, "they can't even begin setting the shot glasses down until we clean up the mess they made when they dropped these." He picks up a plate on the nearest table, which appears to have been dropped from a height of a couple of inches. Cheese and dates have toppled off each other and rolled around the plate. One of the toasts is facedown atop the other and the crostinis have skidded everywhere.

"We've got seven hundred and sixty plates to make perfect in the next ten minutes. So divide up, swarm the room. Do what you need to do. Make every plate perfect!"

I set out for the tables closest to the stage, so I can sweep in one direction. Gustavo's at the far end, closest to curtain, and I work toward him. Only about every third plate is wrecked as badly as the one Chef showed us, but every preset needs at

---

* Close cousin to "brioche toast."

least fifteen to twenty seconds of handwork. I avoid doing the multiplication or thinking too deeply about how much time and labor might've been saved with a short sermon to the service captains about the importance of a gentle drop. I try not to think about how far behind I am now on my peppered beef, how reamed I'll get during hors d'oeuvres serve-out. Instead, since the primping required so little cognition or skill, I begin to revel in the vaguely disconcerting thrill of simply being on the main floor.

Unless a K.A. or chef is working an event with an action station—omelets, say—guests will never see a chef jacket on the floor. A head chef might allow kitchen assistants to steal a peek at the dining room if it's really impressive, or if an uber-A-lister like Beyoncé or the Dalai Lama is there, but to spend a stretch of time like this out here happens only once in a blue moon—usually when someone's fucked up, like now. The longer I'm on the floor, the more I can glean what's happening beyond the kitchen. Who will be eating these serrano-wrapped logs of Manchego we're setting in beautiful crosses, just so?

On the stage, a woman rehearses the beginning of a speech, introducing the charity the event will benefit. Public funding of the arts is imperiled, and her organization raises money to educate children about the visual arts, theater, music. She introduces a film about the charity. The light in the room dims and those gold-streaked curtains turn into video screens on which a short documentary begins. Teenagers from public schools all over the New York area testify that learning about the arts from this organization has inspired them to dream big.

The film ends, then starts at the beginning again. I have one table down and have started the next when a team of servers follows in behind us, working a speed rack stacked with sheet pans of shot glasses holding the rillettes, the tapenade, and the almonds to set down on the plates. The children are inspired all over again. Two tables done. The film stops and the house lights come up. A man in a suit steps forward and introduces a performance artist, who will be honored. Tall, dressed in many black floor-length layers, the artist steps to the microphone: "My mother and father were war heroes in Yugoslavia, in World War II . . ."

We finish fixing plates and the servers have set down all their shot glasses. The floor is emptying—of the production technicians, the kitchen assistants, the servers rolling speed racks back toward the kitchens. Only a few captains remain as I sprint through the archway, down the dark back hallway, to return to the kitchen.

"It was crazy!" I tell Jhovany. "The servers mangled the preset! I had to redo hundreds of plates!" He just shakes his head slowly, shrugs. Each of his hors d'oeuvre stations now has four platters ready to go, and the servers gather around, idling, chatting with their captain. At my station somebody has set up four platters with perfect examples of the beef-on-toast, and Jhovany shows me a near full sheet pan of backup on the speed rack—not enough to cover the duration of the cocktail hour, but I'll be okay if I can keep up. A sigh of relief settles in my shoulders. The captain says, "Go!" The servers descend, and the first platters disappear, toward the early birds in their tuxedos, ambling into the hall.

I reach for a sheet pan, pick up the brioche toasts, and start laying them down. *Boom, boom, boom.* Saori sets up another platter of her shrimp. Jhovany hovers, tells her the stripe of char powder on her plate doesn't look right. The team's in crunch mode. We're not the ones saving kids with the arts, nor are we war heroes. Earlier that day, I learned there's been a flood in South Carolina, a town an hour or so from where Ted and I grew up. A childhood friend's father has lost his home, but at least the family is all safe. Others have drowned, and I hunger to connect with friends there, to find out more. But in these unraveling minutes, the size of the celery-root slaw, the direction of the crostini on the plate, and the angle of the Manchego cross are my world. Because that's why I'm here: to cater.

Pam Naraine

2

Not the Sharpest
Knife in the Drawer

Ted Works the Prep Kitchen

In the weeks after I first met Patrick Phelan, executive chef of Sonnier & Castle, at the James Beard House, I kept up with him online, "liking" his Facebook posts about obscure nineties punk bands and "hearting" the food porn he posted to Instagram—painterly, swooshing abstractions suited as much to gallery walls as dinner plates. That July, he and his wife, Megan, invited me for a simple Sunday supper at their apartment in Greenpoint. Petite and intense, Megan had been a pastry rock star for Michelin-starred restaurants and was now head baker at Sullivan Street Bakery, where she led three shifts of crews baking breads and pastries, 24–7, in two Italian ovens, each the size of a suburban garage. Patrick, it turned out, was an actual rock star—or almost one—fifteen years ago, among the first artists signed to a small indie label in

Richmond, Virginia, that now boasted Grammy winner Bon Iver. He'd recorded three albums before food took over his life.

After dinner, I asked if I could trail him in his kitchen, to find out more about catering, and he was sanguine. My brother and I had logged hundreds of hours in restaurant kitchens with a reporter's notebook in hand, interviewing chefs as they worked, but the loftiest position I'd ever held in a commercial kitchen was porter—summer 1988—bearding mussels, trimming strawberries, and scrubbing pots at my uncle's restaurant in Toronto. I'd ended up metabolizing my love of food in different ways, becoming a food writer and a cookbook author, developing and testing recipes for six or eight people—twelve at the most. All I knew is that I wanted to see firsthand what it took to scale up to hundreds and thousands.

The Monday following our supper in Greenpoint, I emailed Patrick some links to stories Matt and I had written, the kinds of pieces I thought might emerge from time spent in the trenches with him. When I heard nothing back for a month, I assumed he'd gotten spooked. But we didn't waste any time. Matt and I started networking in the catering and special-events world, reconnecting with an old college friend who'd gone to work for a top party planner in Brooklyn designing product launches for Louis Vuitton and galas for the Metropolitan Opera. I cold-called a chef named Robb Garceau, the ace hotboxer the Soto brothers had credited for teaching them the skills that set them on their path. To my astonishment, when Garceau answered my call, he said, "I know who you are." He explained: as executive chef for Union Square Events in 2008, he'd been the chef at my wedding. Our wedding food had been perfection—barbecue served family style—but from a back-of-house perspective especially memorable since a waiter had spilled a platter of chipotle-butter-basted salmon down my suit (the dry cleaner the caterer sent it to worked a miracle!). Garceau seemed intense, unflappable, and happy to talk shop. By that time, he'd held the executive chef position at four of the city's top firms, so we put a date on the calendar.

"You've seen salmon on a seersucker blazer," he said. "Remind me to tell you the story behind the sprinkler head that sits on my desk."

And, hoping to get a head start acquiring skills on the hotbox, I started hunting for one to field-test in my home. I figured I could find something dinged-up and cheap like the one in the photo the Sotos had shown me at the bar after the Beard House dinner. With two hundred dollars' cash that I hoped would cover both the unit and its delivery, Matt and I strolled the blocks of the Bowery where a smattering of restaurant-supply stores hawk their wares—some new, some well used. The nomenclature for these rolling metal boxes, it turns out, is loose. At our first stop, the proprietor spoke only halting English, and when I asked for a hotbox, he pointed to a stack of four or five nesting, heavy-duty brown plastic insulated carriers the size of beverage coolers, but with hinged doors on their sides.

"A proofer?" I asked. He led us deeper into the store to a shiny version the size and shape of the Sotos' hotbox, but with a glass door and a panel of knobs and push buttons across the bottom, like a very tall electric Crock-Pot. Not our quarry.

At the next place, we got schooled by a man in a cashmere mock turtleneck over his huge belly, sitting behind a desk. When I asked for a hotbox "on casters," he countered, "Are you baking bread? Or you want a Cres Cor?"

I described it as best I could and he said, "You need a Cres Cor. Cadillac of sheet pan cabinets." He pulled a thick catalog from a desk drawer and flipped it open to exactly what I'd seen in the Sotos' photo, the header at the top of the page revealing yet another name for these things: transport cabinets.

"This is top-of-the-line brand-new," he said. "Twelve hundred, let's do thirteen with delivery and call it a deal."

Now that we knew the lingo and steep sticker price, plan B was scouring the websites of Craigslist and Amodeo Auctions. Michael Amodeo, king of New York restaurant liquidations, is a Scorsese look-alike who sets up his auctioneer's podium, a paint-splattered ladder, in newly defunct cafés and bistros every day, selling for cents on the dollar the fixtures of chefs' dashed dreams. I'd once scored a nearly new $900 Italian commercial coffee grinder—the kind with the hopper and doser you've seen in espresso bars—from an Amodeo auction for thirty-five bucks. But after tracking online listings for a few weeks, we just couldn't find a used hotbox. Were these things like farm tractors—so durable, so valuable, they maintain their value indefinitely, rarely hitting the resale market?

Then, one Friday on the cusp of fall, I was in my apartment kitchen cleaning up from a lunch I'd cooked for visitors and nursing a midafternoon glass of rosé when the phone pinged with a text from Patrick: "Busy next week can u work prep?"

I didn't even look at my schedule, and in my wine buzz I typed, "Sure."

"K."

My phone was silent fifteen minutes. Then twenty. Twenty-five. I poured another half-glass of wine and settled at my desk.

Ping! "Need u 2 do HR forms ASAP." Then, before I could even tap into the calendar . . . *ping!* The address of Sonnier & Castle, in the West Forties. *Ping!* "3pm, k?"

HR? This was serious. I'd been thinking to trail him for a couple of days, then see how it all shook out. Now I was the one who was spooked.

It was two o'clock, and he was more than an hour away. But I dumped the remaining wine in the sink and texted back: "C u there, 3:15 more like."

This close to the Hudson River, Manhattan had a forlorn, olde New York cast, with battered taxis spilling out onto the street from low-slung garages. I hustled through the neighborhood fast as I could, past a brick barn where the Central Park tourist horses were getting their hoofs reshod. Sonnier & Castle's masonry facade was sleek and matte black, with no signage at all. The central loading bay and the entry doors flanking either side were set with milky opaque privacy glass, all shut tight. I knocked on the door discreetly marked "Deliveries," and in seconds it opened a crack, the toe of a well-worn Air Jordan wedged in at the bottom. I stepped up and found myself on the loading dock, where the shoe's owner, a lean guy in black jeans and a black Sonnier & Castle T-shirt, wrestled a few coolers the size of coffins in front of the bay door. At the far end of the room was a pair of swinging doors whose porthole windows glowed the unmistakable fluorescence of a working kitchen. Just outside the doors, in a small office to the left, was a chef in a white coat, a stocky guy with a shock of sandy hair, staring intently at a computer.

"I'm looking for Patrick Phelan," I said.

He glanced up and shouted, "Watch behind!" Just then the door of a walk-in refrigerator whacked my shoulder and a chef backed out from it carrying a sheet pan of grilled red peppers.

"Sorry," he said.

"Be more careful coming outta there, Gustavo," said the chef from his desk. Then to me: "In the kitchen, door's on the left."

I followed Gustavo into the sharp light and warm hum of a kitchen at full tilt. Nearly twenty people, in white coats and black beanies, stationed around the perimeter of two stainless islands, worked knives and peelers on their boards. Patrick was in his chef's coat, at a computer on one side of an office closet too tiny for me to step into. He introduced me to Casey Wilson, his assistant, and apologized for having gone silent the past couple of months; the company had had their best month ever in June, he said, but then July had slowed down, so there'd been no need for more hands.

He glanced at his watch. "Fifteen minutes 'til pack-out, but I can give you the two-dollar tour." To Casey, he said, "Can you print a set of new-hire forms for me?" And then he stepped out into the kitchen, which seemed spacious enough, maybe six hundred square feet—not the cramped galley I'd seen in many New York restaurants, but there still wasn't room for a fly-on-the-wall journalist in this shop; he needed me to work. Along one side was the hot line: two six-burner ranges, two double-basketed deep fryers, and a stacked double oven. At the far end of the line was a tilt skillet, a heated rectangular pan the size and depth of a baby's crib that I'd only ever seen in hotels.

Once I signed the paperwork, he said, I'd be a K.A., and

by Monday I'd have an electronic time card for the punch clock on the wall. I'd earn ten dollars an hour in the prep kitchen, twenty-five working on-site hours at parties. And I'd need a clean chef's coat. At home I had a rack full of chef's coats I'd been given at festivals and cooking schools, festooned with corporate logos and my name embroidered over the breast pocket. I didn't see anything like that in this kitchen.

"Okay if it's got my name on it?" I asked. "Or a logo?"

"No logos, no colors, no names," he said. "White coat. Black shoes. Black pants. Black beanie. Go to OK Uniform in Tribeca. They'll hook you up."

"And we'll provide aprons. And knives," he said. "You can bring your own blades if you want, but I wouldn't. They tend to disappear."

Come Monday, Patrick said, I'd be working these islands or at the prep table running the length of the wall opposite the hot line—fryers and burners were manned by his senior people. At the kitchen's far end was the dish room, where I'd find clean supplies on racks: cutting boards, pots, plastic containers. The kitchen assistants worked silently, heads down— Chef was roaming the floor. One sliced beautiful beef filets from tenderloins while another belted his rosy pucks with butcher's twine and filled a steel pan with them.

Just then, a third K.A. picked up a full pan of the filets and tipped it up until they all tumbled into the fryer, erupting in a loud white noise of crackle-burbles.

"Wait!" I said. "What was *that*?"

"That, my friend, is how you sear six hundred filets in a couple of hours. A few minutes and we'll have the color on those exactly where we want it."

This sounded like Soto-level intel so I asked, "Where are Juan and Jorge?"

"Sotos haven't worked prep in years," he said. "They've got a daytime gig downtown."

I'm not sure why I'd assumed the cooks who prepped the food were also the ones who cooked it at a party, but this was the first of many revelations about off-premise catering.

We left the kitchen and Patrick showed me the walk-in refrigerator, cool and smelling of fresh thyme and overripe lemons, where racks from floor to ceiling held raw material—bus bins and clear Cambro tubs of vegetables and herbs on the left, ranks of milk and egg cartons along the back wall, steel pans of meats and fish on the right. Past the ingredient fridge was the staging walk-in, a cold room for food already prepped to be sent to parties. Impossible as it had been for me to purchase an affordable hotbox, here were a dozen of them lining each wall, with a narrow aisle down the middle just large enough for two chefs to pass sideways. In the chilly room, Patrick unlatched the hasp of one of the doors, revealing sheet pan after sheet pan of beef filets, burnished brown, with a grayish sheen of cooled fat.

"These'll chill overnight and we'll ship 'em out tomorrow afternoon," he said.

Next, Patrick led me down to the basement and showed me the cage in the men's locker room that held clean aprons and kitchen towels and, beyond the locker rooms, the commercial ice maker, its huge plastic shovel hanging on the side. At the far end of the hallway was a pastry kitchen where two chefs dropped cookie batter onto waxed paper with ice-cream scoops.

On the way back to his office, he said, "It's a bit like *Lord of the Flies* in here—my kitchen production manager's been on vacation this week."

"What does he do?" I asked.

"*She*," he corrected. "Pam's been with Sonnier since day one. She puts the purchasing list and task list together every morning." As we crossed back into the kitchen, he said, "She moves the prep train forward all day long."

Outside his office door was a corkboard plastered with gridded sheets of paper. Each sheet was its own event, detailing in tiny type the client's name, venue address, guest count, run of show, and on every row of the grid the name of a separate menu item with a quantity down a column in front: 200 Mushroom Beggars Purse, 75 Salt-Roasted Salmon, 350 Housemade Marshmallows.

"Pam is a savant," he said. "She can scan six, eight of these grids and know we need three cases asparagus, five of baby carrots, whatever. I forget what a skill that is until she's gone, and I'm looking at all these grids going, 'What the fuck?'"

Just then, Casey proffered the forms—an IRS Form W-9 and a payment authorization acknowledging my hourly wage and one stating that I'd receive no health benefits—and I filled them out. Patrick told me he had a meeting with a party planner Monday morning, my first day, so just to get my time card then from Casey and Pam would put me to work. On my way out of the building, I noticed that the loading bay doors were now open, a box truck was backed up, and the dockhand was moving those coolers and some stacks of soda crates onto the truck.

On the street, I typed the directions for the uniform shop into my phone. Everything had happened so fast and my mind was soupy. I tried to focus on what little I knew: you made the food; you refrigerated it; it got packed onto a truck and sent to a party.

Monday morning, I skittered down the narrow stairs to the basement, shucked my backpack in the men's locker room, and retrieved an apron and clean kitchen towels. I looped the apron's yoke over my head and tied its strings around my waist, cinching the towels against my right hip. I straightened my posture in the mirror. A K.A., ready for duty.

Upstairs, the kitchen was even more crowded than it had been on Friday. I knocked on Casey's door, retrieved my time card, and introduced myself to Pam Naraine. There was no mistaking Pam. One of just two women in the kitchen, and in apparent age and affect the most senior staff member, she perched on a stool at a prep-height stainless-steel counter between the hand-washing sink and the punch clock, hunched over a clipboard.

I swiped my plastic time card through the electronic reader and I scanned the room. At the far end of the hot line, a tall guy paddled something around the tilt skillet—onions and thyme, it smelled like. In the other far corner, Gustavo Zepeda—the guy who'd knocked into me Friday afternoon—worked a meat slicer, his elbow pumping easy strokes, smooth as an oil derrick. I reached between two K.A.s to pull a pair of plastic gloves from a box in the center of the prep island.

"You know where's the walk-in?" Pam asked.

"Yes," I said.

"Find the chives, you're going to cut me three cups fine."

"Yes, Chef!" Easy. Then she showed me the knife drawer, empty except for a crappy industrial number with a white plastic handle and visible chinks in the blade. I immediately regretted not having brought my own kit. I ran my thumb along the edge and inquired if she might have a honing steel.

"It's not in the drawer?" She called out to the room: "*Hello? Who has the sharpening steel?*" All the K.A.s stopped what they were doing and looked up. "Anyone has the sharpener?" she asked. A murmured translation—*afilador?*—shuddered through the ranks.

"Do the best you can," she said, in her dulcet accent.

I found space for a station on the second island, the side farthest from Pam's desk. I retrieved a clean cutting board from the dish room and set up between a guy trimming beef tenderloins and a woman hollowing out blanched fingerling potato halves. I wished to be nearer to Pam's perch so she could monitor my progress and maybe advocate for a better knife, but from what I could tell, the more senior K.A.s worked the island adjacent to her desk, closer to Patrick's office.

I thumbed the knife, found the sharpest two inches of blade, and made sure that sweet spot struck the chives squarely on the downstroke. Still, the pressure of the knife on the gathered stems mashed them flat against the board and the onion bits detached into a dark green, matted mess. Before long, there was a voice over my shoulder.

"Hey, bro, don't crush your product." It was one of the K.A.s from the prep island near Pam. He demonstrated with his own petty knife, fast strokes of a Japanese blade that made a whispery *shin-shin-shin* as he cut, slicing microscopic hoops of chive so perfectly dry they sprang and rolled all around the board.

My neighbor at the table, the one who'd been trimming a

log pile of beef tenderloins and watching me wrestle chives, witnessed the exchange. "*Mira*," he said, and reached for a sturdy long-handled metal spoon from a neighbor across the table. He took my dodgy knife, whipped it along the edge of the spoon handle, ten strokes briskly on each side, then dragged the blade through a clean kitchen towel, and placed it on my board. "More better," he said, with a shrug and a gentle smile.

It *was* better—not by any stretch sharp, but workable—and I continued filling the quart container, little by little. It took over an hour, and when I was done I brought my container to Pam. She had me split the chives into three separate pint deli containers, then label and date them. Above her desk, suspended from a rod, were a dozen spool dispensers of different colored sticker dots. She reached for blue, orange, and red dots and stuck them in a line on the sleeve of my chef's coat. "Each of these is a different party, a different proofer," she said. "One on each cup, then find the matching proofer in the walk-in."

I found the corresponding colored dots on three proofers in the staging walk-in and placed them inside with their labels turned to the front so they'd be easily identified.

I wondered: whose hands would reach for these next? Would they get worked into a dish some other chef was cooking later that day? Or would they remain in their proofers and go to the site as is, for garnish? If so, how would they be deployed once they got there? Over a soup? The main course? On a canapé?

As soon as I walked back through the door, Pam said, "Get two cases of the tricolor carrots. You're going to wash and trim."

Back at my station, I set up my peeling operation. These carrots were slender, pretty specimens—orange, yellow, purple—hanging in small banded bunches. I trimmed the carrot greens, cut off the rubber bands, and fell into an easy peeling rhythm, carrot after carrot, reaching and peeling. Occasionally I looked up, distracted by what everyone else was doing. How did it all add up, fit together? Who makes a party out of all this?

I turned to my neighbor, the guy who'd helped me with my knife, and introduced myself. During my chive trials, I'd stolen glimpses at Wilmer Rodriguez's handiwork, the precision with which he lifted with the tip of his knife the silver-skin membrane off the raw beef in flossy threads, not a trace of red meat attached. He'd been shuttling four or five trays of these—one tray at a time—in and out of the walk-in. Now he was tying the tenderloins with butcher's twine, handling them with firm plumping motions even as he cinched his knots— each loop of twine spaced so evenly from one knot to the next that it looked as if it'd been done by machine.

"*Qué fiesta la carne?*" I asked, a clunky, off-translation of "What party's that beef for?"

"*No lo sé,*" he said, shrugging.

It dawned on me as I peeled those carrots, watching Wilmer's virtuosity with a thousand dollars' worth of beef, that I'd need to get used to the dislocation of task and result, of labor and outcome in this kitchen. It hadn't occurred to me that simply knowing the who, what, where, and why of one's handiwork—information every home and restaurant cook takes for granted—might in itself be privileged information.

Pam came around as I was nearing the end of the carrots, now piled to the rim of a huge plastic lug I'd found in the dish room. She rapped her knuckles twice on the table next to my

43

cutting board. "Now blanch them in a pot of salted boiling water and shock in an ice bath," she said.

The continuity from peeling to blanching felt like a gift. I portioned batches, dunking them with a spider skimmer into the boiling water, not too many at a time, so they turned luminous orange, yellow, purple—tender enough, but still snappy, and they glowed even brighter once they hit the ice bath. When I was done, Pam asked me to label the lug with the date and store it in a staging proofer marked "General Prep."

"What party are the carrots for?" I asked.

"Don't worry about that," she said. "Get me a case of green beans from the walk-in. Trim and blanch, just like the carrots."

"Yes, Chef," I said, but I was thinking: how long could I keep this up? With no outcome to envision, the labor felt robotic, unrelenting. My peers at the prep table seemed unbothered, chatting softly to their neighbors, mostly in Spanish. I introduced myself to Danita Holt, the woman making fingerling potato cups with a melon baller. She had her own business on the side doing wedding and birthday cakes. She'd been working prep for Sonnier & Castle for years. *Years!*

When Patrick returned later that afternoon, I asked him if there were some parties I could work that week, but he said the next few days were slow and he and Juan Soto had to give priority to their "muscle." He explained: Juan's like a one-man staffing agency, Patrick's connection to however many chefs and K.A.s he may need on a given night; on slower nights, he may give first refusal to Sonnier & Castle's top party chefs. I wondered if I'd ever get there: *muscle.* He held out hope: things were ramping up, fall was going to be busy. But during that first week, there were times I thought I'd fold and retreat back to my writing desk. I picked flat-leaf parsley and thyme until my fingers turned green. I halved eight thousand champagne grapes in an afternoon. There was a rhythm to every day: the longest stretch of work got done in the morning, 7:00 a.m. to 1:00 p.m. Then we broke for an hour-long family meal, followed by roughly two or three more hours (after the heavy lunch, these dragged on forever). And then the pack-out began: at around 3:00 or 3:30 p.m., Patrick or Tyler Johnson, his sous-chef, would migrate to the loading dock, often with another recruit in tow, and begin checking, item by item, ingredient by ingredient, that the hotboxes and coolers headed to the parties held every element for every item on the menu. The loading bay doors opened; the box truck backed up. There was some comfort in this flow, and in the serial geography of the space: you made the food in the back; you chilled it in the middle; you packed it out at the front.

Just the moment I thought I'd crack, Pam did something especially kind, or gave me a more challenging assignment, showing she was beginning to have some faith in my work. Her cheeks were high, smooth orbs under her eyes, and with a prominent chin her look at rest was a half-smile. She was a woman of few words and clear boundaries. I'd asked how her vacation was and was met with a wordless, contorted expression: do I *know* you? Still, her eyes sparkled through these corrections. My fourth day on the job, Pam asked me to reduce some prunes in sherry while I was slicing a haunch of prosciutto on the meat slicer. I forgot the pot on the stove until I caught a whiff of burnt sugar in the air. "*Shit!*" I said, a little too loudly. The prunes were ruined. I looked to Pam, panicked that I was going to get reamed, or at the very least a dreaded "Coaching and Counseling" form (for lateness or poor performance). Pam only giggled a little and reached for the pot handle.

"I'll take care of that," she said. "Finish slicing the ham and Wilmer's going to teach you to french lamb chops."

So I learned new techniques, typically overseen by Wilmer. Wilmer, a Mexican American man in his late twenties with a Don Corleone mustache, showed me how to trim fat and fleshy matter from each lamb chop's gently arcing bone so it ends up a lollipop-like bulb of clean red meat. It's a task with its own frustrations, to be sure: sometimes—who knows why—the micron-thin layer of sinew that covers the bone doesn't peel away cleanly and I'm left to whittle the bone bare with the back of my knife. And as much as I try to leave the gummy lamb blood in its package before discarding the plastic, during the time I'm working with the rack it leaches red goo all over my cutting board. Rationed hand towels are the only way to keep my board clean and dry, soaking up the liquid and knots of silver skin, but after about five racks, my first towel is so thoroughly soaked through with blood that it can't absorb any more, and I realize there are twenty-eight more racks to execute. I've completed only four in thirty-five minutes. As for Wilmer, he's done with his and has started in on mine.

The more time I spent working prep, the more I was intrigued by Pam. Her title—kitchen production manager—didn't even begin to articulate the role she played, sitting at the intersection of so much knowledge, materials, timing, and labor. Patrick was in awe of her talent divining yields of multiple ingredients across multiple party menus, but I was equally impressed by her role as living cookbook for Sonnier. There were no master recipes, nothing written down, so from memory she deputized the thousands upon thousands of recipe instructions to her charges efficiently, firmly—*Get me the lamb shanks from the walk-in. You're going to pull the meat and portion it out*—and always with a disarming smile. I never once saw her lose her cool. She was essential to the operation of this kitchen—full stop. How did Patrick manage even a minute without her? I'd later learn the owners could scarcely recall a time when she wasn't in charge: over twenty years ago she'd been operating a Guyanese food kiosk across the street from the warehouse Russ Sonnier and David Castle began renting to create their first catering kitchen, in a former auto repair shop on Forty-Sixth Street. They were customers of her cart, and they saw she cooked with a refined palate and a solid work ethic. So they hired her—this was in the earliest days, before the gas line to the kitchen had been installed—and in a very short time, with just a couple of parties under their belt (a small buffet for an American Movie Classics screening, *The Last of Sheila*, and a cocktail party for two thousand at Saks Fifth Avenue), they found she was a fast prep chef and also a quick study: she needed to be told only once how they wanted something prepared. Moreover, she could delegate and communicate that knowledge accurately and efficiently to teams of young K.A.s. Ever since, she's been at the center of Sonnier & Castle's kitchen, its institutional memory as the executive chefs she works under come and go.

Those first weeks in the prep kitchen I peeled dozens of cases of carrots, chopped quart upon quart of chives, and I came eventually to appreciate something in the rhythm of an endless, repetitive task, one that turns you so inward you forget anyone's there, and snap back to reality only when the timer on the oven buzzes—so loud the sound seems to lodge itself between the back of your neck and your throat. The only silver lining to that panic-inducing reveille was the clock hanging over the door to the dish room, showing three and a half hours had passed in an instant.

At Sonnier, as in many catering shops, the day is divided into a prep shift and an event shift. It's rare that any kitchen worker—the prep K.A.s—would cover a party shift the same day, simply because it's not physically realistic to expect someone who woke up at 5:00 a.m. for a 7:00 a.m. kitchen call to be on his feet all day, slicing and dicing until 4:00 p.m., then roll into an event shift from 5:00 p.m. until 10:30 or midnight.* But I learned those first couple of weeks that the prep/event split went beyond simple logistics and the limits of human endurance. Whether you work prep or event is character defining, it's part of who you are, and you rarely cross over. Working events pays better, but the accordion effect of the party business means you might not work a single event Sunday through Wednesday, but you're booked Thursday, Friday, and Saturday. By contrast, prep K.A.s are virtually guaranteed (except in the barren, wedding-less days of January and February) an eight-hour workday every day, even if all the fiesta action that week falls on Thursday, Friday, and Saturday; with twelve parties crammed in prime time, there will always be something to prepare on a Monday. So prep K.A.s tend to be men and women with children to come home to, or people with longer commutes, or just younger kids in their twenties, who prefer to spend their weekend nights at bars rather than on the job. Event K.A.s are typically more independent, more

---

* And yet some exceptional beings, like Juan and Jorge Soto, are able to perform well under these circumstances. If possible, they catch a 3:30 p.m. catnap in their car if they reach the fiesta site early.

mercenary, and have that improvisational skill set suited to making food happen in makeshift kitchens with rudimentary tools. They typically cover for their fluctuating hours by freelancing for a number of different caterers, or by having a steady daytime gig—assisting a private chef, working a breakfast or lunch shift at a corporate cafeteria, or, like the Sotos, at a so-called drop-off caterer.

During rare moments of downtime during my weeks in the prep kitchen, such as at the lunchtime "family meal"—when the most junior K.A.s sat on upended plastic crates and coolers on the loading dock—they'd say: "Never seen you before, bro. Are you Prep? Or Fiesta?" And even though I was "Prep" in fact and in pay grade, I desperately wanted to be Fiesta.

A couple of weeks into working prep, I turned a corner. I now knew where the parchment, the slotted-spoon drawer, the shelf of red-wine vinegar were, and better knowledge of the kitchen made movement around the floor smooth and intuitive. The names and faces of my prep mates were familiar, and those early days when it seemed to be a roomful of individuals doing isolated tasks for Pam seemed like eons ago. I noticed that K.A.s relied on each other in small, almost indiscernible ways. If you went to the recycling closet with an empty cardboard box, you grabbed your tablemate's cardboard, too. If you were closest to the oven when that deafening alarm went off, you silenced it, yelling, "Ti-*MER*!" at top volume to signal whoever's pan of lasagna or tray of crostini was in there. You saw the communal lug of ice almost empty and took the initiative, hustling down to the basement ice machine to replenish it, because you knew the other K.A.s and Pam were watching and would have your back next time you were in a bind.

One Friday Pam's realm morphed into a test kitchen, and became almost silly with happiness. A meatball party had been booked for the following Monday; we needed to R&D eight different meatballs, including a lobster meatball, a chicken cordon bleu meatball, a lamb gyro meatball. Pam spent the morning sketching out each recipe, and then after family meal she assigned each K.A. a meatball to test. I got the chicken cordon bleu and I experimented with ratios of ground chicken, egg, panko bread crumbs, salt, black pepper, and poultry seasoning, bundling the mixture around cubes of prosciutto-wrapped Gruyère. I fried them in batches of a dozen or so, then distributed each iteration to Pam and my prep mates. We all tasted each other's handiwork. Miguel's first try on the lobster meatball was decent, until he toned down the lemon zest a bit. Then it was superb. Danita hit the lamb gyro meatball on the nose her first try. Pam high-fived everyone as they turned in their recipes—they wouldn't get produced 'til later—and then asked if I'd prewrap the prosciutto-cheese cubes so they'd be ready to go Monday morning. It was a fingertip-minuscule, sticky-dreadful task, cutting the prosciutto and wrapping it, and by four o'clock I was only 100 cubes in. I needed 350. Michael and Adolfo were about to punch out, but they both stepped up.

"Stay on the ham," Adolfo said. "We'll wrap." We spent the next hour wrapping and chatting. His parents worked the kitchen in a restaurant near where I lived; he'd been their delivery guy for years, knew every building in the neighborhood. When we were done, I started to thank them, but Adolfo cut me off.

"Naw, man," he said, untying his apron, reaching his fist out for a bump. "In here? We work as a team."

Still, the disconnect between prep and party wore me down. The following Monday, those sheet pans of prosciutto-wrapped Gruyère had disappeared and Pam proffered two bunches of rosemary for me to strip and mince. Over the weekend, another K.A. had pattied up the cordon bleu meatballs, par-fried them, and by the time I'd caught up with them they were already being packed out. Where every challenge and triumph at the cutting board at home yielded a sensual or social gratification, fulfilled within a few hours, here every sheet pan and quart container vanished into a box truck, driven to some ballroom or library or museum. Yes, it ended up on somebody's plate—I knew the work we were doing here was the engine of the operation—but the lack of closure, not knowing the who-what-when-where-why, was like flipping a novel open, reading halfway through, then throwing it away. And repeating the exercise, ad infinitum. Could I possibly last another week at this? *Two?*

For vegetable crudité for 1,000 guests at a Sonnier & Castle event, number of pounds each of carrots, celery, haricots verts (green beans), and fennel required: 50. Number of pounds of red peppers: 60.

Pounds of lamb shanks needed to yield 400 five-ounce portions after trimming and cooking: 250.
Pounds of short ribs required to yield the same number of portions: 400.
Pounds of beef filet to yield that number: 200.

Pounds of veal bones needed to make a 12-gallon batch of red wine sauce: 150.
Number of 750 ml bottles of red wine: 24.
Ounces of red wine sauce yielded per batch: 1,536. Ounces, per portion, sent to parties with main courses requiring it: 1.

Pounds of white onions Pam orders to yield 1 gallon caramelized onions: 20.
Pounds of white onions Neuman's Kitchen chef Robb Garceau orders to yield the same quantity: 22 pounds.

Number of 2.5 ounce balls of burrata, an Italian cheese made of mozzarella and cream, sold to Neuman's Kitchen clients in 2016: 325.
Number sold in 2018: 12,388.

Piece count of baby lamb chop hors d'oeuvres sold during the 2017–18 holiday season: 7,832.
Number of lamb entrées sold during the same period: 0.

Number of homemade pig-in-blanket hors d'oeuvres sold in the first seven months of 2018: 24,991.

Number of lobsters cooked in a calendar year for Neuman's Kitchen mini lobster-roll hors d'oeuvres: 3,500.
Yield in lobster meat of those lobsters, in gallons: 89.
Yield in mini lobster rolls served: 28,493.

Percentage yield of a trimmed and cooked boneless pork butt for pulled-pork barbecue: 50

Percentage yield of a trimmed and cooked bone-in pork butt: 65*

Yield, in portions, of a 2.5 lb Florida Red Snapper: 2.

Yield, in portions, of a 5 lb one: 3.

Sources: Pamela Naraine, Sonnier & Castle; Robb Garceau, Neuman's Kitchen

---

* Moisture retention is better with bone-in meat, resulting in a higher yield despite the bone waste!

3

The Client Is (Almost) Always Right

Ted Investigates the Sales Function

Late into my fourth week working prep, I was in a post-lunch daze slicing Yukon Gold potatoes on a mandoline when Patrick burst into the kitchen. He carried a hotel pan* of pearly white, raw fish fillets. Sous-Chef Tyler Johnson and a senior K.A. followed close behind, bearing their own Cambro buckets and sheet pans. They dropped everything on the stainless prep island opposite the grill and, as if on cue, the K.A.s stationed around that island began silently packing up their boards and knives, Pam lending a hand as she ushered them toward the far end where I was, closest to the dish room.

Patrick pulled down a printed grid from the corkboard outside his office and caught my eye. "Off-load those potatoes,"

* A stainless-steel pan about four inches deep, for storage, transport, and serving from at a buffet.

he said. "I need you on this tasting. You're on garnishes and plate wipes."

A tasting! A few weeks back, he'd told me he'd been "killing it in the client tastings," a forecast of how busy fall would be. "The tasting" was where a party was sold—or wasn't—and the more he spoke of it, the more I imagined a tasting to be as potentially humiliating as a casting call. You cooked for a bride and groom, or a hostess with her event planner in tow, or a half-dozen members of a nonprofit board—and after some ruminations on the savor and texture of the fish, you immediately were gonged or you won the job. Patrick loved them, since a tasting was catering at its most controlled, most restaurant-like level: one end of the prep kitchen was transformed into a hot line; proteins were cooked to order; a garde-manger station was set up—where the plating of cold dishes like hors d'oeuvres and salads happened. And there were none of the wild cards of being off-site, no thunderstorms, tents, dodgy generators, or Sterno—he was cooking with natural gas, the stove bolted to the floor. The food porn he shared on social media mostly emerged from these tastings, since the comparatively small number of guests served meant he could nurse every plate until it was a photograph. The challenge was typically in the number of different dishes you had to present, an array of options showing off the range of the kitchen's talent—more hors d'oeuvres, first courses, entrées, desserts than anyone would ever serve at an event, much less eat; the point was to push the tasters to say yes, and to zero in on whether they'd prefer the branzino or the short rib.

Here also was Sonnier & Castle's best opportunity to express its personality, its brand. Of course Patrick would want to dazzle the judges in an audition like this, but it's also, just as crucially, the optimal moment for the chef to plant ideas and set expectations. It's the first skirmish in catering's ongoing negotiation between what the client wants the food to say about her and what the caterer wants the food to say about the firm. Patrick's confidence, charm, and gifts with the English language, I suspected, would put him at an advantage in this early stage.

"Make me a pint of plate wipes for serve-out, and get these spotless," Patrick commanded, pointing to stacks of white platters and round salad and dinner plates on the prep table. Pam, assuming correctly that I didn't know what a plate wipe was, pulled a basic white paper towel from the dispenser above the hand-washing sink and showed me how to fold it into sixteenths, the size of a matchbook, and to wet it with tap water but then wring it as dry as possible by squeezing it like a vise between two palms.

By the time I'd made the plates sparkle, Pam's end of the prep island had been organized into a pickup line. The client was a theatrical-marketing company who'd never heard of Sonnier before it booked this tasting. It was a long shot, Patrick surmised, but if he won the job the fiesta would be a dinner for nine hundred in the Temple of Dendur* at the Metropolitan Museum of Art. The menu seemed straightforward: two different buffet sets, each in a theme the client had chosen: "Little Italy," in Patrick's interpretation, featured a salad of favas, pecorino, and mint and branzino with fennel. "Uptown," which included beef short rib with black truffle

---

* Among the first nontraditional event venues in New York City, opened in 1978, it became synonymous with conspicuous-consumption parties of the eighties after the 1987 Tisch-Steinberg wedding, a $3 million affair (roughly $7 million today, adjusted for inflation).

bordelaise, Patrick apparently had read as defining the luxurious zip codes surrounding the Metropolitan Museum. Each buffet had two plated salad options, a fish, a meat, and two side dishes, all to be served family style. Twelve items in all, not including the three desserts.

"Pull me some mint, oregano, and marjoram," Patrick ordered. By the time I got back from the walk-in, some prep angel had placed a pair of small, sharp scissors on the island, and I set to work cutting the innermost, brilliantly green upper leaves of each frond of mint. After the previous weeks in the prep kitchen wondering where in the cosmos my labor was headed, these clear parameters were a relief. I was in a story with a beginning, a middle, and an end—and it was in development at that very moment! There were deliverables, and an audience arriving imminently to consume our food and render judgment. I understood my role in the operation—small as it was—and my scissors quivered with the anxiety of the curtain raiser.

A service captain in suit and tie rolled a half-proofer into the kitchen and parked it at the end of the table. "I've got some news: they're early," he said. "They're only three, not four. And they only have an hour for us."

"Grid says two," Patrick said.

"I'm telling you what Sales just told me. They have to leave at three."

"Tyler? Ted?" Patrick called out. "We're on."

And then everyone was in motion. In ten minutes, Tyler had all four salads plated and on sheet pans and the first two options—a beet salad with shaved sheep cheese and an asparagus/smoked salmon combination—in the proofer and headed up in the elevator. I'd never been to the floor above, where the tasting room and the Sales Department were—a kitchen assistant had no reason to go. I'd seen men and women who worked upstairs because they came down for lunch each day, chatting mostly among themselves (much louder than the K.A.s). It had been a warm fall, and they talked a lot about the weather—rain plans were enacted or not based on the forecasts of a party-rentals guru they knew, a sailor who lived on the East End of Long Island who had the latest information from maritime sources.

Patrick and Tyler were side by side at the stove now, each wielding four pans, a hot blur. Patrick crisped skin on the branzino in butter, Tyler glazed short rib in a glossy brown goo. The platters filled, then I scattered my pretty herbs. After the first buffet dishes went upstairs, there was a pause in the action. In Patrick's office, an ancient monitor the size of a loaf of bread broadcast a fuzzy black-and-white overhead shot of the tasting room. I recognized a man on the Sales team from family meals downstairs, but no expressions were discernible—just amounts left on plates and platters that, in concert with strategic calls on the phone above Pam's desk, determined the timing of the next dishes. Deliberations over the first buffet items took longer than anticipated, well beyond the half hour they'd claimed as their limit. They had yet to taste "Uptown" or the desserts.

On the monitor, the waiter and captain began to clear plates and platters, and we sprang into action. The half-proofer came off the elevator and I ferried the dirty china and cutlery into the dish room to make way for platters of the new buffet dishes. By then Lucy Astudillo, the pastry chef, had come upstairs and was tending to desserts. Once those had gone out, Patrick asked Tyler, "Landmark Tavern when this is over? I'm ravenous."

"Sure," Tyler said. "I missed family meal, too."

Just then the phone above Pam's desk rang and Patrick picked up. "Be right back," he said, and he flew out of the kitchen and up the stairs.

I wasn't hungry since I'd eaten some rice and beans and leftover chicken wings at the family meal, but I wanted to be present for their postmortem. It was nearly 3:30 p.m. K.A.s were wiping down their stations with sanitizer, streaming out of the kitchen to the locker room, heading home. A cocktail reception later that night had already been packed-out, and there were no other fiestas on the calendar for the evening.

While I waited for Patrick to finish, Pam and I butchered a few pineapples and skewered them into kabobs for a luncheon the following day. Twenty minutes later, Patrick had yet to come downstairs, when Tyler emerged from his office.

"Check this out," he said. He was watching the tasting room on the monitor. On the screen, Patrick was gesticulating animatedly, in an intense conversation with the clients, whose body language did not read favorably to us. Tyler smiled wincingly, shaking his head. "I'm starving. Let's go," he said.

We headed south a few blocks to an Irish pub on Eleventh Avenue, a last vestige of the old neighborhood. Tyler ordered a burger and a beer. I ordered a beer.

He'd grown up in Seattle, majored in biochemistry at Evergreen State College, and worked at a pharmaceutical company for a few years. But his creative spirit rebelled against corporate life, so he'd checked out, enrolling in cooking school in New York and finding work in the kitchens of Gotham Bar and Grill and Momofuku. Sonnier & Castle was his first stint in catering; he'd been there almost six months. What he missed most about working in restaurants was "owning" your mise en place, he said; in catering, someone else always performed the basic prep tasks for you, and you didn't necessarily know who'd done it, or even when. You'd reach for a container of washed, picked mint from the walk-in and there was a decent chance it might be dried out or slimy. In my brief prep experience, the greatest hazard of communal ingredient ownership seemed to be more quantitative than qualitative.

Then Patrick walked into the dim bar, still wearing his chef's coat. "Done deal, guys," he said.

"What?" Tyler asked, incredulous.

"They asked a shit-ton of questions. It was brutal," he said. "But we got the job." Then he waved the bartender over and ordered a basket of fries and a Stella Artois. When his beer arrived, he hoisted it and said, "Here's to making the sale."

61

That first tasting, at least from the prep kitchen perspective, made the genesis of a party seem so simple, so routine: Chef conceived the food and cooked it, and the clients tasted it, approved, and signed the contract. But Sales, I'd soon learn, was a more layered enterprise, with salespeople typically playing educator, nanny, shepherd, and diplomat, too, in a perpetual struggle to keep the stakeholders in alignment and the party on track from birth until the final guest departs. Just as the menu for a sales tasting may evolve in the run-up to the audition, the menu for the event itself is an ever-evolving document. Revisions are inevitable, typically coming down fast and furious in the last months, days, even hours, before a party. They can be as random as a host deciding he wants to add a crudo (raw fish) course; or that he'd prefer key lime pie rather than strawberry rhubarb. Changes related to vegetarianism and allergies are common, as guests in recent years have become increasingly expressive of preferences and intolerances in their RSVPs. And the purchasing landscape may change in an instant if, say, a hurricane takes down the Florida stone crab crop for a week or two. The local strawberry season may peak two weeks early. Apropos of nothing, the party planner could add a bright new idea—s'mores station, anyone?—at the last minute.

But the first principle I learned about sales is that repeat business prevails and sustains the industry. The cold-call tasting for which I'd been herb wrangler is relatively rare, except in catering shops that specialize in weddings. It's the reason that the business of corporate and nonprofit event sales is especially insular, almost like a guild, with client relationships that span decades. These relationships take finesse to maintain but, once secured, some sales experts are able to carry those connections wherever they go, to different catering firms. Patrick knew one salesman who'd closed a deal by finding out the prospect's shoe size and delivering to her office a $900 pair of Manolo Blahniks.

"In the context of a hundred-thousand-dollar booking, that nine hundred dollars means nothing," Patrick said. "It's good business. And it would be penny-wise, dollar-dumb for the CEO to take issue with that on his expense report." Especially if that one booking leads to the event taking place every year for a decade.

For most of the salespeople and chefs we polled, 80 to 85 percent of catering clients are repeat customers; 10 to 15 percent more are referred from that original clientele. In twenty tastings, they might have one or two clients who simply stumbled upon the company's website and got inspired to call.

You'd never guess those odds by browsing caterers' websites, which tend to be lavish productions with alluring slide shows designed to reel in that rare fish, the new-new customer. There's a striking similarity to all of these sites. You'll see the close-up of a sexily perspiring cocktail rimmed with a colorful garnish, party guests laughing across a tablescape dappled by incandescence, a dessert that's a miniature marvel of modern architecture, the uniformed server proffering a platter of something with a winsome smile. There might be a slogan: "Life Happens around Food." "Food. Service. Style." You may detect subtle differences—some offer menu items in descriptive terms; others are more coy, leaving the images to stand alone. Prices will never be quoted.

The sameness of tone and content in the advertising materials obscures the grievous stresses at the heart of fashioning menus for special events and seeing them through to showtime. The primary tension is between what the client desires, your culinary dreams brought to life!, and the food-technical limitations of site, season, and available equipment—the dishes the firm knows it can execute best, most profitably, in a given situation. Another tension exists in sustaining the fiction that your party is the most uniquely important event on Earth when it's likely one of two or three the firm is producing that very same night—fifty that month. The salesperson (in fact, "event producer" and "event director" have become more common on business cards) manages these tension lines. But the term "sales" doesn't begin to describe the nature of the relationship that develops with the client. Should you decide to call a caterer, don't be surprised if the sales agent who answers wants to spend hours talking about *you*—your journey and story are precisely what make your party different from every other one on their calendar.

"The product is the same thing night after night—a meal of some sort," says Collin Barnard, an independent event director who worked for Sonnier & Castle for ten years. "But it's not just a meal, it's: 'Why is this meal important to you?' We need to make sure we are catering to you, specifically. Everything has to be personalized."

How personal?

A bride and groom recently tasked Barnard, now freelancing, with creating a dessert tribute to the meet-cute moment of their first date, years ago, in Rome. The groom had ordered an *affogato*—an Italian dessert consisting of a scoop of vanilla ice cream with a shot of espresso poured over it. The waiter, not quite understanding the groom's accent, and seeing plainly that he was American, brought over an avocado!

Ergo, their idea to serve an *avocado ice cream affogato*. The executive chef would need to devote talent and labor to researching and developing this mutant dessert. The avocado ice cream had to be scaled, cost-effectively, for eight hundred servings and—most important—it had to taste delicious with the shot of coffee.

And if the avocado ice cream *didn't* taste delicious in the R&D phase?

"You have to be brave and tell your client, 'We tried it, it didn't work,'" he said. "The worst thing in the world would be to say to the client, 'This is what you wanted. Taste our failure.'"

Fortunately for Barnard, his chef loved this sort of challenge. But I was aware that not all chefs do. By the time I'd met up with Robb Garceau, the Soto brothers' mentor, he'd just jumped firms, to his fifth executive-chef position. And one of the reasons he'd left his prior position was because Sales at the previous shop kept saying yes to customized items requiring research and development, or prodding him to come up with novelty food. Garceau was at a stage in his career when he wanted to make simple, beautiful food that told the story of its origin; he was fine meeting a client halfway, but he felt gimmicks diluted his employers'—and his own—brand.

"Most salespeople won't say no to a client," he said. "And that's where a lot of integrity gets lost in catering."

But not all of Barnard's clients are looking for menus composed of tributes to moments in their lives. Some are more reasonable, willing to choose seasonally appropriate ingredients, and who understand, for example, that if there's a loose run of show at their party, with plenty of speeches and toasts, they'll need to choose food that can idle without degrading. A fifteen-minute delay in serving fish is the difference between fantastic and lackluster. By the same token, ice cream has exactly ten minutes to temper to perfection; any more, and you're looking at four hundred bowls of ice-cream soup.

As conduit between kitchen and clients, a salesperson is uniquely positioned to observe and respond to changes in the food culture, staying on top of what's trending, gauging which ideas might be fads and what's everlasting. "I've sold more pigs in a blanket than anything," Barnard told us. "Every wedding has them—doesn't matter if it's a million-dollar wedding or not. Gluten-free and seasonality are here to stay. Molecular gastronomy was hot for a second but that's over. We tried matcha—didn't work!—but comfort food is perennial. People want their mac-and-cheese cups. Beef filet is still king."

He prods his chefs constantly: what's the next beef filet? The next salmon? The next duck? In the past decade, short rib became a new beef filet alternative. And to date, he has never sold a single pork entrée. He's tried to encourage vegetarian brides to embrace a vegetarian dinner menu but never had any take his counsel, though they do tend to demand more substance and complexity in their vegetarian options. "It's no longer okay to just have a salad, or a portobello mushroom thing," he said. "The veggie option has to be equally as thought out and as excellent as the meat option, even though we may only serve 10 or 15 percent of them."

Understanding that percentage of *options* the kitchen needs to prepare is also within the salesperson's purview. Having just enough of each on hand keeps costs in line and waste to a minimum, at the same time ensuring guests receive the entrée they want—without an embarrassing shortfall. The art involved in these calculations favors an experienced salesperson with sociological savvy bordering on clairvoyance. For example, if it's dinner for five hundred on Wall Street with beef filet as the main course, he may specify that the kitchen prepare just 10 percent of total attendance for the vegetarian option—even a bit less if spouses aren't expected, vegetable love was ebbing editorially in the previous quarter, and it's an R month (which favors meatier choices); if it's a luncheon for Planned Parenthood with a thousand attendees, he may feel confident requesting 25 percent as the vegetarian option, year-round.

Barnard aims to maintain a mix of different types of clients—corporate (product launches, movie premieres, awards shows), nonprofit (fund-raising and charity galas), and social (weddings, bar/bat mitzvahs, birthdays, and anniversaries)—to insulate himself and his firm in economic downturns, when corporate money becomes scarce. Although the portfolio of clients may be diversified, he concurred with Patrick that the clientele, by and large, is women. "Whether she's the hostess of the event or the director of events at MOMA, we're always asking: how do we cater to *her*?"

Through a friend, I reached out to one of those women soon after meeting with Barnard. Gina Rogak has spent twenty years directing events for museums—the first ten at the Guggenheim, the last ten at the Whitney Museum of American Art, and we met in her light-filled office in the Whitney's massive, Renzo Piano–designed building overlooking the Hudson River. Rogak resists calling herself the caterer's client—that would be her board of trustees, the event chairs, and guests. But to the catering firm, someone in Rogak's position is Client One, and caterers will do virtually anything to charm her. While Whitney gala committee members are invited to tastings, they rarely show: it's typically just Rogak and a few interested curators. A straight-talking native New Yorker, she never skimps on criticism. A recent tasting she found "so unimaginative it was painful. It looked beautiful, but I told them, 'You're selling that fresh-local-aw-shucks experience; we're selling *glamour*!'" She insisted the caterer change the entrée from beef filet to one from the caterer's repertoire she found far more appealing, a slab of halibut draped with an electric-yellow zucchini flower.

For dinners celebrating exhibition openings, Rogak wants the menu to be inspired by the art on display, and she often requests themed menus—but nothing too ham-handed or literal, lest the food trivialize the art and, by proxy, the institution. Rogak nixed the corn bread for an opening of a show of Grant Wood paintings (too corny), but approved it for an

Edward Hopper exhibition, since it seemed to her like classic diner fare. She's put on countless Pop Art parties, including a Warhol show where a soup bowl was preset and waiters circulated, pouring the vichyssoise out of Campbell's soup cans. For a surrealism exhibition at the Guggenheim, the appetizer appeared to be a dessert, and the dessert an appetizer.

One item Rogak will never serve: chicken. "It's the old 'rubber chicken' joke," she said. "I just can't."

I also reached out to Susan Holland, whom I'd seen profiled in the *New York Times* as the go-to planner for gay weddings with budgets starting at $1,000 per guest (and rising to sometimes three times that). Holland abandoned a painting career in the late seventies to become a caterer, added florals to her repertoire, but then dropped both those pieces when she realized she didn't need to be creating the food and flowers to practice her craft. In her own broad terminology, she's a producer, working with teams of "artists" (including caterers) to stage extravagant and ephemeral "art installations" (events) designed to be experienced in a single night. She designed several state dinners during the Obama administration.

Holland's fairly unique in the event world for having been on both sides of the tasting audition. For years, she cooked the tastings for her catering firm herself; now she's accompanying her clients as they make the rounds of caterers. Every customer is different, she says, and caterers need to adapt their sales pitches accordingly.

"Some clients want a laundry list presented to them," she said. "Forty-five thousand different items from four traditional caterers, with their prices." She prefers to work with those who view a party more holistically, as a collaboration with the chef: "Who's being celebrated? Where's it happening? What do they like to eat?" For those who are less rigid, she'll try to steer them to the young, independent caterer Yann Nury, a French chef who worked for five years for Feast and Fêtes, the catering arm of the French restaurant Daniel. Nury insists on an initial consultation with prospective clients, to divine their preferences and parameters, and he won't take the job unless he senses they're giving him the freedom to bring his talents and creativity to the table.

"The interaction doesn't always work," Nury told me. He was conducting a tasting of his latest creations for Holland and me at her apartment, an open-plan glass box at the top of a skyscraper in downtown Brooklyn, with a view west, toward Manhattan. Nury's been successful enough that he has the luxury to pick and choose. He'll only work with a select few party planners, because he's found that the extra layer between the host and the chef can spell disaster for both. For a New York baby shower, a well-known musician couple recently flew in a party planner who revealed to Nury that the menu would be kale salad, lobster rolls, and mac and cheese.

"I was like, *Jackpot!*," he said. "I'll do my version of these, it will be so fun!" He accepted the job, but it didn't go as he'd expected. The party planner sent him recipes from the couple's favorite restaurant in Los Angeles, along with photographs of exactly how the dishes should look and how they should be served—a mimicry job that he ultimately fulfilled but was none too thrilled about.

"Why would someone choose to spend so much money on a creative caterer and then try to impose a recipe?" he said.

Then, there is the opposite situation, which he adores. "Some people absolutely don't want any control," he said.

"They're like: July thirteenth, a hundred people, a hundred-thousand-dollar budget, I'll see you on the twelfth!"

Whether a client is pushy, or a pushover, catered events are always expensive. And even when the budget is stratospheric, the imperative for discounts and savings is likely hovering just overhead. Collin Barnard had said, "I've never had a client tell me: 'Spend anything you want, our resources are unlimited.' There's never been a time when money's not been an object."

Though many of Holland's clients may be multimillionaires and billionaires, she occasionally has to remind them what they're paying for when they complain about the price tag.

"I tell them, 'You're not buying a diamond. Having a party designed and curated—everything brought in just for that one moment and then disappearing—just for you? A special event is the most extravagant thing you can do!"

Whether it's selling cars, diamonds, cosmetics, or ephemeral parties, the salesmanship of luxury products is similar: you seduce by appealing to the buyer's needs and aspirations. But for the catering salesman, "closing" the deal doesn't end the process, it's only the beginning. He will work his cell phone to the bone in the months between the sale and the event, playing intermediary among the hosts, their event planner, and the chef, trying to broker to satisfaction the inevitable changes as a party evolves. Everyone will have to compromise.

Some of the most horrific stresses in the process, in fact, may be lurking beneath the surface of that 80 percent repeat business, the part of the catering picture that seems so safe and secure. These events, often annual, like a holiday party, a new-product launch, or a dinner after the trustee board meeting, are booked by the event director/party planner. It may be a regular event, but there's a tacit novelty imperative: the menu can't remain the same year after year. The salesperson and the party planner work together to invent ways to make each successive party more successful than the last, and thus pressure builds as their relationship grows. The Gina Rogaks of the world take tastings seriously because there are no minor details for her—anything that goes wrong at the party (a salty soup, rubbery salmon, a humid dining room, a warped dance floor) she hears about the next morning. The salesperson and the planner are locked in a mutually beneficial, and perilous, embrace. As Danny Meyer, one of the nation's foremost restaurateurs and owner of Union Square Events, told us in a moment of candor: "With catering, you're basically selling security. There's one person who books a party for five hundred people," he said. "And if it sucks, their job is on the line."

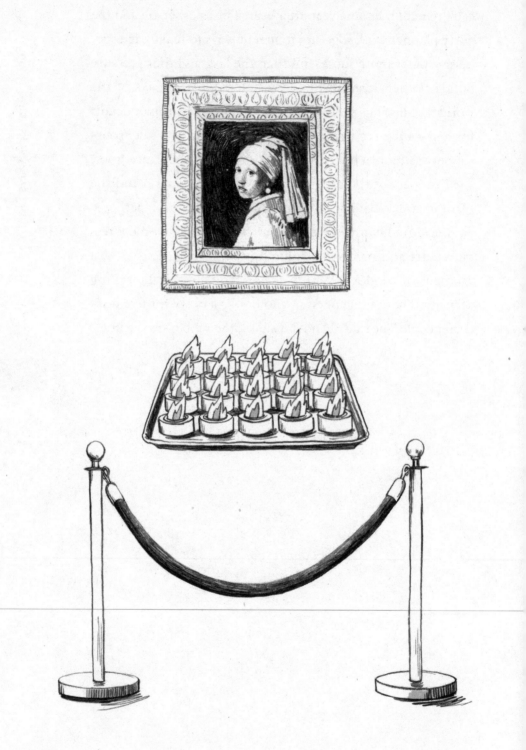

4

Fiesta in the Palace

Matt Works His First Event

Ted preceded me into the prep kitchen at Sonnier & Castle and helped fill me in on its general layout and key players. Still, I felt compelled to work overtime to reach his level of knowledge, to prove my mettle and commitment to Patrick and the team. So on busy days, I clocked in the prep kitchen at 7:30 a.m., then worked past pack-out, to around 7:00 p.m. One such day, heading into my eleventh hour, I began to lose my equilibrium as I broke down whole chickens. The stainless prep counters and chickens started spinning around me; I didn't hit the tile, but I quit working extended shifts. About a month after I began working prep, Patrick tapped me for my first fiesta gig, the Frick board dinner, on a brisk Tuesday in October. The Frick Collection, as it's officially called, is a grand museum that sustains the quirky residue of a great American steel fortune on a prime stretch of Fifth Avenue. Metal magnate Henry Clay Frick built his palazzo in 1913 for $5 million (in those dollars), with every intention of furnishing and bequeathing it as a museum, applying to its walls Grand Tour plunder of the highest sort, works by Titian, Velázquez, Vermeer, and Goya, as well as all the porcelain and other decorative baubles that attend high taste. It's a paroxysm of Beaux Arts limestone, gilt, and curlicue, suitable backdrop for any royal drama.

At lunchtime during my prep shift, Patrick had asked if I wanted to help him pack out and work an event that night, and I said yes without hesitation. And when I found out it was at the glamorous Frick, I was even more stoked. My earlier inklings of a career using my degree in art history might have had me working at an institution like this, sweating the provenance of a Renaissance chalk sketch instead of writing about country ham or catering. This event would be the last to load out, Patrick said, and super low-impact from his perspective: a CR & D* for just fourteen guests, staffed by two chefs—himself and Juan Soto—with me as the sole kitchen assistant. It seemed easy from a logistical perspective, but he said there was a lot at stake: the employee at the Frick who booked the party was, according to Patrick, a germophobe who took her job seriously and loved nothing more than to call out the catering team on something, typically when someone's taken off a latex glove to perform a fine-fingertip task like pinching thyme leaves from their stems. As for me, with such an intimate event, and without a cloud of other kitchen assistants

---

* Cocktail reception and dinner (seated, plated); CR & BD is cocktail reception and buffet dinner.

hovering around, my performance was likely to be much more closely scrutinized.

Over the course of that morning and into the afternoon, under Pam's watchful eye, I ripped a couple of pounds of prosciutto di Parma thin as onionskin on a meat slicer, peeled a forty-pound box of Yukon Golds, sliced them, then blanched them in salted water. At around 3:00 p.m., about the time I was cleaning up my station, things got busy on the loading dock. I checked the corkboard outside Patrick's office, saw he'd be packing out four cocktail parties—for a cosmetics company, a leveraged-buyout titan, a French champagne brand, and the ex–Spice Girl now fashion designer Victoria Beckham. Patrick's usually level temperament gave way to high pique as he checked off items on his clipboard, his handcrafted, leather-soled shoes slapping through the tile corridor between the prep kitchen and the loading dock. "Pam! Who has the tuna for the tartare? I can't find the fucking tuna in the walk-in." "Tyler! Where are your chicken skewers? This should have been loaded out fifteen minutes ago!"

By the time he told me to clock out from prep, the truck had circled back from delivering those four catered receptions around town and the loading bay had a calm-after-the-storm aura. The sun dipped over the Hoboken cliffs, darkening the street, and most of the kitchen crew left for the day. Only the provisions for our museum dinner party were left to pack and the handful of re-runs already called in from two of the other parties. So I helped Patrick roll the top-heavy hotbox on its janky casters across the metal tailgate and onto the truck. We wheeled it into place against the back corner, alongside a giant white cooler, a red plastic dry pack, and a bunch of milk crates with the bar items. We locked the casters and he strapped the proofer against the wall to minimize movement over the potholes. "Fuck it," he said. "No point taking a taxi, let's ride with César."

So we hopped up into the cab of Sonnier & Castle's white truck, an Isuzu Turbo Diesel with the company logo emblazoned on its flanks alongside a larger-than-life decal of smiling servers in gingham shirts. I settled into the sticky vinyl bench seat and then César pulled us out into traffic, trundling east—haltingly, it was rush hour—along Forty-Eighth Street, toward Times Square. I felt the diesel engine idling inches beneath us, the seat warming, and I thought about the ice melting in the cooler that held the tuna tartare and the Parmesan cream sauce. Eighteen (four extra, for safety) perfectly portioned pieces of Atlantic salmon and the three orders of yam dumplings—the vegetarian option—were back there, on separate sheet pans, beneath tight layers of plastic wrap, slowly but inevitably entering the zone. Patrick pulled out his file folder with the event brief to check who the service captain would be and how many servers under him—there would be two. For fourteen guests, we'd have a total of seven employees on-site. As for the pairs of hands that had gone into prepping and loading all the material we've got on board? Easily thirty, maybe even forty.

I ran some numbers in my head. Weren't there dozens—maybe even hundreds?—of restaurants in New York City that could accommodate these fourteen guests comfortably, in a private room, with exquisite food, impeccable service, a beautiful environment? Wouldn't it be more efficient, safer, more sustainable (in terms of all kinds of resources, but especially human ones), and even less expensive to hold this dinner meeting at an acclaimed restaurant? How many years had this gig been Sonnier & Castle's?

Patrick tapped the directions into his iPhone and the map of the route pulsed into view, its traffic grid settling dark red, and he sighed heavily. I didn't think it was the time to pepper him with these kinds of questions, so I asked him how he got into cooking.

As we sweated it out in Midtown traffic, he told the story. In 2000, a buddy in his band got him a job washing pots at a cozy, drug-addled Richmond, Virginia, bistro. Even from the dish pit, he found the food culture of the indie restaurant riveting. Before then, Red Lobster had been the most ambitious restaurant he'd ever dined in. In his first year, the chefs taught him the basics of cooking and soon moved him from dishes to garde-manger. One day the grill chef went MIA for a stretch and Patrick stepped up. He loved the energy of the line, so after releasing his second album (well reviewed, a U.S. tour, but no breakout hits) he returned to the grill, but found that the place was going off the rails, with waiters and waitresses sneaking shots during service. When one late-night shift ended with a brawl between a friend of the owner and a customer under the streetlamps outside the front door, Patrick stood on the bar and instigated a staff walkout.

When the owner regrouped, months later, she forgave him his insurrection and brought Patrick back into the fold under a new head chef, Andrew Manning, a tattooed badass unlike any of the narcotics-fueled kitchen grunts Patrick had met before. Andrew immediately instituted an all-new menu, with pastas made by hand. He got rid of bread deliveries; they baked their own every morning, and he showed Patrick how to shape his first fresh loaves. Andrew retaught him the basics—blanching vegetables, making sauces, breaking down whole animals. From Andrew, Patrick learned a new way to be a chef, both scrupulous and punk-rock at the same time. You could work in a bistro in Richmond and cook like you were on a world stage, as long as you had the chops, the self-discipline, the drive. I'd seen those kitchen ethics on display, in the care Patrick took dialing in the skills of his prep K.A.s, and in his Instagram photos of tweezered food. Here was a chef gunning for Michelin stars in a Sterno world. How did catering fit into that career trajectory? Was there something—anything—about the hotbox hustle keeping him from his goals?

As we pulled up to the stairs of the Frick's main entrance on East Seventieth Street, Juan Soto was waiting on the bottom step. It had been months since we'd met each other at the James Beard House, and we bumped fists in greeting—there was no time for pleasantries. He unlatched the truck's metal tailgate, as Park Avenue dog walkers hurried by. Patrick and Juan jumped up into the truck, slid the cooler and the dry packs, a large roll of brown kraft paper, and a twenty-four-can crate of Sterno to the edge of the tailgate. The last thing they fetched, together, was the hotbox. Once it'd been lowered to the ground, one of the tuxedoed servers and I rolled it over to the front steps. I grabbed for a handhold on the slippery aluminum angles at the bottom of the heavy box, and—careful to avoid tilting it more than a few degrees—the four of us duck-walked it up the six broad, shallow marble stairs of the front entrance. God help us if someone stumbled and this thing tumbled. Every particle of food for this dinner was inside there.

Juan took over the hotbox once we got it to the entrance

landing, rolling it past two security guards who held the doors open. Our polyester black pants, black clogs, and untailored white chef's jackets were the only credentials we needed to enter this palace. I returned to the curb, grabbed the case of Sterno, about thirty pounds of ethanol fuel, and marched into the building, past the grandfatherly security guards, and past several old master paintings—a Vermeer and Rembrandt exhibition was under way, on loan from the Royal Picture Gallery in The Hague. Heading into this dinner, I was concerned not only about Juan and Patrick calling me out on some flub or amateurish technique, but about a consequence more major than that: if I accidentally light the joint on fire with a hotbox full of Sternos, hundreds of millions of dollars' worth of art and a handful of billionaires would be toast.

The vestibule provided for our kitchen was just off the central courtyard, not far from the entrance, a utilitarian junction where loaner wheelchairs are stored and where a service elevator empties out next to a drafty fire exit. Juan, Patrick, and I unrolled brown kraft paper and covered the floors and halfway up the walls, taping it down with blue masking tape. We set three folding tables in a U against the walls and centered the hotbox in the middle of the tiny room, close to the corner where servers would pick up finished plates. The dry pack and cooler of ingredients we slid under the tables. I opened a brand-new box of purple food-service gloves and set it out to appease the germophobe, if she came around.

While Patrick set about assembling the platters of hors d'oeuvres (Tuna Tartare with Dijon and Diced Celery on Round Potato Crisp; Curried Chicken with Black Currant and Toasted Coconut on Bite-Size Papadum; Peking Duck Roll with Cucumber, Scallion, and Hoisin; Mission Fig Puree with

Candied Walnut and Whipped Boursin on Brioche), Juan began to organize the proofer. He cracked open twenty Sternos in short order, using the outer lip of one can to open the inset metal lid of the next—*ker-POP, ker-POP, ker-POP*—setting each on the sheet pan until he had a full tray. He then scooped a tiny dab of the ethanol gel with the handle of a serving spoon, ignited it with a Bic from his back pocket, and proceeded to light the entire tray in ten seconds by kissing the flame on the spoon handle to the open top of each can. He then portioned the lit Sternos out onto two pans set in the bottom of the hotbox. He said he was creating a warm zone at the top for wicker baskets of bread (ciabatta piccolo, multigrain, olive, purchased from Sullivan Street Bakery) cocooned with plastic wrap; later he'd move the trays of Sternos farther up in the box, creating a hotter zone in the upper middle where the first course—Wild Mushroom Ravioli with Mascarpone, Sweet Onion, and White Truffle Cream—got finished, and afterward the main protein, Atlantic Salmon with Creamy Parmesan Orzo, Roasted Tomato, and Crispy Phyllo. The rosy fillets of salmon in the proofer had already been seared to a nice chestnut brown in a few places back at the prep kitchen, but they were rare inside. The only other flash of color among the ingredients we unloaded from the cabinet was the magenta red of the loin of tuna, for the tartare.

I set up a small electric hot plate at one corner of the U and, after filling a handled pot with canola oil, began to fry yam dumplings—the "silent"* vegetarian option—in olive oil until brown, flipping once and then setting them out on paper towels on a tray, which we wrapped tightly in plastic

---

* Not printed on the menu; offered to guests only upon request.

twice for reheating later in the hotbox. It took me several wontons before I got the feel for browning without scorching the
edges of the wontons black.*

The tuna didn't have a trace of fat or sinew, and its almost
plastic uniformity and otherworldly hue told me it was institutional quality, gassed with carbon monoxide to hold a vibrant
color in the freezer for many months without any signs of oxi-
dation. But when Patrick cubed it into tartare, the translucent
rubies looked beautiful against the matte black of the slate
serving stone. With five minutes to go before the 7:00 p.m.
start, he'd set out three platters, one of each type of hors
d'oeuvre, with only the curried chicken yet to finish. By now,
the trustees' dining table had been arranged upstairs and the
butter pats preset. The two male servers and the captain began
to hover, one eye gauging our readiness, the other eye on the
door, and ears alert to the tinkle of coat hangers that would
announce that first guests had arrived.

Once the yam dumplings were fried, I reached down into
the cooler for the Parmesan cream sauce for the first-course
ravioli. There were two quart containers of it, cold and dense
as a milk shake, and I had to prize it out of the plastic with a
metal spoon. I dialed up the electric burner underneath the pan
and as it heated up the sauce began to loosen and pool. Juan
looked over my shoulder, concerned it was breaking—oil was
puddling on the surface. I wasn't convinced, and kept whisking to re-emulsify the oil. I took my eye off the now-bubbling
sauce just long enough that it scorched on the bottom and
telltale flecks of black began to show. *Fuck*. I stirred now,
careful not to scrape the bottom of the pan, to see if the flecks

---

* Alas, this wasn't a vegetarian crowd; the yams were never called for.

could be hidden or quarantined somehow. Juan and Patrick swooped in, conferred, and said it looked like the prep kitchen had over-reduced the cheese sauce (I sensed they might be giving me a bye). Juan spooned out some of the brown flecks and captured others with a paper towel twisted into a pointer. I attempted a hybrid resurrection of the sauce, with the good half of what existed, plus new cream and cheese, whisking to melt it through. I thought that what we had was adequate in supply and commendable in flavor, but Patrick said even that appeared broken. Patrick called the driver, César, to deliver more cream, pecorino crumbles, and shaved Parmesan, a quart of each, along with the white cranberry juice for the bar—whoever packed out this party forgot that the Frick outlaws red wine and red cranberry juice on the premises. (I could only imagine the Aubusson-staining catastrophe that had occasioned the rule!)

We busied ourselves on other tasks, boiling ravioli and setting out the garnishes and components of the main course, and replenishing the hors d'oeuvres platters as we waited for the re-run. When it finally arrived, Patrick remade the sauce in the nick of time, simmering it down and then adding in two whole quarts of Parmesan crumbles. The sauce was basically melted cheese—nobody would complain. And then—from my perspective at least—he ruined the finished sauce with a dash of truffle oil, a chemical fabrication widely reviled by restaurant chefs with integrity, but evidently not yet verboten in catering.

Throughout the machinations and deliberations over this damn sauce, Juan, Patrick, and I were dipping the tips of our pinkie fingers into it, scrutinizing them closely as gemstones under a loupe, tasting, then sticking fingers back in for a second and third appraisal. Honestly, if the germophobe were around, we would have needed a bucket of spoons for the number of times we had to sample that sauce. A bare finger—touch and taste in one—is the perfect tool. If you ever dine outside your home, you've tasted someone's pinkie—and a molecule of saliva—a thousand times and lived to tell about it. And thankfully the person for whom this news would be the greatest living nightmare was, at least up to that point, nowhere to be seen. I really couldn't blame her—the job-ending prospect of an ill trustee the morning after the board's annual repast (whether or not the food was causal) might give me bleeding ulcers for days leading up to the event.

Juan warmed up everything for this dinner simultaneously in the hotbox: the bread in the convective heat at the top, caramelized onions for topping the salmon, and ravioli (at the appointed time Juan ripped a two-finger-wide porthole in the three layers of plastic encasing the sheet pan and ladled a few tablespoons of cream sauce onto the ravioli to moisten and re-energize them for the ride). The stacks of plates were warming in there, too, gaming the distance the food had to travel—about forty yards—to reach the upstairs salon where the table was set. Directly below the plates was the salmon, finishing over Sternos in the bottom-middle of the box.

Few guests ate the hors d'oeuvres—in fact, they were quite a tough sell. Was it the presentation, I wondered, on black slate and a bed of black lava salt? Too modernist for these antiquarians? Would a Sèvres platter have been more reassuring?

Now, all eyes turned to Juan, whose job it was to get the

eighteen portions of salmon perfectly cooked, plenty warm, but not overdone, with no flecks of white protein goo.

At one point, during the lag between pasta and main course, as he was juggling scalding hot sheet trays in the box, the normally tranquil Juan muttered under his breath, "Fuck cater."

Patrick laughed. While Juan bore the logistical brunt and burns of this event, Patrick functioned as landing guide and stylist, ensuring each plate lived up to his vision. As the crew member with the least experience, I garnished and swabbed fingerprints off the plate rims.

Miro Oliveira, the amiable service captain with graying temples, perfect posture, and an unflappable air, reported that there were thirteen diners present, of fourteen expected. Patrick and I stepped in to assist the two waiters, running trays of four plates to the bottom of the Whartonesque sweep of staircase and pausing so they could stack two on each arm and ascend. Clinking of glasses and murmurs of conversation trickled down from above.

The dessert, round lemon tarts, bedazzled with rare salts and crushed candied violets, was so attractive that I started for my phone to capture a photo. These beauties were, I realized, a parting shot that set Patrick's food apart from any clubhouse dinner, and the moment they went upstairs we began closing down the kitchen.

I felt relieved—I'd screwed up under pressure and survived. And hadn't set the joint on fire. Adrenaline dissipated, then exhaustion set in. Just as I truly ached to quit, Juan was in highest gear, figuring out what materials and recyclables could be shoved back into the still-warm hotbox—converted now to a refuse wagon—and what to junk in stiff black garbage bags. It wasn't obvious to me among the china what was Sonnier & Castle's and what belonged to the rental company—and they had to be kept separate. So I folded up the tables, ripped the paper off the wall, and set out some aluminum pans of hors d'oeuvres, leftover salmon, and yam ravioli with plastic forks for the service staff and security guards. Once everything was packed up and locked down, the service captain and servers would load everything out and into César's truck, now circling back to Seventieth Street for the pickup.

One of the museum guards, a woman in her sixties, encouraged us before we left to take a good look at Vermeer's *Girl with a Pearl Earring*, perhaps the artist's most famous painting, on loan for the special exhibition. Juan and Patrick were still busy, so I walked through a central hall of the mansion, alone, and regarded the girl. And as she glanced back at me, over her shoulder and through the centuries, her scrutiny seemed almost more real to me than the guests that night (and certainly more real than the putative germophobe). The entire evening we never set our eyes on a single trustee, nor they on us. A moment of melancholy washed over me, but it soon ceded to a more thrilling sensation. Nobody else was in the hall and I was carrying a tote bag big enough to steal the painting away. It was the first time I'd thought about the perils of granting strangers the kind of access we enjoyed that night.

On the sidewalk outside we regrouped. Juan said he had to get back to the Bronx; he was facing a 4:00 a.m. call time. Patrick suggested that he and I repair to the restaurant Daniel, a few blocks south, for a nightcap. As we approached, the enormous brass revolving door sent forth a rogues' gallery of Upper East Side denizens: many furs, suspicious tans, walking canes. The bar cleared out soon after we arrived, and waiters hovered, delivering to our table jewel-like *mignardises,** gratis, with impeccable timing, justifying in an instant the $22 cocktails we'd ordered.[†]

"I'm like a hummingbird," Patrick said, swooping in for a pomegranate jelly drop. As far as I could tell, he'd consumed no food the entire day except for the pinkie sips of pecorino-Parmesan cream. I knew he must be exhausted, too, but I asked him to pick up the thread of his story, back at the Richmond bistro with the cool new head chef and the faltering music career. By the time he'd finished a third album, the record company expected him to go out on tour again, but Patrick couldn't afford the time or the expense. He was breaking up with a girlfriend, and Andrew had left town a few months before for Italy, to be chef at a trattoria in the village of Grinzane Cavour, in Piedmont. He asked Patrick to come to Italy and be his sous-chef, and Patrick hopped the next flight to Torino. In Piedmont, Patrick's mind was blown every single day: by the glistening eyes in the fish market, by eggs with yolks the color of navel oranges. He worked double shifts for Andrew, back to back, 10:00 a.m. to midnight with no break, and learned to be uncompromising in a totally new way. When you had the best raw materials at your fingertips, if you fucked something up, even slightly, you didn't put it on the pass.[‡] It went in the trash. And in time you learned to fuck up less.

He lived a life as artistically pure as a chef could in this village perched on a hill above Alba, where wild caperberries

---

* Miniature finger desserts typically presented as a gift from the chef and served after the dessert course, along with any coffees.

[†] I was earning $25 an hour for my labors that evening.

[‡] The place in a kitchen where completed dishes are presented to be picked up by servers and delivered to diners.

grew out of walls of the castle that housed the restaurant. He slaughtered his own chickens, rolled his own pasta, and haggled with old ladies over eggplant at the market every morning. He shaved white truffles over eggs for breakfast and drunk-drove a Fiat Panda at night with his kitchen mates. Piedmont was the experience that instilled in Patrick the values of chasing world-conquering food whatever the circumstances. But after six months of living the slow-food-focused life, he decided that what he really wanted was an education.

"But that's a story for another night," he said, just as the check arrived at our table. He put a corporate card down on top of the leather folder without glancing inside it.

I was bone-tired, but before we left I had to ask Patrick about the compromises and fudges we'd made at the museum this evening, fixing the broken sauce with a rasher of cheese, pushing hot salmon up two flights of stairs, hoping it made the journey safe and satisfyingly onto the plates and into the bodies of people we'd never meet. I wanted to know: was he exhilarated or demoralized by this—by all accounts successful—evening?

His eyes leveled on mine and his hands came together, the hummingbird still, for just this instant. "I've never gotten used to cold orzo," he said. "To bullshit fish cooked at four p.m. and reheated.

"It drives me *insane*!"

5

The Telephone Chef, the Glorious Guys, and G.I. Joe Veterans Frankfurter Service

Modern Catering's Origins

How did we *get* here? How did producing lofty feasts in the lowliest of circumstances—at a premium over the cost of a similar restaurant meal—evolve into a multibillion-dollar industry? As soon as we began moonlighting as K.A.s, a natural curiosity took hold that developed to fever pitch the first few times we watched Juan work the hotboxes at Fifth Avenue palaces. We also began to feel an obligation to our coworkers in the trenches: why are we contorting ourselves like this? Why is an emo rocker slinging bullshit salmon in a gilded cage? Who *started* this?

Granted, catering isn't the only time people travel with food and must consider time, temperature, perishability. Consider a picnic in the park, a camping trip, the bag lunch. Sandwiches assembled and wrapped; carrots peeled, cut into sticks, fruit washed. Pattied ground beef for burgers packed in a Tupperware container, in layers, with sheets of waxed paper between. Portable grills and beach chairs (*rentals*, in the catering analog). Packing frozen cranberry juice boxes, the child's lunch kept cool 'til just after noon, that meat loaf sandwich with mayo more or less safe. "Planning" is what this amounts to in the civilian world; in catering, the reductive slang for strategic food movement is "meals on wheels."

We began our quest simply tracing the lineage of hotbox skill—which seemed the most critical and unusual talents of modern caterers. Robb Garceau, now the executive chef of Neuman's Kitchen, a top firm in New York City, had been the Sotos' teacher; he'd only ever worked in restaurant kitchens (mostly the innovative Southeast Asian fine-dining Vong) before assuming the executive-chef mantle at Sonnier & Castle, so he'd been schooled in Sternos-in-proofers by David Castle, one of the firm's founders. We made an appointment to meet with Castle and we talked about catering history in the reception lounge on the second floor, an open-plan room overlooking the street that also housed the tasting room that had appeared on the monitor in Patrick's office. It was the only time we ever went up there.

Castle's mentor in all things hotbox was French-born Jean-Claude Nédélec, executive chef for the pioneering New York City firm Glorious Food, founded in 1971. Castle had started as a waiter there in 1983, a kid fresh from Saratoga Springs with a degree in business and $300 in his pocket, and then migrated into the kitchen under Nédélec's tutelage. "I know that Jean-Claude *perfected* the hotbox techniques," Castle told us. "But I'm not sure whether he invented them or not."

We'd need to ask the master himself, but Castle wished us

luck in that endeavor: the chef was notoriously press-shy, hard to pin down. He said we might have an easier time with Glorious Food's founder, Sean Driscoll, but he, too, could be prickly and discreet. "Flatter Sean a *lot*," Castle said. "Tell him I told you he's the founder of modern catering."

And then Castle gave us another valuable lead: the *true* founder of contemporary meals on wheels was in fact not Driscoll but a man a generation older, Donald Bruce White.

With our marching orders, we reached out to both Nédélec and Driscoll separately and, not surprisingly, got no immediate response from Nédélec and a polite phone call from Driscoll saying he was too busy. It was nearing the first weeks of May, when Glorious Food catered the two most important events of New York's spring social calendar (the Metropolitan Museum's Costume Institute Ball, a.k.a. "the Met Gala," and the American Ballet Theatre Gala at the Metropolitan Opera). After that would be a full roster of Memorial Day parties in the Hamptons, he said, so something might be possible after then—but not too far after, because they'd already be in production for July Fourth parties in Southampton.

In the meantime, a few trips to the New York Public Library revealed that Donald Bruce White had died in 1986, and the more we dug into his biographical details, the more we learned about off-premise catering history in general. In the decades immediately preceding the 1970s, a small party like a museum's trustees dinner would typically have taken place in a restaurant's private room, at a hotel restaurant, or at a trustee's private club. Larger, lavish events—like weddings and birthdays—went down in those same private clubs or in the banquet rooms of hotels, church parish halls, and fraternal organizations (and in fact many still do). At these occasions, the restaurant, hotel, or club's own kitchen prepared food on-site, from the chef's own repertoire, in the chef's native work environment, his comfort zone. Hosting a customized, off-campus party wasn't even considered back then because the equipment and techniques for producing events in kitchenless venues didn't exist. And dining in a dusty library or museum, no matter how grand, at that time would have violated some sense of decorum. Dinner-where-you-wished wasn't yet an entitlement; the resident chef in his fully equipped kitchen still held sway.

The traveling circus model of catering—an independent operator offering ultra-personalized service, who brought with her the kitchen, the chefs, the waiters (and often props and flowers) to wherever you wanted to be—arose in the early 1960s, incidentally not far from the Frick Collection. Individual caterers of quality (including James Beard, who specialized in hors d'oeuvres) had existed on a small scale throughout the midcentury, but the person who truly revolutionized the way New Yorkers celebrate, who in fact brought the category of off-premise into being, was Donald Bruce White.

White didn't start out working in food. He was born in Brooklyn to parents who ran a nursing home, later attended boarding school in Connecticut, and aspired to be an actor. He was just twenty in 1945 when he made his Broadway debut, in the role of a cad who punches the daylights out of a theater critic. (The real critics, as it happened, punched back, and the play closed after three nights.) White fled New York, spending four years in traveling productions including a USO tour of the Pacific, but his return to Broadway in 1949, as Charles Dickens's son in a plodding, two-act staging of thirty-five years in the English novelist's life, was not much longer-lived than his debut—the show closed after just five days.

Two years later, White landed the role that would launch him into the world of food, a bit part as a real-life errand boy, delivering the ingredients to the kitchen set of *Josie's Kitchen*, a stand-and-stir cooking show that ran for ten years on New York's NBC affiliate. Its host, Josie McCarthy, went on air nearly a decade before Julia Child debuted *The French Chef.* McCarthy was skilled at breaking down cooking processes into simple terms and adept at extolling both the shortcuts of the postwar era—the canned goods and jarred mayonnaise— but also the fresh herb garden she kept in the Manhattan skyscraper where she lived. Her example and guidance inspired White to cook, and he found he was more comfortable cooking than acting. After a few years preparing small dinners for his friends in their apartments, he renovated a shabby storefront at First Avenue and Fifty-Third Street that for decades had been Caldeiro's Fruits and Vegetables and hung out his shingle: THE TELEPHONE CHEF.

The shop's services would barely merit a mention today, amid the sheer numbers and varieties of competing meal-delivery services—from Uber Eats to Caviar to the thousands of brick-and-mortar restaurants offering customers the ability to order in. But in 1962, White's notion of delivering *escalopes de veau à la Marsala, duck à l'orange,* or *boeuf bourguignon* for two people, or twenty-two, after placing a brief call, was a new app for the old phone. "In this incredible age," marveled the *New York Times* in April 1962, five months after he opened, "the mere dialing of a number can obtain a weather forecast, the state of a World Series baseball game—or a fully-cooked meal delivered to the home." In those early years, the Telephone

Chef was strictly a prepared-meals delivery service. Customers called between 11:00 a.m. and 8:00 p.m. to place their orders for dinner that evening; White delivered the entrées with vegetable side dishes in colorful casserole pans, with a salad and dinner rolls. Prices ranged from $3.00 to $3.50 per person, depending on what main dish you chose, and White took a $5.00 deposit for each casserole pan, which he came around to pick up the next day.

The *Times* writer mostly enjoyed the Telephone Chef dishes she field-sampled: "chicken tarragon . . . proved to be delicious"; "the salad had unusual merit . . . composed of a variety of greens, such as Boston lettuce, escarole, and endive." She did, however, find fault—in a line that will resonate with any caterer of any kind in any era: "The noodles that accompanied the dish did not survive the reheating too well."

Straight out of the gate, White's concept was a hit—so much so that eighteen months later two rival companies emerged, Pantry East and Casserole Kitchen, also offering chef-prepared meals delivered to the home. Whether White felt pinched by this burgeoning competition for Upper East Side hostesses' attention or was simply eager to innovate, by 1965—the same year he moved to larger premises on Third Avenue in the Nineties and expanded to a second location in a sparkling skyscraper at UN Plaza—he'd added a new service to his business, one that would become the model for off-premise caterers to the present day. Now, instead of simply delivering a casserole, White brought to your Park Avenue apartment or limestone town house the entire party, as well as the French chef, the servers, and the kitchen equipment required to run it. Your Roper stove remained cold and clean!

White became known for his "crepe parties," and the paper

of record was on the scene for one of his early ones, the pre-view for a fashion show. An employee, Louis Retailleau, a French chef with the requisite tall toque blanche, worked four propane-powered burners, turning out feathery pancakes filled with truffled chicken, seafood, or sweetbreads and ham in Madeira sauce, for white-gloved waiters to pass around to guests. But for the period-piece cast to the menu (and the fact that propane has been illegal to deploy indoors in New York since the 1980s), the crepe party reads as an "action station" that could appear in any town in the twenty-first century. Toward the end of these events, Retailleau would delight guests by asking if they'd like to have their own turns at the pan. White broke down the ossified world of venue-dependent events—the one that put control in the hands of the banquet manager of the Yale Club or the Plaza Hotel instead of the host or host-ess. He sold his clients the values of consumer culture, the personalization of celebration: if you wanted a raw bar in your living room, you could have that, and he'd provide not just the clams, oysters, and someone to shuck, but an antique pewter-lined dry sink to display the shellfish on ice. His own English Coalport dinner plates were available if the occasion called for them, but if your party was downright casual, he had a street vendor's hot-dog cart, too. He had huge polished copper chaf-ing dishes. A silver-domed carving station. A doughnut machine. Having a picnic? He'd pack each lunch in its own hamper lined with a red-and-white checkered linen.

A Don White party had theatrical flair, just enough and not too much for the LBJ era, and, as Gallic as his menus were, the way he contextualized his food took the starch out of the routines and aesthetics of the Franco-laden food of the time. His attention to design forecast transformations twenty years later, as "catering" became "Special Events" in the 1980s, a shift that coincided with the explosion of the charity gala as a fund-raising tool. No longer would a party be flowers and food and a band if the occasion required it: *Design* emerged as the first principle in the creation of a meaningful celebration; everything else proceeds from there. And in the process, every business in service to design—from florals, to furniture, to lighting, to food—would change substantially.

In the late sixties, catering became a form of culture in the United States. A new national magazine, *Catering*, emerged, devoted to the then billion-dollar national industry. Nearly two dozen businesses competed in the New York market—an assortment of drop-off shops, off-premise and on-premise firms (the banquet halls, and businesses with an exclusive on a party space), and several chefs-for-hire working out of their apartments. The Telephone Chef opened a branch of his business in Southampton, Long Island, summer playground for the set who were his bread and butter (this milestone still marks a New York City caterer having hit institution status). In 1968, he catered Thanksgiving dinner for comic heavyweights Anne Meara and Jerry Stiller (and a three-year-old Ben Stiller) at their Riverside Drive apartment. Not long after, he orchestrated a surprise birthday party for *Catch-22* novelist Joseph Heller at his apartment in the Apthorp, with Mel Brooks, Anne Bancroft, and 132 others in attendance, entertained on piano by the movie-music titans Burton Lane and Saul Chaplin. By 1970, White had dropped the "Telephone Chef" from his listings in the Manhattan White Pages and renamed the business "Donald Bruce White Caterers."

The *New York Times* began to publish, every five or six years, listings of caterers, with capsule reviews of each firm, its strengths and its prices, and *New York* magazine followed suit with the kind of overview of a food culture now common in every city in the country. *New York*'s first catering round-up, "Don't Cook Tonight: A Catering Guide," appeared on news-stands on November 8, 1971. "12-PAGE PULL-OUT GUIDE TO CATERERS" shouted the cover line, and perhaps to justify devoting so much space to such a rarefied service, the editors assured readers: "You don't need a million dollars to be able to afford the cost of having your home-entertainment chores done for you, nor do you have to be planning a blow-out for hundreds of guests." Food writer Mimi Sheraton's gonzo takes on the various firms zeroed in on their repertoires with a sharply tuned palate and rapier wit. The firms ran the gamut, from G.I. Joe Veterans Frankfurter Service at 370 West Eleventh Street, specializing in Sabrett hot dogs and ice-cream parties (she notes the principals can dress in army fatigues, clown costumes, or tuxedos, according to clients' desires) to Cleo's La Cuisine, of Maplewood, New Jersey, run by the pioneering African American caterer and North Carolina native Cleo Johns, whose corn pudding Sheraton loved so much she confessed to having traded Mrs. Johns three cookbooks for her recipe.

That same month in 1971, *Vogue* devoted a two-page spread to recipes and entertaining advice by White that confirmed his status as a catering trailblazer. "Reality Food: Menu, Recipes, Tips for an Organic Dinner" foreshadows themes that would inundate the industry forty years later, when "organic," "sustainable," and "green" became unavoidable. Seek out "fish from clear, unpolluted water," he recommended, "poultry . . . grain-fed, not shot up with unnatural things," and wine from "good vineyards [that] grow grapes without chemical sprays." White's recipes included rocket (arugula) canapés, zucchini with brown rice, poached pike with yogurt sauce, apricot mousse, and organic Jamaican coffee.

We felt we'd gotten some measure of Donald Bruce White, but in all our research we found no mention—beyond Chef Retailleau and his propane burners—of hotboxes and scaling-up techniques. He'd done ever larger parties as his business grew, but there were few clues as to how he'd accomplished them behind the pipe and drape.

But by then, Driscoll had called us back and offered up time on a sunny day in early June. Glorious Food had recently vacated the building it'd inhabited on the Upper East Side since 1981, so he was working out of a rental office overlooking Madison Avenue in the Twenties, with barely enough room for a chair for a guest. Driscoll looked like a sporty granddad, wearing a seersucker blazer over an untucked blue oxford, a fitted navy-blue Lacoste ball cap, and chunky black glasses. We'd read a few profiles of him and knew we'd get nowhere inquiring about clients, though we spied a smattering of names from the fashion and art worlds (Missoni, Burch, MOMA) and East Coast high society (Weymouth, Lindemann, Tapert) on file folders in a standing sorter on the window ledge. In any case we were more interested in his own story, and in having him connect us to Nédélec.

In 1971 (the same year White appeared in *Vogue*), Driscoll was a thirty-two-year-old former ad man, trying to move from producing TV commercials into moviemaking. When catching up with an old friend, a well-connected editor at *Glamour*, he told her that while his script was making the rounds he was helping his boyfriend, Christopher Idone, open a restaurant in Soho. She told him they were crazy: first, because she'd never heard of Soho and, second, because there were already too many great restaurants in New York and too few caterers of distinction. She said she'd make a few phone calls, and that's how Idone and Driscoll began routinely catering small private dinners for eight to ten people, working out of their Forty-Eighth Street apartment, and starting the firm, Glorious Food, that would dominate the New York catering scene for two decades. Driscoll was salesman and accountant. Idone was chef and food stylist: he'd spent a couple of years cooking in Italy and France, and during his time in Paris he had been taken under the wing of the cook for the family he lodged with, who'd shown him how to shop the markets and prepare impressive meals from what he found there.

Word of mouth spread about these elegant young men doing French-style,* white-glove service, and then one day in 1972 Driscoll got a phone call from a woman representing Fieldcrest Mills, who told him the North Carolina company was launching a new line of sheets, and she needed them to cater a cocktail party with a raw bar at the Cooper-Hewitt Museum of Decorative Arts. The event was larger than he and Idone had ever attempted before, and there was an unusual catch: she wanted an ice sculpture of an American eagle.

"If you can't do the eagle," she said, "you don't have the job."

Idone said, "*What?!* Ice is what falls on the floor when I open the freezer!"

But Driscoll had a showman's mettle. He'd been an Irish step dancer growing up and majored in theater at Emerson

---

* In "French-style" service, a large platter of food is brought to a table by a waiter with serving utensils, who serves each person in turn from the platter (as opposed to the food being pre-plated and the plate simply dropped in front of the guest).

College. Like Donald Bruce White, he'd also performed for U.S. soldiers in traveling productions, having served in the army in the early sixties as a song-and-dance man. In his advertising days, he'd grown accustomed to never saying no to a client. He told her they'd do the job.

Driscoll made a few phone calls and soon had found a master of ice sculptures in New York, the twenty-two-year-old banquet chef at the Plaza Hotel, Jean-Claude Nédélec. He asked if Nédélec could carve an eagle for them.

"How big do you want it? Do you want lights?" Nédélec replied.

"Just get me an eagle," Driscoll said.

When Nédélec pulled up in front of the Andrew Carnegie Mansion in an old station wagon, with three hundred pounds of ice hand-chiseled into a perfect bald eagle, Driscoll had no idea this diminutive Frenchman would not just become his new partner in Glorious Food's rise, but end up devising and codifying most of the techniques for large-scale cooking that became standard for all caterers in New York City and beyond.

To learn that part of the story, we had to get a conversation with Nédélec. Driscoll warned us that an appointment with Nédélec was highly unlikely, the chef was just too busy. But we knew Bob Spiegel, cofounder of Pinch Food Design, whom we'd interviewed for this book a year earlier, had worked in the early eighties at Glorious Food. We knew we were getting somewhere when we contacted Spiegel and he said that for him Nédélec was like a father figure. Spiegel brokered a joint meeting exactly three months after our session with Driscoll, at a bar around the corner from Pinch, in far West Chelsea.

In that meeting Nédélec confirmed, almost word for word, Driscoll's ice eagle story. But in his telling, he knew almost immediately after that first greeting outside the station wagon that they'd be working together again soon, because Driscoll seemed to be making it up as he went along.

"Where do you want me to set the eagle down?" Nédélec asked him, and Driscoll's face went blank. He'd forgotten to order a table to display it. They called for a re-run from the up-and-coming rentals firm Party Rental Ltd., and Nédélec told Driscoll, "Listen. Next time you have a party, call me. I freelance, and I'm going to help you out."

Nédélec had grown up in the tiny Breton town of Coray, a military brat whose father was transferred with the family, first to Germany and then to Paris. In 1963, just fourteen years old, Nédélec apprenticed in the kitchen of the grand Paris hotel Le George V, the 1920s white art deco palace steps from the Champs-Élysées where Eisenhower had lodged during the liberation, where Marlene Dietrich lived for most of the fifties, and where John Lennon and Paul McCartney would, a year later, write "Can't Buy Me Love." During Nédélec's short tenure there, the hotel held a cooking competition among its apprentices, grand prize of which was six months' tuition at L'École Hôtelière de Lausanne in Switzerland.* Nédélec won, and he excelled at the school, especially in ice-sculpting classes. Shortly after graduation, he left Europe to visit an aunt who lived in Queens, New York, and to attend the 1964 World's Fair. He was so taken by the lifestyle, and the directness of Americans, "how they tell you everything on their minds right now," that he stayed.

---

* Then and now considered among the top culinary schools in the world.

Nédélec found a tiny apartment in the East Village and bounced around the kitchens of small French and German restaurants in Manhattan for several years until his aunt secured him an interview at the Plaza with executive chef André René.* Nédélec started as *chef-rôtisseur* (the meats station) but was soon promoted to banquet chef, a position that came with a forbidding spatial challenge: the banquet rooms at the Plaza then were hundreds of yards away from the kitchen. The hotel had been getting by serving lukewarm food and using electrified proofers, but Nédélec hated these flame-free warming boxes: they took hours to get to temperature, and when they did they still weren't hot enough. He was concerned, from a safety perspective, that the food was spending too much time in the bacteria-friendly danger zone, so he started experimenting with a prosaic aluminum transport cabinet—no cord or electricity required, used primarily for moving large amounts of room-temperature or chilled food around a huge kitchen—and Sternos. And what he found was that this hotbox, properly loaded with little flames above and below the food, was very effective at getting fillets of salmon to temperature and holding them there. Using sheet pans, you created zones in the box, and controlled the heat in each zone with the number of Sternos you placed on each pan. The only other major variable was the door—it had to be left ajar to get enough oxygen to feed the flames, but not so far open that the heat you needed was lost.

Nédélec taught himself—using only his senses as guides—

---

* The same man who would, in the late 1970s, become the founding chef of Windows on the World, the marquee restaurant at the top of the World Trade Center.

the temperatures and times it took to rewarm various browned meats and fish and par-cooked side dishes like grains and vegetables, and he perfected techniques of modulating and controlling the heat.* It's an insanely analog system, a bit like piloting a hot air balloon, but it's ruthlessly efficient, self-contained, safe, scalable, and cost-effective to run.

When Nédélec began freelancing for Glorious Food, Idone and Driscoll were still schlepping supplies on the subway in baskets, mostly catering parties for eight to twelve people. And they'd only accept one job every few days, to ensure they had time enough to recover from the previous event and to prep for the next. Nédélec's banquet intelligence allowed them to increase their workload, and they started catering parties for the Fifth Avenue retailer Henri Bendel. Through that contact, they made inroads into the fashion industry, luring in Bill Blass, Ralph Lauren, and Calvin Klein as clients. They brought Nédélec on board full-time in 1976—incidentally, the same year former model and stockbroker Martha Stewart opened a catering firm out of her home kitchen in Westport, Connecticut. With Driscoll as pitchman, Idone as food stylist, and Nédélec as production genius, Glorious Food was unstoppable. There was a youthful, upstart, cheeky charm to the firm; when Driscoll cold-called event planners at department stores and they wouldn't take a meeting, he'd leave a brown paper lunch sack with a bouquet of fresh parsley and his phone number.

Glorious Food had by no means usurped Donald Bruce White's dominance. In fact, as they still struggled to produce ever larger events out of the Forty-Eighth Street apartment,

---

* The cold, too—a hotbox loaded with sheet pans of crushed dry ice can be used to keep desserts cool.

White had bought a grand, Italianate four-story 1890s town house at 159 East Sixty-Fourth Street and installed his business and residence there. (Although it can't have escaped White's notice that Glorious Food soon moved into a carriage house just eleven blocks north, with a similar arrangement to his own: a ground-floor commercial kitchen in a residential neighborhood, for easy loading in and out; instead of a residence above, there was an event room. This arrangement would become a midcareer model for quite a few New York caterers who rose from apartment-kitchen industries to become mature businesses, hauling in millions of dollars a year from industrial warehouses with loading docks.)

By 1977, the year Studio 54 was founded, Donald Bruce White was a bona fide personality, and his catering company a $750,000-a-year concern ($3 million, adjusted for inflation). Hallmarks of his style proved influential and enduring in the business, and primary among them was discretion. White dropped the names of a few key clients—including three First Ladies of the United States and a smattering of Fortune 500 companies—but he made absolutely clear there would be no dish. "It would ruin me," he said. In the press, White deftly channeled queries about certain clients to the subject of *trends*—another front-of-mind theme for caterers operating at the top of the New York City market—declaring that his best customers were wanting "simpler food . . . fewer sauces, less beef." Veal and chicken were his most popular main dishes, and he thought people might be surprised to learn fried chicken was all the rage. Spirits consumption among his clients was way down, he reported in one interview, and a full 50 percent of them drank only white wine. "But the idea that people have given up rich desserts is ridiculous," he said.

"Everyone wants one." Fueling White's attention to trends was the pressure to deliver some degree of novelty while catering ten dinners a night: "I see many of the same people at the same parties. I have to stay innovative." And as for those signature crepe parties, he scoffed. "That was in my show-off period . . . I flambéed everything in sight!"

White struggled to manage his clients' desires while maintaining his own distinct style as it developed into a brand—a dilemma that would become more difficult as time went on, as the sheer number of caterers in the marketplace grew and clients felt empowered to seek ever-greater customization (precisely the dilemma Robb Garceau had articulated; you lose your identity if you're always saying yes to a host's desires). White told *People* magazine in 1977, "The client is always right. If they want finger bowls and white gloves, that's what they get." But he drew the line at a few elements of a party he would not abide under any circumstances: salad courses at seated dinners ("It keeps people at the table too long") and pistachio ice cream for dessert ("Can you imagine?").

White projected a seen-it-all bemusement in that *People* profile, chain-smoking and rolling his eyes while fielding telephone complaints from a client (the nuts and the coatrack had arrived late at a party the night before). The name-dropping increased with his years, and as the industry he had created engulfed him.

"There is nothing that can faze me now. Nothing," he told the reporter, relating the story of scrambling eggs at 5:00 a.m. at Woody Allen's, when the director's New Year's Eve party ran into the wee hours. That weary edge might be familiar to any caterer operating in the upper end of the market, honed by the relentlessness of delivering "the best" at whatever cost, striving every day to avoid a disaster and to make each party unique and special, knowing full well that there will always be another (possibly several more) tomorrow night. And the next night. And the one after that. When Donald Bruce White died in late May 1986, at the age of sixty-two, in St. Vincent's Hospital, his obituary in the *New York Times* named cancer as the cause of death and noted that he had "dissolved" his business the prior September on account of the illness. His name would vanish from the New York entertaining scene, but the theatrical precedent he set endures, in the roving mobile oyster shucker, the Baked Alaska action station, and any time the food steals the show.

As for Glorious Food, it brought a style and sophistication to events in the mid-seventies that hadn't been seen anywhere in the United States. Jean-Claude Nédélec had connections to supply chains for international luxury ingredients virtually unknown in American catering circles: Vacherin cheese, Iranian caviar, white truffles, scallops with the orange roe still attached. True, their dinners were in the laborious French style, with white-gloved waiters serving portions from silver platters, but if you looked closer there was a streamlined modernity to its operations. Nédélec and Driscoll dispensed with bread plates altogether and pushed clients toward an all-purpose glass, a stemmed wineglass that could be filled with white or red—or Coke, or a cocktail. Nédélec and his team were regularly using hotboxes behind the pipe and drape. Sean Driscoll had done casting for commercials in his days as an adman, and Glorious Food was the first firm to hold waiter castings, with an emphasis on attractive male* models and actors. But the partners went a step farther, developing an in-house waiter-training program, with a Frenchman, Serge DeCluny, in the role of headmaster.† The firm hadn't existed when Mimi Sheraton wrote *New York*'s first catering guide; by the time *New York* published its second, in 1978, Glorious Food was named, along with Donald Bruce White and Cleo Johns, among "the establishment" in New York. Jacqueline Kennedy Onassis, Brooke Astor, and Pat Buckley were regular clients.

Where Donald Bruce White had once been the innovator, now Glorious Food was doing what had never been done. In September 1982, ten years after the firm opened its doors, Idone published the lavishly illustrated cookbook *Glorious Food*, which not only showed how much the look and the presentation of the food mattered, but also became a game changer in publishing. Released by art-book publisher Stewart, Tabori & Chang, *Glorious Food* was among the first coffee-table cookbooks (Martha Stewart's *Entertaining*, published by Clarkson Potter, and also hugely influential, appeared in bookstores three months later), and it set a standard for design-centric cookbooks to come.

As it was broadening the reach of the catering business, Glorious Food also revolutionized related industries: where Donald Bruce White had prided himself on providing props

---

* In 1998, Glorious Foods settled a class-action discrimination suit brought against them by women waiters, filed by the American Civil Liberties Union.

† It is rumored the comedian Bronson Pinchot, who worked as a Glorious Food waiter, based the character he plays in the movie *Beverly Hills Cop*, the art dealer Serge, on DeCluny.

and service items from his personal collection of antiques, Nédélec returned from trips to Europe with a sample of a particular platter or serving piece, and he cajoled Party Rental Ltd. (which had become the go-to firm for most Manhattan off-premise caterers by then) into purchasing three hundred of the item for their inventory. And Party Rental Ltd. made that purchase, because keeping Glorious Food's business was, by then, essential.

The cover of the cookbook *Glorious Food* expressed in a single photo the food values of the enterprise—a simple, deconstructed *salade niçoise*, its elegance and modernity displayed in the abundance and rare variety of ingredients—two kinds of lettuces, yellow and red cherry tomatoes, haricots verts, *jaunes*, and *violets*, the olives and nest of pickled red onions arranged in a palette-like composition. Inside, the photos, many taken in their clients' grand apartments, immersed the reader in a tableau of seventies high-decadence (hold the polyester). If the cookbook reads as a period piece today—the comically abundant buffets, the artificial lighting, lemon sorbet served in hollowed-out lemons—*Glorious Food* fixed the firm's status as the go-to shop in New York, a city about to greet the boom economy of the 1980s with gusto.

In the early eighties, the stress of the parties began to weigh on Idone, so Driscoll bought him out of the business. He made Nédélec executive chef and co-owner and convinced the shy Frenchman to appear in a full-page Dewar's scotch print advertisement—one of the "Dewar's Profile" series that ran from the late seventies to the early nineties. In the close-up black-and-white portrait of Nédélec that appeared full-bleed in numerous magazines and newspapers in 1984, he leans insouciantly, chin in hand, over a well-worn cutting board, in his tall paper toque blanche and chef's jacket, a bottle of Dewar's and glass of scotch on ice perched at his elbow. This was several years before the dawn of the celebrity chef, and even the top chefs at the best restaurants in New York were not household names—to say nothing of catering chefs! The text that appeared alongside Nédélec's portrait gave a national audience a glimpse at the rigors of event catering, with a gloss of self-mythologizing:

> *LATEST ACCOMPLISHMENT: Catered the Museum of Modern Art's reopening, with more than 10,000 people in six days.*
>
> *PROFILE: Energetic. Thrives on what the rest of us might call chaos. Sees a sit-down dinner for two thousand as an intimate little gathering.*
>
> *HIS SCOTCH: "Dewar's 'White Label,' on the rocks. Its taste blends perfectly with the sense of accomplishment I feel when five parties have gone well. On the same night."*

By that time, Nédélec had proven himself to be gifted not only in the kitchen operations that enabled the firm to throw so many parties on such a large scale, but also as a mentor to a squadron of chefs who executed his vision from one night to the next and allowed "Glorious"—the shorthand moniker by which the firm came to be known in the industry—to expand to Washington, D.C. They opened a restaurant in Georgetown, Glorious Café, and ingratiated themselves to hostesses and institutions in the nation's capital. They catered the Hot Mousse of Sole with Lobster and Truffle Sauce, as well as Veal Medallions with Morels, at Ronald Reagan's second inaugural luncheon and the National Gallery of Art's dinner for Prince Charles and Princess Diana during the royal couple's first visit to the United States, at which dessert was, in impeccable eighties style, an apricot mousse served in a hollowed-out pomegranate.

Perhaps more than either Driscoll or Nédélec anticipated, they trained many of the same chefs who would emerge less than a decade later as the second generation of catering innovators, with their own competing firms. In 1990, a few years after his tenure at Glorious, Bob Spiegel founded Creative Edge with Carla Ruben, and, twenty years after that, Pinch Food Design (widely considered the most avant-garde of catering shops). Spiegel remains awestruck by his time at Glorious Food: cooking for David Bowie and the Queen of England, hotboxing a party when Andy Warhol sauntered in the kitchen to snap Polaroids. David Castle, who opened Sonnier & Castle in 1997 with Glorious alum Russ Sonnier, recalls his tutelage under Nédélec in the high-flying Reagan years as foundational from a career-knowledge perspective, but also fun. Following a particularly profitable season, Castle packed it up with the firm's other chefs for a summer sojourn through France. The group traveled from Cannes to Lyon to Paris, guzzling Château d'Yquem and inhaling foie gras at Michelin-starred temples of haute cuisine. For his part, Nédélec refers to his former charges as "my kids," and yet competes head to head with them every day—he remains actively engaged as executive chef at Glorious Food.

Sean Driscoll died of cancer a year and a half after we interviewed him, in January 2018, at the age of seventy-seven. A small paid notice appeared in the *New York Times*, but we were surprised there hadn't been a full obituary by the paper, given how extensively it'd covered his work during his life. He was so discreet and private, perhaps he would've preferred no fuss; still, his central role over the decades in building the catering business from a cottage industry into the juggernaut it is today seemed noteworthy. A nonprofit he was involved with hosted a private memorial reception that spring that was, according to an event director who attended, thronged with "all Sean's women." After learning the news that he died, we returned to the notes from our interview. What struck us first upon re-reading them was Driscoll's sharp wit.

When we'd asked him how he felt about Glorious having trained so many of the succeeding generation of New York caterers, he seemed magnanimous. "Sure, you start with us, and then you go off on your own . . ." he said, trailing off. Then he'd pulled his glasses down to the bridge of his nose, locking eyes over the top of them and pretending to seethe: "And. Then. I. *Kill*. You!" He doubled over in laughter.

Driscoll had admitted his mordant sense of humor didn't always translate. A woman in New Jersey once asked him if Glorious Food might cater a party in her home and he'd replied, dripping mock-condescension he assumed she'd heard: "I've only been known to cross the river on occasion." He sent her a price list, but never heard back. Years later, she was the chair-woman of a Manhattan charity gala that Glorious Food catered, and she asked him: "Do you remember telling me you'd never come out to New Jersey?"

We also found in this reading more than a few lines echo-ing the weary resignation Donald Bruce White showed report-ers toward the end of his career.

"I have two mottos," Driscoll told us. "Every night is open-ing night; and, you're only as good as your last soufflé." Then he added, "Because if there's not enough salt in the salad dressing—or too much—there's nothing I can do the next day except apologize. That's why everything *has* to be perfect. Every night."

Primarily, our journey into the past solved the riddle of who created the pattern of our nightly tent campaigns and this insane cooking style. But we also gained some new perspective on our earlier question: why endure the hefty price tag that goes with a dinner for fourteen produced in the splendor of the Frick's Gilded Age mansion, easily $500 per person, and possibly twice that?* Why not a fancy restaurant instead for the trustees? Because when Donald Bruce White and Jean-Claude Nédélec enabled dining inside the kitchenless museum, it was suddenly *possible*; and not long after that, someone empowered by the Frick Collection's board decided that the value of meeting for dinner inside the old pile was priceless. And who's to say it wasn't? (We'd later learn that among the board members likely to have attended the dinner that night was the billionaire Stephen Schwarzman,† chief executive officer of the Blackstone Group; Emily Frick, grand-daughter of Henry Clay Frick; J. Fife Symington IV, a greenhouses and cannabis magnate; plus several other bona fide billionaires besides.) It isn't that far-fetched to presume that if our team did our jobs making that evening magical, a board member's heart might swell so large at the majesty of this

---

* Which is pretty close to the New York average for an event when all expenses, including decor and rentals, have been factored in.

† Whose seventieth birthday party, in 2017, for five hundred guests in Palm Beach, was widely reported to have cost $5 million, or $10,000 per guest.

occasion—the heady blend of wine and sumptuous food, the Gilded Age setting, flowers, and lighting, the proximity to all those Vermeers—that he or she might decide to bequeath an extra ten or twenty million to the collection. Play with billionaires, and the cost of dinner becomes near irrelevant. *Just make it perfect.*

Control of such an evening, of course, might be paramount—the ability for the Frick event director to nuance these crucial details, while keeping the proceedings on known territory, far from the variables one might find in even the most hushed private restaurant dining room. And yet who was truly at the controls during that night's dinner? As far as the food the guests were about to ingest, it was just us: an exhausted, frustrated indie rocker, a freelance writer working his first fiesta, and the best proofer in America, Juan Soto.

6

Dinner in Light and Dark

Ted Grows Up as a Party Chef

The call for my first fiesta came in much the same way the call for prep had, with scant notice. One of Juan Soto's guys texted in sick at the last minute, I jumped at the chance, and thereafter Casey Wilson seemed to reach out to book me often. That fall and winter I worked a dozen or more parties and I looked forward to them: with each one, you stepped into a different world, with a new venue and vibe. Juan and Jorge took me under their wing and, especially at those early fiestas, it seemed like I was in perpetual motion from the moment I set foot in the venue until Juan or Patrick cut me from the clock. If I stood idle for even a second, Juan had some task to fold me into. He and Jorge were great teachers. Since they were kids, they'd worked together for their parents, who sold shoes at street festivals and markets in Mexico; they'd been immersed in a life where you packed things up and moved from one place to another. They showed me how to tape down a room with paper to protect floors and walls, position the proofers according to the site plan, box out the tables and nap them with linens. With every large party I worked, the more the routines of massive, military-grade load-ins became intuitive, and I fell easily into the rhythm of the team. We were a random group of people, but we seemed to compete only to out-support each other with superior anticipatory skills and experience.

Jorge was slighter in build than his older brother, with a more laconic, New Yorkese accent, a great ability to delegate, and with a better command of English than Juan. But he wasn't as generous with instruction. Juan gamely narrated aloud for me whatever he was doing on the fly, in the sweatiest heat of battle, shouting above the clank of plates and proofer doors. His goal is for each of his charges to become what he calls "*chef completo*," a philosophy of catering that applies the same expectations to every individual on the team. Juan's charges (generically referred to as Sotos* by everyone on the crew) begin working for him at the rank of *manos*—"hands," with the most rudimentary skills—but as soon as you've acquired some aptitude, and proven reliable, he wants you to be able to step in for anyone, to perform any role in the kitchen, from sanitation on up to main protein chef, running the hotboxes. Each team member is a complete chef.

Once a kitchen was built and assignments delegated, the focus narrowed to the food torture, and here the tasks tended to be so varied, solutions so on the fly, it could be riveting.

---

* Fiesta workers, largely of Mexican and other Central American descent, booked through Juan.

Once, plating up 280 yellow beet and burrata salads for a gala, I opened the proofer to find the luminous yellow, jewel-like diced beets, preportioned into small foil cups, had leached a couple of teaspoons of bright yellow liquid into their cups. The contents of each needed to be inverted into the center of the salad plate, and Juan said those beets had to be perfectly dry. There were five sheet pans of these suckers to drain—three hundred cups total—before we could even start plating. I found an empty deli container and began, cup by cup, draining that beet water. Two cups in, I saw Juan nod to a super-young Soto, Pélos.

"My friend," he said. "Watch me." Lightning quick, Pélos stretched a triple thickness of paper towels over the top of my sheet pan of cups. He snapped a second sheet pan down over the top, flipped the sandwiched beet cups, and set the contraption upside down on the table. All sixty portions of beets drained into the paper towel, and in a minute or two K.A.s were inverting those cups onto the plates, building the salads. Sheet pan magic!

There were other ways Juan's *chefs completos* watched out for amateurs like me. The *Wolf of Wall Street* premiere was the first giant buffet party I'd worked in the city, with every dish on the menu set out in a large bowl or platter at long tables on the floor. Behind a black curtain were stations, each manned by a K.A., who refilled the empty platters and bowls as the servers returned them, in a constant stream. Being a newbie, I got assigned to the station entailing the least finesse—opening towers of cardboard boxes of four different varieties of *pizze rustiche* brought in from Sullivan Street Bakery. Here's where I first witnessed how a crowd of six hundred could demolish food so fast that the back of the house had to struggle to keep up. Early in the party, I fanned out the pizza slices, making beautiful, Escheresque tessellations of every platter; an hour later I was tossing them into floppy heaps as fast as I could.

But more astonishing than the gluttony was the condition of the venue, a setting almost too fitting for a film about the seamy underside of extravagance. The party happened to be one of the final events in the Roseland Ballroom, a former ice-skating rink on Fifty-Second Street that had hosted everyone from Madonna to AC/DC to Hillary Clinton (and has since been rebuilt from the ground up as an apartment tower). Our kitchen was erected on a stagelike, raised platform stretching clear across one end of the ballroom. When I first arrived, I'd launched up onto the stage, slung my backpack off my shoulder, and started looking around for the stash of workers' belongings. An older kitchen assistant I didn't recognize ripped a clear plastic garbage bag from a large roll and offered it to me.

"No, thanks," I said. I had no idea what he was suggesting. We typically used these bags for recycling plastic and foil containers.

"*Sí, sí*," he said. "*Ratones.*" He snapped open the bag, grabbed my backpack, dropped it in, and tied a loose knot in it.

"*Ratas y cucarachas en todas partes.*" He pointed to a railing, where a dozen similar-looking bags of people's belongings were tied up, suspended off the floor away from the mice, rats, and roaches. Margot Robbie and Martin Scorsese were in the house that night! Leonardo DiCaprio and Matthew McConaughey and Jonah Hill! And the place was crawling with vermin.

Also that fall, a level of trust developed between me and Patrick as he grew comfortable with my skill set. I made up for my shortcomings by projecting an ever-ready eagerness to learn, and we became friends during our commutes back to Brooklyn. And he showed me the tumultuous range of fiesta styles that catering chefs had to roll with from night to night. After a string of large events I'd worked, Casey emailed, asking me to meet Patrick at 4:45 p.m. at an address on Park Avenue, an ornate building with a coterie of liveried doormen. I waited for him outside the service entrance, marveling at the scale of the buildings and the streets in this part of town, their manicured tree pits rimmed by wrought-iron fences and brimming with winter pansies. But once Patrick arrived with the truck and another K.A., and we'd wheeled the proofer down into the dark, leafless service courtyard, the scene became relentlessly grim. An ancient, yellowing Jacuzzi was tipped on its side like a boat beached at low tide. Around the perimeter of the courtyard, spaced every few yards, were traps for killing extra-large rodents. A snowy-haired gent wearing epaulets and white gloves met us at the back door and escorted us up, his Aqua Velva like a weather system in the narrow, creaky elevator.

And once the service door opened, the color meter flipped again, and we were in the kitchen of a radiant apartment that opened out into further rooms of amber light, laughter, and what appeared to be hundreds of millions of dollars of modern paintings and sculpture. A philanthropist was having a small cocktail reception for a friend. By New York standards, the kitchen was ample, but there was only room enough for us and our half-proofer. (It was the one time I ever used a client's home oven.)

A man in the kitchen introduced himself as the host's secretary, requested all the names of the kitchen and service staff, and recorded them in a notepad. I suspected this was a security measure, but he emerged twenty minutes later with a stack of checks. Before I'd assembled my first platter of Diced Lobster, Lemon Mayonnaise, Fresh Dill on Brioche Round, I had a tip for two hundred dollars in my breast pocket.

"Old-school," Patrick said to me in a hushed tone. "Before 2008, a lot more people rolled like this."

The hostess's staff had worked with our crew dozens of times over the years and they chatted as if this were a family reunion—about their various auditions, children, hairstyles changed since the last event. This kind of bonhomie was atypical; that night New York City felt more like a village, if only for a couple of hours. Most private parties this small brought with them an extra level of scrutiny and anxiety.

But by far the most memorable party that first year was a large gala that threatened to jump the shark in its sophistication and theatricality. At $2,000 a head, it was designed to inspire "disorientation and fear" in its 465 lucky guests. Patrick had asked me to come before the prep shift ended to help him pack out, and in the taxi to the venue he filled me in on the particulars. It was the most extravagant party of New York's fall social season that year and, he believed, the most important of his catering career. But he had legitimate fears that it would be a cringing, career-ending shitshow, despite numerous planning meetings he'd taken with the designer David Monn and his team. Monn, one of New York's most prominent and extravagant event designers,* was calling this party

---

* "The Three Davids," in New York City, refers to three designers, all competing for the same high-end, high-concept business: David Beahm, David Monn, and David Stark.

his first-ever performance art piece, evoking "the darkness of the moment before creation." As we crept across town in the cab, Patrick handed me a copy of the program, a sleek black pamphlet with the words "IN THE VOID" printed in bold block capitals. I opened the cover and read:

> *We begin life in the ultimate void, a womb . . . "In the Void" is an artistic expression of inevitable voids we encounter throughout our lives. Dark lonely periods, surrounded both by nurturing forces and the surprises we encounter, as we struggle, work, and evolve toward the light of self-actualization and connection.*

"It gets better," he said. "There's a six-hundred-foot-long table snaking across the room that represents your umbilical cord. To remind guests of their journey from 'the ultimate void—the *womb*!'"

The menu opposite these notes was more grounding than the précis: Frisée Salad, Pecorino, Cipollini Onion, with Bacon Marmalade; Braised Lamb Shank with Winter Greens and Huckleberry Jus; Vanilla Bean Pot de Crème. The three courses seemed straightforward, bordering on safe, to me, but Patrick broke down the daunting and odd logistics he was confronting: the table effectively divided the room in half; so, to find their seats, each couple had to split up at one end of the room and take separate paths, following the umbilical cord for several minutes until they found their place cards, rejoining each other across the divide of the tablecloth. This choreography was guaranteed to inflate the usual fifteen minutes it takes to get chatting guests seated (without taking into account the dining room being nearly pitch-black). As for the waitstaff, the poor souls would be covered head-to-toe in black body stockings, Morph-automatons instructed to march out from the east entrance to the floor—without speaking, without changing stride—drop their plates, and exit at the opposite end of the hall. Patrick had calculated the pickup/drop/pickup round-trip as nearly six minutes, so even with twenty waiters working each side, the first guest would get her lamb shank nearly a half hour before the last—making dining together on warm food and leaving before midnight virtually impossible.

The dark cloud hanging over all catered dinners is *simultaneity of service*—the expectation that everyone in the room will be served the same thing at about the same time. It's the unavoidable compromise every catering chef has to embrace, knowing that everyone will most likely *not* be served at once, but within a twenty-minute window, more or less (ideally less). Guests shouldn't be put in a position to envy one another any more than they already do, lest mutinies develop. At the very least, those who can see others dining before them become disheartened, and at the worst they cause a ruckus—if word makes it back to the hosts, then caterers may get excluded from the running for next year's gala. In preproduction meetings with Monn's team, Patrick had raised the potential doomsday scenarios, trying to get everyone reckoning with reality. For starters: wouldn't visibility be a problem for the servers? With catsuit-covered eyes, in a hall dark as the womb, wouldn't they bump into one another? And their mandate to be mute— what if a guest had an allergy or a question? On top of all that, the dessert course was to be served by waiters on Citi Bikes—imagine the potential accidents there!—followed by a sudden and deafening *CRACK!*, like thunder and lightning, at the same time a wall of fog two feet high would envelop everyone, along with 180 dancers from the Alvin Ailey American Dance Theater streaming into the room to perform. This amount of raw stimulus-in-the-dark could not end well.

"This is not a young, hip crowd," Patrick pointed out. "One of these geezers is going to have a heart attack. I just know it."

As if on cue, he started punching his own chest with his fist—which I recognized was Patrick's pneumothorax acting up. After the first couple of parties I worked, I asked how he and Juan Soto projected the utmost chill even in super-stressful situations. Patrick explained: a catering chef quickly learns that an expression of panic is like a drop of blood in the shark tank. As soon as a party planner, or a host, or the people on your crew see you sweat or lose your cool, *they* start freaking out, and then their coworkers, until the entire system breaks down. He said the only sign he was really stressed was a mild swelling in the lining of his lungs that sent sharp pains through his chest. These shallow thumps he self-administered to his thorax, just beneath the notice of most of his staff, helped ease the pain.

I also knew that underneath his cool demeanor Patrick was warm and earnest, almost to a fault. On one of our subway trips back to Brooklyn, he'd filled me in on how he'd transitioned from cooking in a trattoria in Italy to catering. After the Piemontese idyll assisting Andrew, Patrick returned to the East Coast, to Trinity College, where he was an older student on financial aid, devoted to social justice, hanging out with professors who'd been South African dissidents and lobbying Connecticut legislators on behalf of food banks in Bridgeport. Upon graduation he was awarded a fellowship at Amnesty International in New York and moved to Brooklyn with Megan Fitzroy, whom he'd met at the Hartford brasserie where he grilled thousands of rib eyes and strip steaks to cover tuition bills. She'd been the pastry chef and had caught him stealing a chocolate truffle.

Soon after they'd moved to Brooklyn, Meg—fastidious, disciplined, talented—found a position at a four-star French restaurant. When Patrick's fellowship ended, he hoped to find a job in advocacy, but in the meantime he needed money for living expenses, so a colleague of Meg's secured him a meeting with Neal Gallagher, Sonnier & Castle's executive chef at the time.

Patrick's interview with Gallagher was extremely short. "Do you work fast?" he asked. "Do you use both your hands?"

Patrick nodded.

"Great. Don't fuck up," he replied. "You start tomorrow as a junior chef, $13.50 an hour."

His first day there, a sous-chef dropped a case of butternut squash next to him and said, "Dice this." He hadn't held a knife for a few years, so within an hour he developed a blister, and by the afternoon it had burst, spattering blood all over his cutting board. Nevertheless, within days, Gallagher assigned him to pastry and bumped his pay up to $15 an hour. Once he saw Patrick's work ethic, Gallagher piled on responsibilities, like programming the kitchen assistant, chef, and driver schedules. Patrick and Meg both kept crazy hours, hauling back to Brooklyn on snowy nights at two o'clock in the morning only to get up and start over again at six. Just eighteen months later, Patrick would replace Gallagher in the top job.

When we arrived at the site, we met up with the Soto brothers' crew, watching through the massive open loading bay for Angel's white box truck to appear on Lexington. We were thirty-odd souls in black rubber clogs, puffy parkas with backpacks, jittery as a pail of eels—and I was the only one, besides

Patrick, who knew what insanity awaited us. Every minute the truck wasn't there was a minute of setup time we were losing. Patrick called to Juan, "All right, let's do assignments. Get everyone close."

"*Ven aquí! Muchachos!*" Juan shouted out, and our crew shuffled in tighter.

"This is the most important party you'll work this fall," Patrick called out to the team. He ran down the play-by-play, pausing every so often for Juan to finish translating. There'd be three kitchens tonight—the hors d'oeuvres and two mains. Each main kitchen would serve exactly half the room, 235 people: salad, main course, and dessert. He handed the lead chef for each kitchen—Wilmer Rodriguez in hors d'oeuvres, Juan Soto in Main 1, and Jorge Soto in Main 2—their own folders with the kitchen layouts and party grids (the dish descriptions, with notes on ingredients, allergies, and substitutions).

"*Marilu!*" he shouted. "You're in H.D., good to have you back. *Pélos!* Where are you, Pélos? You're in Main 1!"

Patrick knew he had a reputation in the business as a decent guy to work for. He chalked it up partly to the social-justice training at Trinity, but beyond the bona fides was a bottom-line benefit: being a good guy lowered his labor cost. He knew half a dozen competing shops run by screamers and psychos and believed his being humane resulted in savings: "You'd work for me for two, three dollars less an hour," he told me, "if the other guy's an asshole, right?" And since his own end-of-year bonus partly depended upon meeting labor-cost targets, his management style not only saved Sonnier & Castle money—it put more cash in his own pocket.

That didn't mean he was above a little fearmongering,

especially when the stakes were high. Once he'd finished up the assignments, he held up his phone and turned to Juan.

"Make sure they get this," he said, and then louder, addressing the whole crew: "If I see you touch your phone from now until load-out—I don't care how long you've worked fiesta for me—you're *gone*."

Assigned to Jorge's kitchen, I was slightly chagrined, partly because Juan's the better teacher and also because Juan's kitchen was the one Monn's team was working out of. Kitchen 1 was Mission Control and I wanted to be there. Over the course of a dozen parties, I'd witnessed some hairy moments—a dolly with hundreds of parfaits in glassware crates toppling over; a mid-gala text to Patrick from the client: *If this is S&C's idea of service, maybe we're a bad fit.* As an employee, I dreaded the disasters, but as a student of catering, I found them just the kind of high drama that can ensue only in off-premise work. I wanted to be there when this careening shitshow of a party plan came crashing down. Fine for someone as well compensated as Monn to dream big and tip at windmills, ignoring the cautions of a practitioner with Patrick's experience. But for him to do so over the bodies and livelihoods of the servers and catering workers seemed to me to be sadistic. From what I'd learned thus far, "In the Void" looked to be particularly jejune and ill-conceived.

Scattered whistles and applause rang out when Angel's truck at last clattered into view, backing up ever so carefully into the bay—its piercing *beeeep-beeeep-beeeep* amplifying as it finally crossed the threshold into the venue. The crew swarmed the tailgate and, in short order, Juan and Patrick were inside the truck, sliding first the giant white coolers and red plastic dry packs to the edge of the box, shouting out the locations written on their labels: "Kitchen 1!" "H.D.!" "Bar 3!" A service captain showed up with a gang of waiters—their limp black body stockings hanging over one shoulder, or tied like scarves around their necks—to collect coolers of ice and plastic crates of bar equipment. From their nervous laughter and banter, I could sense they dreaded their transformation to come.

When it was my turn at the tailgate, Juan spun a tall hotbox around. "*Virginia!*" he said. "Kitchen 2, right?" He held the cabinet, labeled "Carne—Kit 2—235," in place at the edge of the lift gate as Patrick rolled a second into position, then lowered hundreds of pounds of food to the ground. Valentìn and I moved 235 portions of lamb shank through the building, seesawing the proofer's clattering casters over electrical cables, maneuvering around the black-clad lighting crews and Monn's squad in their party-dresses-with-shouldered-cardigans. Curtains separating the floor from the wings were pulled back in places and I could see silhouettes of figures out on the floor, carrying penlights to find their way around. Hundreds of near-invisible wires hung from above, each strung with white oak leaves, which, illuminated by pinpoint spotlights, appeared like a screen of falling snow, frozen in a moment. In the minimal light reflected by the suspended leaves, I could see that the scrim of leaves traced the undulation of that single, serpentine dinner table Patrick was so concerned about. Whatever it was, it was breathtakingly awesome, and my pulse quickened a beat.

We rolled the hotbox into our kitchen, where prep tables were arranged in three long parallel lines at one end of the room, with narrow aisles in between. Eddie and Marilu were laying down the first-course plates on the tables three across, so the rims of outer plates hung over the edges by an inch or more. We rolled our hotbox down one aisle, careful not to hit any of those cantilevered plates, and parked it at the back of the room with the others.

Jorge Soto had tapped Luis to be his hotbox deputy, so Luis stayed close to the proofers containing the main-course items, shuttling sheet pans of the preportioned lamb shank, spaetzle, and winter greens in their foil cups, spacing them out into zones, like with like. He stacked all 235 dinner plates in a single proofer and fired it up with three or four Sternos to take the chill off. The rest of us fell in on the salad-course coolers, pulling out plastic quart containers of pecorino shards and aluminum pans of greens, shouting out their contents as Jorge checked items off the party grid.

Patrick appeared in our kitchen to build the sample plate of the first-course salad. A walkie-talkie hung from his hip pocket, its earpiece coiling up to his cranium, a microphone clipped to his placket. His shoulder clapped his cell phone to his other ear, checking in with somebody—likely sous-chef Tyler, helming an intimate dinner that night at the town house of a star architect in Greenwich Village; or Ryan, a junior chef leading a cocktail reception for 130 in the lobby of a skyscraper in Jersey City. Jorge had set up a station for Patrick, who holstered his phone, then tossed handfuls of frisée and arugula into the bowl. He teased a glob of bacon jam on top, rubbing it around the bowl with bare fingers until it warmed up and slickened the greens.

Patrick layered the leaves on the sample plate just so, a cascade of greens that appeared to have dropped from the very air but took twelve steps to prepare, an organic sculpture about six inches tall: a tangle of frisée; scattering of arugula; three half-moons of shaved Granny Smith; the dressed frisée-arugula mix; two more slices of apple; more undressed arugula; three thin shavings of pecorino over the top. As he laid the elements, his hands gently plumped and primped. He lifted the plate to eye level, stared at it from the side, set it back down, and pulled out an errant stalk of frisée. Then garnishes: a pinch of smoked Maldon salt, a scatter of purplish micro-amaranth, a drizzle of electric-green olive oil. He seemed to be in another world as he belabored this little salad plate amid the motion and chaos, and I recalled that discussing his music career, he professed to prefer recording in the studio to performing live. *Pitchfork*'s review of his album *Cost* (7.1 out of 10) had praised the minimal, essential, deliberate character of his music.*

For a second he gazed upward toward the ceiling, as if trying to remember something; overhead, paint peeled precariously in sheets and a few missing panels exposed a snarl of ducts, wires, and insulation. He thumped his chest, tapped the mic on his lapel: "Forty-five minutes 'til H.D. serve-out, Wilmer. *Rapido!* Copy?"

He turned back to regard his salad hero. "Okay, guys, we have our sample."

Jorge motioned for all the K.A.s to come take a look. "*Hermosa, señor!*" he said, a blade of sarcasm in his voice.

"Key here is lift," Patrick said. "Throw out any slimy arugula leaves. And don't crush the greens when you drop the apple and pecorino. *Lift.*"

We set to work on the salad in pairs. First course is almost

---

* "Phelan gives no quarter to superfluous vocals or disorganized arrangements. He lays out his quietly dissonant melodies in transparent, sequential lines, and his vocals—stoically emotive and unapologetically human—become the centerpiece of any song they inhabit."—Brian Howe, *Pitchfork*, March 22, 2006.

always a room-temperature dish—it has to be. Because unlike an hors d'oeuvre or buffet, where you can assemble your dishes in groups on platters, continuously, over the duration of service, a plated first course is the same dish served simultaneously. When the dish involves numerous elements, like this overthought salad, it has to be assembled layer by layer, by a team. It requires coordination and mobility—and plenty of real estate.

Standard prep tables are twenty-four inches wide and most first-course plates are nine inches in diameter. You can fit three across and eight down the length—twenty-four per table—if they're laid down so the outer plates hang a couple of inches off each side, an element of risk that makes the entire enterprise more compact, flexible, and fast. If you have 235 plates to serve, you need room in the kitchen for at least eleven tables with enough space in between for your workers. If there's room for only a table or two, workarounds exist, like transferring plates as they're completed to jack-stands, a.k.a. "plate towers"—six-foot-tall, four-sided racks on casters, that will fit a total of 104 plates vertically in three square feet of floor space. A far more risky option is to stack standard prep tables on top of tables, double-deckered, but this latter scenario is beyond dangerous: an errant elbow would take down not only all the plates of the table above, but also those on the table below. Still, I'd seen it done.

Jorge assigned me and Mini the shaved Granny Smith apple slices, and we got in sequence with the pecorino droppers and frisée slickeners. It was repetitive, but there was a certain satisfaction in the exactitude and the continuity, the plates gradually building up in my field of vision. Valentìn and Marilu swept behind the apple crew with huge salad bowls, setting down tufts of dressed salad, the core of the dish. The labor calculus of all of this was extraordinary, eight or ten K.A.s building salads leaf by leaf. Why not a fall *soup*? All you'd need to garnish would be drops of a finishing oil, maybe a scattering of spiced pumpkin seeds—most of the labor would be concentrated in the prep kitchen at only 10 bucks an hour instead of $25 per for the eight people we had. Maybe this was too extravagant a ticket for guests to encounter a soup? I guess at some point a kitchen has to deliver on the expectations of a $2,000 seat, whatever the labor cost. Still, at this rate, getting 235 hand-crafted salads, with *lift*, took ten K.A.s more than an hour.

The team had moved on to garnishes—the purple amaranth sprouts and olive oil—when a piercing cackle-shriek of laughter erupted at the far end of the room. Servers streamed in wearing black bodysuits, the goth-Martians gathering in the area where the sanitation crew had set up coffee stations in front of a wall of pink plastic glassware crates. Their form-hugging body stockings left nothing to the imagination, and the entire room—the kitchen assistants, sanit guys, the waiters themselves—erupted in guffawing and whistling, until a service captain, Michael Alge, suddenly appeared on the scene.

"*PEOPLE! PEOPLE!* I need you to be *adults*," he bellowed. "Five minutes 'til the floor opens and I want it *quiet*!" But even he couldn't suppress laughter; it was absurd and it took several minutes for the room to settle.

Patrick arrived to check on the first course after peace was restored. He walked down the length of the tables, scanning plates and squatting down every so often to survey the lift.

"What happened here, Jorge?" he asked, picking up two plates that looked flat. "These won't work, my friend." He dumped them in a trash barrel and handed the dirty plates to Jorge. "Redo these two and you're fine. I'll get Michael to call for the pickup."

Patrick started toward the doorway, eyes on the ranks of the salad plates, nary a glance toward the *zentai*. Then he abruptly turned back. "Jorge, I need one of your guys to expo* Juan's kitchen," he said. Jorge surveyed the available talent and nodded toward me. The word "expediter" sounds impressive, but I'd been in this role in a main-course plating line several times before. In a restaurant, an expediter is typically the most senior chef on the premises, standing at the pass adding final garnishes and making sure everything heading to the floor looks the way it should. In a plating line for a catered dinner, where speed is paramount, the expediter typically wipes errant smudges and fingerprints, a position you give your lowest-ranking *manos*. I didn't care; it meant I was headed to Kitchen 1, exactly where I wanted to be to observe this party at full tilt.

I caught up with Patrick in the wing and kept pace with him, walking around the perimeter to Main Kitchen 1. When we passed in front of the loading bay, the Party Rental Ltd. box truck was parked outside and a runner was shuffling in from the truck carrying two pink crates full of plates.

"*Hey, buddy!*" Patrick called out. "Is that my re-run? Dessert plates?"

He grabbed one crate; I grabbed the other.

When we arrived in Juan's kitchen, a line of tall, sleek, black-clad servers were waiting, a salad in each hand, listen-

---

* Expedite: in a restaurant, the expediter hands a completed plate from the kitchen off to the waitstaff to deliver to the table.

132

ing for the captain's signal. The audience of gala-goers in their black dinner jackets and dresses had been seated without a hiccup. As we headed to the back of the room, I said something in Patrick's direction to the effect that it all appeared promising to me: the pieces of this catering puzzle seemed to be fitting into place.

"Let's not get ahead of ourselves," he said after dropping the crate of plates, thumping his chest, and swallowing hard. "Shit doesn't hit the road 'til they start picking up the main."

I watched in silence with Patrick for a few moments as the first salads went out, the Martians silently goose-stepping into the hall with their lofty charges. Then I fell in with the kitchen team, sliding plates down the tables to the pickup, where the stream of returning waiters grabbed for another pair and peeled off toward the floor. And once all 235 frisée salads were gone, the crew transformed the room into the main-course plating line, pushing tables to form a large T that extended out from the proofers lined up against the back wall of the room.

"*Chilango,*"* Juan Soto called to me. He opened one of the proofers, where the Sternos' blue flames wobbled beneath sheet pans. The last event we'd worked together, he'd shown me how to preheat a pan so a sheet of plastic wrap pulled across the top shrank on contact with the hot metal rim, sealing the food in a steamy bubble that brought everything to a safe serving temperature. He slid a sheet pan halfway out; beneath its ballooning, steamed-up wrap were the main-course lamb shanks

---

* A term of endearment he used with all his charges that literally means "resident of Mexico City."

in their preportioned foil cups. He poked an index finger at the tensioned plastic. "You see," he crowed. "Perfect."

Juan knew dozens of clever hotbox tricks, fixes, holds, and fakes, and often had to utilize them to solve the prep crew's mistakes. For this fiesta, they'd packed out the lamb with so much *huckleberry jus* in each cup that it would have flooded the plate when the K.A.s inverted it. So he and Geronimo had had to strain the 235 portions of almost all their purply-brown gravy. And the pieces of lamb in some cups were thick as loins, so they'd had to pull each one apart into smaller morsels. How could anyone stay ahead of all these details, on deadline, in real time? For Juan, every save, every errant detail remedied, was an energizing point of pride.

"Donde micros?" he asked after a while. He'd mapped out the plating line and assigned me microgreens—garnish. No surprise there; I was still *"manos"* to him. I fetched two small plastic clamshells of arugula sprouts from the cooler and set them at the end of the line closest to the entrance to the floor. He scrawled in black permanent Sharpie directly on Party Rental Ltd.'s tablecloth everyone's name and their "drop," starting closest to the proofer and moving down the line: *Sergio/Spatz; Pelos/Carne; Roxy/Verduras; Dutch/Salsa; Virginia/Micros.* He marked up the opposite side of the long table and all ten of us fell into our positions.

The black catsuits began filing back into the kitchen, dropping dirty, mostly empty salad plates at the sanit station—a sign we were near go time for the main course. Dutch tightened down the valve on his German funnel—the finest of catering tools,* an ingenious conical "sauce gun" with a

---

* Also called a "confectionery funnel."

spring-loaded valve for drip-free pouring with a trigger thumb. Across the table, Marilu folded paper towels into plate wipes, dipping them into a container of water, and passed me a stack. Juan reached into his proofers to retrieve a clean plate and three foil cups and began building the sample: spaetzle first; lamb shank jauntily on top and to the side; winter greens in the crook. A squirt of sauce from the funnel made a gentle arc over the top. I sent a few pinches of microgreens down the line and Juan plucked a pinch for his garnish and popped the rest in his mouth. He walked the plate down the line so we could all inspect it and dropped it at the pickup just as Patrick appeared.

"*Bueno*, my friend," was Patrick's judgment.

A service captain nicknamed Panda herded his troops into a single-file line down the hall from the pickup and passed out black napkins to protect their hands from the lava-hot china.

Geronimo hoisted a stack of plates out of the proofer and clanged them down at the top of the line. And then everything happened fast. Patrick said, "Go!" and Geronimo and Juan passed sheet pans full of food down the line. All heads bowed. Sergio picked up the first plate, inverted his foil cup of spaetzle, nudged it to his left, reached for another. Patrick got into position at the top of the "T" to watch the first plates come off the line.

"Lighter on the garnish," he said.

Only about five plates had gone out when we heard a shout—"*Shit!*"—followed by a deafening crash. Two plates of the main course had smashed to the floor at Patrick's feet.

Everyone froze, focused on a waiter whose face we couldn't even see.

"Plates are too *hot*!" the waiter squealed.

"Did you double up the napkin?" Panda shot back at him. A sanit guy had already swooped in to clean up the wreckage.

"Nothing to see here," Patrick said. "Keep the line moving, people."

"Make sure your linens are doubled up *before* you pick up, please!" Panda shouted.

The assembly line started up again and kept moving, twenty more plates or so, until Patrick shouted, "*Stop!*" There were no morphs to pick up plates, and about a dozen main courses partially assembled on the line. Patrick looked down the hall, looking for servers, and pinched his mic. "Chef to Michael. Your servers need to be *sprinting* back here, okay? Food's not getting any warmer."

A minute or two more ticked down, and then a gaggle of morphs appeared in the distance. Patrick shouted down the hall. "Pick *up*, please! You guys need to get back here faster!"

More waiters appeared and our plating line lurched back to life.

Patrick looked at me, said sotto voce, "If they start returning plates to be rewarmed we're fucked."

As if on cue, one of the party planner's associates, a willowy blonde with an English accent, called from the threshold of the kitchen door, "*Chef!* We've had complaints of *lukewarm* food!"

Patrick thumped his chest. "*On it!*" he shouted back.

A few minutes passed, and she stepped back through the door again. Our line had paused again, waiting for servers. The British woman called out, "Chef, can we *please* hurry this along?"

"*Speeding up!*" he replied, then tapped the mic on his lapel: "Chef to Michael. Your waiters need to *run. FASTER!*"

Moments like this, as I sprinkle sprouts, I return to a nagging question: what kind of person *chooses* this as a nightly drill? Why not work in a restaurant, where the challenges are in a barrel for the shooting? Sure there's a ticket printer spitting out orders, slamming a line for a time, but at least the pressure to deliver food gets spread out over a bell curve each night rather than a few hair-raising, all-or-nothing spikes. As I got to know Patrick better, I sifted his background for possible answers. His father was in army logistics and quite the martinet; before Patrick was fourteen years old, they'd moved twenty-three times—to places as different as Hawaii, Germany, and Kansas. But he claimed that hadn't fazed him.

"I loved the idea of reinventing myself," he'd told me in an off-duty interview. "By the time I'd made close friends, I found myself in some sort of trouble and it was time to move on." And he noted his early exposure to a withering form of discipline might be why he stayed sure-footed amid the chaos of high-end catering.

He was keenly aware of the wages of the itinerant life. By Patrick's junior year of high school, his family had seemed to finally land somewhere permanent, in a D.C. suburb in Virginia. His three older siblings graduated and gone, Patrick and his mother began unpacking, but within a few months his father announced he'd been denied promotion to general by the army, and he departed the following day for a United Nations posting in Cambodia. At first, the commander communicated sporadically, then never. One day Patrick was mowing the lawn, listening to the Melvins on his Discman, when a Jeep with a "UN" logo on the door, driven by a guy in a blue helmet, pulled up. His father got out of the passenger side, gave him a cursory wave, and walked inside the house. Patrick continued mowing until his father emerged, walked back to the Jeep, and with a single word, "Good-bye," left his son's life for two decades. His mother told him they had four days to pack up the house. She left for California to live with a sister there for a stretch, and Patrick moved in with a friend's family and threw himself into making music. He'd started a band, Plush Velour; they had a killer light show and were playing regularly, opening for his heroes Slobber Jaw and Pope Joan.

Numerous times I'd seen Patrick make the best of a situation that might easily crush someone lacking his drive and resilience. As much as he could get frustrated, infuriated even, by catering, he also professed to having big ideas for the industry's future. He'd met a software developer about an app that centralized chef, waiter, and kitchen assistant bookings and leveraged social media to incentivize worker performance and team building. But there was another dream in play, too, as the intermittently flailing plating line of "In the Void" threatened to derail his career. He'd confessed that he and Megan had a yen to quit New York City entirely, to settle down and start a family. Andrew had by now married an Italian woman, Valentina Giordano, and they planned to move to Richmond in the coming summer to raise their child. Patrick and Meg had a dream of partnering with them on a restaurant—a warm, glowing, modern room in an old brick building.

"*Chef*, we need special meals now!" It was the British woman again, like a bullhorn. "Twenty-two vegetarian!"

Patrick looked to Juan.

"I got you, *Papi. Tranquilo.*" Juan had set up a couple of proofers' worth of the silent vegetarian option, Acorn Squash with Moroccan Vegetables, Spiced Tofu, and Israeli Couscous, plated, ready for its pinch of sprouts and squirt of apricot sauce.

And in the meantime, the waiters in their black Lycra had found their stride. Patrick cajoled our plating line to a faster rhythm. He needed the guests to love this food and this party so when the gala board met for their postmortem, they'd sign on with Monn for next year, and Monn, if things went right, would book Sonnier & Castle.

Despite the evening's numerous risks and absurdities, at the end of the night Patrick's team had, in his own parlance, *crushed it.* No mutiny had broken out, no bicycle accidents, no heart attacks—no guest had suffered an indignity worse than lukewarm lamb. By 10:30 p.m., Patrick dismissed most of his crew, and only he, Juan, and I remained to serve dinner for Monn and his team. They were loudly delirious with happiness, even the Brit. Everything had been *brilliant*: food, music, dancers, the harpist on the platform spun around the room by dancers, the Citi Bikes, the *CRACK* of lightning, the fog machine. And when the room settled, Monn called Patrick over to talk with him privately. He told him they'd reached a new height together. Monn had pushed himself to become the artist he always knew he could be, and he was grateful to have a chef who understood and could execute his vision. New meetings were already in the works. There was plenty more business to come.

But by 11:30 p.m., with only a handful of union electricians

139

and Sonnier & Castle's three-man sanitation crew left in the building, Patrick and I were still there, checking the numbers and condition of the hotboxes, the coolers, the dry packs of utensils, towels and aprons, making sure everything would make it back to the prep kitchen. Two large plastic lugs the ice arrived in had gone missing. Party Rental Ltd. would be collecting its stuff first thing in the morning.

I'd heard that most executive chefs leave parties as soon as the last main-course plate hits the table, but Patrick wasn't that guy. Still, it seemed that any sane person might weigh the value of a couple of plastic containers against a food and beverage budget of hundreds of thousands of dollars (which on that successful night would yield donations of hundreds of thousands more) and have left those lugs behind for the angels. Nearing midnight, the heavy black curtains came down, revealing the snaking table taken apart, in pieces stacked on the floor. The chairs were in neat towers in a corner. And Patrick finally found the lugs. So we left.

By the numbers, "In the Void" was an enormous success. Media coverage and word of mouth were unprecedented for the charity, and Monn got contracted to do the gala the next year. He rebooked Sonnier to do the food the following October for a guest count that had nearly doubled, to 785, on the success of "In the Void."

But as it happened, by then Patrick and Meg had already been in Richmond for a few months, focused on their restaurant dream, and with a child on the way.

The term, used since the 1980s, refers to the art of improvisation in the catering business. Here are a few of the classics used in the heat of battle.

Forgot a strainer?
Poke a bunch of holes in the bottom of an aluminum foil pan with a skewer or a ball-point pen.

Forgot the whisk?
Flatten a foil pan lid. Roll it up lengthwise into a dowel shape. Cut strips in one end with a chef's knife or kitchen scissors. Splay ends slightly.

No foil? Head to coat check and grab two metal coat hangers and reshape into something resembling a whisk.

Forgot a flour sifter? Or a shaker for confectioners' sugar?
Find a wicker bread basket or a basket from a floral display.

Pots and pans already packed on the truck and you need to cook a parting snack for the host?
Place a sheet pan directly over the lit Sterno for searing or reheating, and cover the food with an upturned mixing bowl or sheet of plastic wrap.

No rope or string?
Scrunch and twist plastic wrap, of the length you need. It's even flame resistant after an initial shrink.

No refrigerator?
The bottom shelves of a hotbox, with a sheet pan of crushed ice or dry ice placed just above the food, will keep very cold, even with warm zones operating above, in the same box.

No honing steel?
Run the edge of the knife briskly along the handle edge of a metal serving spoon or ladle.

Meat slicer overheating?
Drape two plastic bags filled with ice and tied together over each side of the slicer's motor.

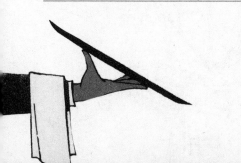

7

The Big Pink Hippo

Taking the Measure of Event Rentals' Category Killer

Long after the conversation dies and the valiant caterers have gone home, there's a final act that truly signifies the party is over. A truck pulls up at the site in the middle of the night (or the next morning) to haul away the borrowed tables and chairs, dirty plates and linens, glasses and other hardware that helped transform an empty space into something resembling a restaurant. You've seen a truck like this, even if it escaped your notice. Those who live anywhere on the Eastern Seaboard of the United States, between Portland, Maine, and Virginia Beach (and back a good two hundred miles inland from the coast), may in fact be familiar with this specific truck because the category killer in party rentals in that region is represented by a large cartoon hippopotamus a shade lighter than Pepto-Bismol. Written alongside the hippo is PARTY RENTAL LTD., an anodyne name that doesn't even begin to reveal the encyclopedic range of *things* you can have dropped on your doorstep tomorrow. Need a cotton candy machine? How about white leather lounge seating for 250 people? A commercial refrigerator? Four—or four thousand—gilt forks? A fifty-foot extension cord, a coatrack, a FryDaddy? It's got tablecloths and tables, platters and plates, in a riot of styles and colors, one hundred or more of each pattern.

Party Rental Ltd. has built its lending business to serve virtually everyone. For a generalist in such a giant business, there's no approaching this halfway or even three-quarters: your stash of stuff has to be the Mount Everest of inventories, an old-school Amazon; you have to offer *every damn thing* a client would need—except tents, it doesn't rent tents—in every possible color and quantity, deliverable in one order. Human nature favors single sources for the boring necessities like chairs, trash cans, and plates; there isn't a party planner in the world who would prefer to make four phone calls, place four orders, if they could get it all affordably with one. Party Rental Ltd. is the leader in rentals in its lucrative chosen region, and has by its massive scale—built up steadily since 1972—prevented any meaningful competition. To re-create its inventory would require a capital investment too large to contemplate.

Another secret to its success is being warm and cuddly to clients—accommodating and personable, and permissive, willing to work with ridiculously last-minute orders and to overlook a lost ice lug or two. Customers spending $250,000 and up in a year represent 80 percent of its business, but Party Rental Ltd. is nevertheless more than happy to deliver to *you*, too, any of the more than ninety thousand separate SKUs (stock-keeping units) in its catalog. All it takes to rent from the company is to meet the minimum order of $325 and to pay the delivery-and-pickup fee—a flat $100 surcharge to most locations in the ten states serviced. To give you an idea of how much $325 represents in rental terms, let's create an imaginary event: you're cooking a special supper at home for a friend's fortieth birthday. There will be sixteen diners (including you) and it's a cocktail reception and dinner, with some easy hors d'oeuvres you've prepared, and four courses—a first course, a main course, a salad, and dessert. You're serving sparkling wine with the hors d'oeuvres and there will be a choice of red and white wine on the tables, and water. For $394.06, you'll have almost everything you need save the food and drink: two round tables for eight plus the tablecloths and matching overlay, all the chairs, the cloth napkins, the plates, the flatware, stemware (four glasses per person, including champagne flute, water glass, and two wineglasses), and the paper cocktail napkins for the canapés you're serving during the first hour. And the champagne chiller, of course!

A total of $494.06 ($30.88 per person) gets you a lot of material hauled to your door, clean and ready for party time, and then picked up the next day. And if that sounds pricey for rentals—it's not *nothing*, after all, and you don't get to keep any of it (except any unused paper napkins)—bear in mind that the fact that you don't means you also weren't obligated to store it, either. And there's this: you don't need to clean any of it! You don't even have to scrape the plates—although the drivers who pick up the rentals the day after your dinner (not to mention the warehouse team that receives those food-slickened plates) would very likely appreciate it.

"You talk about a *dirty* job?" Jim McManus bellowed, as he ushered us across the noisy receiving floor of PRL's 275,000-square-foot warehouse in Teterboro, New Jersey—the company headquarters and the largest of the company's five warehouses from D.C. to New England. It was late May 2016, spring gala season was mostly over, but as he waved his arm languidly across ten loading bays, half a dozen trucks were backed up, feasted upon by forklifts and warehouse workers, unloading the last of the previous day's parties, pushing battered proofers and rolling round tables into the warehouse. "*Everything* needs to be cleaned. Everything," he continued. "And you should see the caked-on dirty dishes—the *shit!*—that our people have to deal with, day after day. We clean it, pack it, count it, wrap it—those dishes gotta be ready to go again for tomorrow."

McManus would be a shoo-in to play Santa Claus at the mall, but today he's playing the role of salty warehouse guide and rentals ambassador, wearing a voluminous pink gingham shirt over his Falstaffian frame. His thirty-year career as a rentals salesman—eighteen of those with Party Rental Ltd.—has revealed to him the full contours, and every nook and cranny, of this invisible business. Moreover, as someone playing a supporting role to every caterer's daily grind, and with an essential monopoly on party rentals in this part of the country, McManus knows virtually everything about everyone who caters. By processing their orders, he's privy to caterers' income and expenses. He knows who your clients are, and who your competitors' clients are. And that's just from the data in his phone; his gossip networks are unparalleled.

As the point person equipping the region's largest parties since the 1980s, Jim McManus has met everyone: chefs, event designers, lighting designers, florists, the hosts and hostesses. He's experienced every conceivable circumstance in catering—witnessed all the epic failures, all the bad behavior—and it doesn't diminish his excitement about rentals one iota: he thrills to the minutiae and the splendor, fueling story upon story, which he offers up to us freely while cursing like a sailor.

In fact, McManus is a sailor, and spends most weekends piloting his twenty-eight-foot sloop, *Sea Yanker*, with his mutt, Rodney, and a crew of pals around Peconic and Gardiners Bays on the East End of Long Island. The son of a dentist, he grew up in West Hampton, where his first job as a kid was delivery boy for a gourmet grocer, ferrying caviar and prime meats to mansions in the Hamptons, kibbitzing at the kitchen door with the personal chefs for New York's wealthiest. After studying ancient religions as a philosophy major at the University of Wisconsin, he moved to New Orleans and washed dishes in the kitchen of Paul Prudhomme at the fabled Commander's Palace. With a letter of recommendation from Commander's owners the Brennans, McManus attended Cornell School of Hotel Administration. In 1990 he got his first job as a salesman in party rentals, working for Broadway Famous Party Rental, in Bedford-Stuyvesant, Brooklyn. Riding out the 1990 recession at Broadway Famous Party Rental, he learned an important lesson that would allow him to weather rough times—9/11, the collapse of Lehman Brothers—with relative peace of mind: because party rentals serves catering and events, primarily a luxury industry, it can endure rocky economic cycles more easily than businesses dependent upon a wider segment of the marketplace.

"When downturns happen, the mid-tier may taper off—the corporate stuff," McManus said, "but the social business continues. People who have money are still getting married, they're just much more private. In the Hamptons, they call it 'behind the hedgerow.' They're cautious about being grossly rich in front of people who are struggling. But what happens behind that hedge? *You. Don't. Know.*"

McManus worked for Broadway, the number two firm in the market at the time, doing roughly $1.4 million a year in sales, for ten years before being hired away by Party Rental Ltd. and witnessing the largest period of growth in the company, and in catering as a whole. Jim won't quote exact figures—PRL is still privately held—but in 1999, PRL was doing close to $15 million a year in sales; today, it likely logs well over ten times that, every year.

That's because, in addition to delivering the champagne bucket and the rest of your needs for the hypothetical birthday dinner for sixteen, once that truck leaves your house, it's throttling on to the next of literally *hundreds* of events PRL is supplying that night. There are approximately 170 trucks total in the company's fleet, and while six or eight parties' rentals may be packed onto the single truck that delivered your goods, there could also be one whopper on a given night—like the Robin Hood Benefit at the Javits Center, a cocktail reception and seated dinner for forty-four hundred, 440 round tables for ten—that alone requires twenty trucks' worth of rentals, four of which will be tractor-trailers carrying nothing but chairs. (The right to sit down in one of those chairs starts at about $3,000, and the evening will raise in the neighborhood of $50 million.)

Our tour through PRL's Teterboro warehouse began in the open office pen, where sales representatives guide customers through their orders and troubleshoot the balky ovens or cracked tureens that require a quick replacement—almost always at the witching hour, 4:30 p.m., when waiters and chefs show up at parties all over the city and begin to assess the rentals that were dropped off earlier that day.

The biggest change in the business in recent years, McManus pointed out, is that orders are coming in at the last minute instead of months ahead of time. As soon as he'd estimated that 60 percent of first order calls to PRL come in within three days of the event, a saleswoman overheard him and interrupted, pointing out that fully half of all orders come in just forty-eight hours before the equipment is needed. McManus acknowledged the role the company played in that reality.

"We created that need by being able to execute at that level, so now the industry just expects us to be there," he said, putting his hand on his hip. "'It's New York, baby, I want what I want and I'm willing to pay for it.' And that's why we are all so haggard."

Before passing into the working floor of the warehouse, we bumped into Franklin Brooks, the chief technician charged with overseeing heavy-duty items including ovens and refrigerators, the kinds of equipment that wasn't available to rent for the evening until McManus made it a priority nearly fifteen years ago. McManus introduced us to Brooks and launched into a story, which he punctuated with repeated jabs at Brooks's shoulder.

"Chefs are cooking a dinner, fifteen hundred people. They've got all the ovens, but ovens ain't fucking working. The party's in two hours, none of their food's heated up yet. These chefs are losing their minds! So they give him a call."

Brooks pointed out that the all-electric ovens ($425 to rent for a day; about $5,000 to purchase) are often the culprit, drawing too many amps—15—for the already overburdened electrical systems of ancient New York City buildings and household extension cords. Even the propane-powered ovens, deployed outside the city, require 6 amps just to power the fans and release the gas, which might be a tall order out in a corn-field, when the tent lights and the coffeemaker are sharing the same extension cord and breaker.

"They're not even thinking about it until the line goes *whoop!*" Brooks said.

"That's why even the greatest caterers, when they run into that, guess what they do?" McManus added. "They whip out the proofers and the Sterno and they cook it in the box, just like they used to. And the show goes on!"

The warehouse McManus led us through had no coherent sense of flow or scale—it was Wonkaesque, with narrower chambers at right angles to larger ones, open corrals set within truly gigantic spaces, and areas defined by walls of things, rather than actual walls. In one area a circular apparatus, a sheet-metal trough the size of an aboveground swimming pool, contained millions of silvery beads—it was a burnishing device that restores the glossy finish to tons of flatware every night. Just beyond was a room crisscrossed by poles, tracks, and sloped rods overhead, moving linens on hangers, essen-tially the largest dry cleaner you've ever seen. Some rooms were wide open—a cement football field with wooden chairs stacked twelve to fifteen feet high on the floor, most stacks sleeved in black cotton, some arcing slightly over the aisles.

Other halls contained racks twenty or thirty feet up, holding cubes of palletized chair cushions of a single color ("Bengaline Cerise" read one container of 288 purply-pink cushions), each tightly bound in plastic wrap. A room the size of an aircraft hangar was a babel of tablecloths sheathed in plastic, row upon row, on racks four rows high. The only organization to the tablecloth storage was the one remembered by a computer server: each tablecloth has a radio frequency ID chip sewn in that can be scanned to transmit its location, size, and details to the system. The 120-inch blue tablecloths aren't stored adjacent to each other, just where they happen to find an open spot on the way back into storage; the computer crafts a pick itinerary for the person assembling each outgoing order. On one long side of the same room are bolts of new cloth, tens of thousands of them, stacked to the ceiling, awaiting a custom cut and sew.

McManus paused for a moment, noting the sheer volume of options, and their insufficiency.

"As far as you can see, row after row after row. And even with all this shit, they want something *different*? That we have to *make*? We have all these other options that are right here in this warehouse, but *nooooooooooo*."

By "make," he meant custom tailor, which was the next stop on the tour, a room with a low ceiling and bright lights, where eighteen women were hunched over sewing machines, cutting and stitching up the hems of new tablecloths and napkins, to serve the clients for whom the selection of colors and patterns and weights and fabrics Party Rental Ltd. offers was simply not enough.

"I remember the meeting in 1989 where the question of the day was: can we introduce royal blue as a color in our cotton line?" McManus said. "The only options were white! And all square—we didn't even have round tablecloths in 1989, because they only rented the square overlays." Back then, he said, people who hosted grand parties owned their own antique tables, with beautiful wooden legs to show off. Today they're renting tables with steel legs that need to be hidden, so the tablecloths drape all the way to the floor.

As we exited the sewing room, his tone turned more conciliatory.

"Look, if I'm doing an event that's got fifty thousand dollars' worth of rental equipment and they need one tablecloth specially made to fit a special table? We're gonna do it. We'll say yes, but it'll cost you," he said. "And they'll say, Great! Because at the end of the day, the daughter only gets married once, and they happen to be very wealthy people, and they don't care to compromise. They just want what they want."

We passed the staging area where orders of chairs and crates of glasses were lined up and ready for loading onto trucks backed up to the twenty outgoing bays. "From three o'clock in the afternoon until six o'clock in the morning, we load, load, load," McManus said, raising his voice to be heard above the forklift backup sirens. We saw bar stools and martini glasses labeled for delivery to the Century Club in Midtown; Chiavari chairs and wineglasses for fashion designer Tory Burch's apartment; there were orders for Vassar College, the New York Public Library, Tarrytown Music Hall, the NeueHouse museum. Hotboxes were headed to Neuman's Kitchen's headquarters in Queens, and to Great Performances' exclusive site Caramoor, an estate in Westchester.

At one corner of the complex was something that felt like a country carpentry shop, where a man wearing a face respirator was sanding some age and rustication into a long, rectangular wood tabletop. Elsewhere, hundreds of spindly table bases, all stacked on each other, had their own room (the tops are stored elsewhere). A loft above us on the left held a thousand coatracks in their summer slumber.

Party Rentals Ltd. can't rest on its inventory. Items disappear* and depreciate, but most important, the customers drive a relentless quest for the next differentiating design that makes this party better than the last. So PRL has its own buyer who travels the globe, to factories in India and China and eastern Europe to source (and customize, if needed) furniture like the plastic mesh outdoor lounge seating that was so au courant in 2016. Moreover, Party Rental Ltd. also has its own in-house furniture fabrication department. To remain competitive, the company has to stay ahead of the latest trends in every element of event design—especially furniture—and the vogue in dining tables the summer we visited was rustic, long, farmhouse-style ones—a huge win for the company, because the tables are fairly inexpensive to make and look fantastic in the right setting. Since they're so unwieldy (compared to a 72-inch plywood round table that can be rolled into place and covered with any linen), PRL can charge a premium for these: the rustic farmhouse-style table seating ten people doesn't require a tablecloth, but it costs $225 to rent; a round table seating ten people is less than twenty bucks and the linens for it around $45 more. The day we visited, all of PRL's farmhouse tables were out on delivery and it was clear there wouldn't be enough coming back to supply the next day's

153

---

* In the fog of war that follows an event, ownership of unmarked items especially can become unclear.

parties, so the carpentry department was building a half dozen more on the spot.

Immediately adjacent to the carpentry shop was the spray-paint booth, where ranks of white Chiavari chairs* were stacked outside a curtained-off cube. A painter, partially obscured by the booth's curtain, was turning white chairs a kelly green. What happens when a caterer rents eight hundred green chairs the same night as another event that's already booked six hundred of the one thousand green chairs already in stock? No problem! The paint booth will convert white chairs to green. Or perhaps your event requires a tone of green so customized PRL doesn't stock it? No worries! They'll custom match it and paint it. "It'll cost you, of course," Jim said as we moved on to the heavy cooking equipment—propane-powered ovens, deep-fat fryers, and outdoor grills. "But we will do it."

"I'm taking you to the brain," McManus said, as we entered a low-ceilinged room with aggressive air-conditioning, a taxi company's worth of CB radios, and an array of screens mounted high on the walls.

Every delivery truck on every route is plotted on a map, its location updated in real time via global positioning systems. The dispatch crew knows when a truck diverges from the route—the drivers generally favor Malecon Restaurant at 175th Street and Broadway, not far from the George Washington Bridge, for a lunch of rice and beans, mofongo, or maduros. A computer plans each truck's route to minimize distance between stops, and each truck holds two helpers and one

---

* The turned-stick style of side chair invented in the Italian town of the same name in the early 1800s and dominant in the events business ever since. It's stackable, and the overbuilt, ladderlike construction makes it especially sturdy and durable.

driver. On a typical day there are about a hundred routes; on a busy Saturday during high season (June and October) there are twice that. It's a twenty-four-hour-a-day, seven-day-a-week operation, and the company's trucks are served with over $600,000 worth of parking violations in a typical year. About 175 drivers and 450 employees overall work for Party Rental Ltd., but that expands to 1,700 during the busy months.

The hippo wasn't always so big. Just a seventeen-minute drive from Party Rental Ltd.'s Teterboro warehouse is an unassuming liquor store, Oprandy's, in Englewood, New Jersey. A squat, two-story stone-and-brick office building from the fifties with a period neon sign stretching over the facade, it looks like the kind of place Don Draper might score a fifth of vodka to drink in his car, his puffy mug illuminated by the sign's flickery light. Almost forty years ago, Oprandy's owner, responding to the demands of his customers, opened a sideline business, renting glasses and paper napkins to his customers for their cocktail parties. He soon added tables and chairs, filling a six-car garage on the site of the store with the rentals business. Demand was so strong that he couldn't keep up. And he was a liquor guy first. A local couple, Sunny and Mike Halperin, saw that his rental business was brisk—and that he was struggling to keep up—so they bought the business and the inventory from Oprandy's. Within a year, they'd left the garage and moved the rentals into a warehouse big enough to house a small fleet of school buses. The year was 1972, the same year the Telephone Chef was renamed Donald Bruce White Caterers.

By expanding upon the old Oprandy's network of local clients and reaching out to Manhattan caterers like Donald Bruce White, Party Rental Ltd. was able to hitch its own success to the explosive growth the New York City catering business experienced in the seventies and eighties. PRL maintained its momentum by keeping trucking operations nimble and storage and maintenance facilities clean ("Look how clean this floor is," McManus said. "Could you *imagine* what would happen if a cockroach crawled out of one of my orders? In somebody's *house*?"), but especially by responding quickly to whatever needs caterers—and, as time went on, event planners—were demanding, whether it was elements of design (stemless wineglasses, Lucite "ghost" chairs, farmhouse tables) or restaurant-grade kitchen equipment. When McManus came on board with PRL in the late nineties, he knew that some catering chefs bristled at the limitations of the hotbox. They wanted to be liberated from rewarmed filet and salmon and to create fresher, brighter food—the kind restaurant chefs such as Rocco DiSpirito, Anita Lo, and Marcus Samuelsson were earning accolades for—which meant cooking proteins to order whenever possible. McManus responded by purchasing those energy-hogging electric and propane ovens, fabricating steel dollies for them with pneumatic wheelbarrow tires to make them mobile and wooden exoskeletons (painted pink!) to minimize dents and dings. They wouldn't be the right equipment for every event because the size of these monsters isn't well suited to the measly space typically designated for catering "kitchens." (Remember propane's forbidden indoors at any New York City venue.) But having an oven that could, say, roll across a gravel driveway in Bedford, New York, or the lawn in Greenwich, Connecticut, made it perfect for certain outdoor events, including the New York City Marathon, another PRL customer, which rents fifteen of them every year to serve ten thousand portions of lasagna in Central Park.

The ovens don't even come close to being the most expensive equipment depreciating in a PRL warehouse. Before the tour wrapped up, McManus collared a black-shirted employee with graying hair and a clipboard, Kevin Garlasco, the laundry manager. (Black shirts are for supervisors, red for upper management, pink for sales.)

In a building just down the street, Garlasco oversees the operation of a Pellerin Milnor Continuous Batch Washer, a million-dollar apparatus made in Louisiana that launders 1,600 pounds of dirty linens per hour, injecting solvents and rinses at just the right time as 130-pound loads inch through the machine, emerging damp and ready for ironing on the other side.

"Every dirty piece of linen from the East Coast that we have, from Delaware to Boston, all gets cleaned in that warehouse," said Garlasco.

Sometimes other linens, chefs' jackets, and even costumes make their way into the machine.

"Customers call us in a panic," McManus said. "They used Grandma's Irish linen napkins that have sentimental value 'cause they were trying to save money, and then their caterer puts it in a bag with our linen and I get people crying to me on the phone: 'You have Grandma's stuff! We really want it back!'"

"We call it N.O.G.—not our goods," Garlasco said, and explained they're cleaned and hung on racks just as they would be in a dry cleaner. "And we do get a lot of items back to their owners. We have a good percentage."

"But it's a needle in a haystack," McManus said. "I tell people all the time: Don't use Grandma's stuff! *Please!* Do yourself a favor, just pay for the rentals!"

- Most commonly rented item in the Party Rental Ltd. product catalog: 10.5-ounce all-purpose stemmed glass.

- Cost to Party Rental Ltd. of that glass: Fifty cents.

- Price to rent: Eighty-three cents.

- Cost of the pink heavy-duty plastic PRL-branded protective crate in which 25 of those glasses are shipped: $75.00.

- Average number of glass rentals per year: 3 million.

- Quantity of 10.5-ounce glasses in stock at any one time at the Party Rental Ltd. Teterboro, New Jersey, warehouse: 100,000.

- Quantity of that glass lost to breakage annually: 100,000.

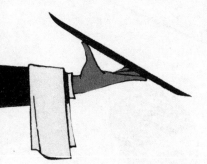

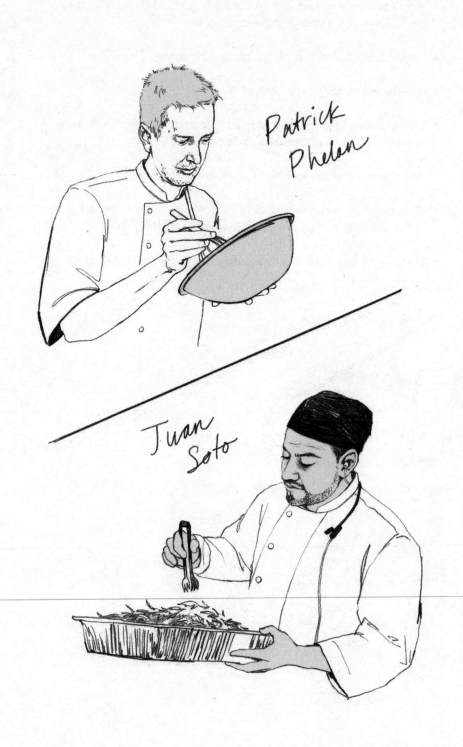

Patrick
Phelan

Juan
Soto

8

Sixteen Hundred Deviled Eggs

Ted Rolls with the Changing of the Guard

Despite the unlikely, outsize success of "In the Void," as fall turned to full-on winter, Patrick's tolerance of the grind was waning. "You have six great events one weekend and you get home to a ton of emails about the next six," he told me. "No time to reflect, to debrief, to bring the staff in for a toast."

Andrew and Valentina's arrival in Richmond was now imminent and Megan ached to quit the city. And Patrick had become resolute that he'd yet to realize his greatest potential and was ready to move his creative energy to a higher plane. Sonnier's owners deserved a chef excited by the prospect of designing ten new salads each season that could sit on a table for an hour and a half.

He wanted to leave honorably, on the best terms with the company that had facilitated him paying off all his student loans and credit card debt, their wedding and honeymoon expenses. So he gave David Castle more than three months' notice (even though his contract stipulated only sixty days). He said he'd help with the search for his replacement and see the firm through a huge event already on the calendar—the Royal Caribbean launch—which would be his swan song.

It was almost too poetic. The client was Cornelius "Neal" Gallagher, the chef who had first interviewed him at Sonnier & Castle ("Do you work fast? Do you use both hands?"). When Gallagher left S&C, he'd opened his dream restaurant, Dragonfly, in Manhattan, but he split with the other owners after just two months* and soon ended up in Florida, where he became director of culinary operations for the Miami-based Royal Caribbean cruise line. Years later, he was throwing a party in New York City to launch nine new restaurants on the ships, a tasting-station event for fourteen hundred guests—the company's best customers and international travel media. Spread out across the upper floor of a building overlooking the Hudson River on Thirty-Fourth Street would be simulacra of the nine different concepts, each serving a limited tasting menu. Since Gallagher was based in Miami, he needed Sonnier to provide ground support—well, nearly everything.

Patrick convinced me to work both prep and fiesta on the days leading up to the event, and I'd never seen K.A.s so packed into Pam's kitchen. Since each of the nine restaurants had a different flavor (Silk served Asian food; Wonderland, the gee-whiz factor, something like molecular gastronomy; Chic was

---

* "I think this platform may have been too small for Neal," one partner was quoted as saying.

anyone's guess but menu items included pasta primavera and shrimp cocktail), the tasks were, accordingly, all over the map. I trimmed a dozen pork bellies the size of car hoods for Jamie Oliver's Italian Kitchen and peeled eight hundred hard-boiled eggs for Michael's Genuine Pub. The walk-in refrigerator filled, and filled up more, and we got creative, utilizing space we'd never tapped, between the tops of the proofers and the ceiling.

The day before the event, the out-of-town chefs descended on the prep kitchen to review our work: first Gallagher, then two of the three celebrity chefs whose franchises would grace these boats (Jamie Oliver sent an underling). Patrick pulled Cambros, pots, and sheet pans from the walk-in, and the chefs tasted, seasoned, tasted again. They were generally pleased by the Sonnier team's work. Oliver's sous-chef, with sleepy eyes and bed-head hair, a dead ringer for his boss, showed up, tied on an apron, and demonstrated for Patrick how he wanted his porchettas skinned, scored, stuffed with mortadella, and tied. He took a selfie with his handiwork and said, "Sending that one back to Jamie, yeah?!" Then he clapped Patrick on the shoulder and stripped off his apron. "Do the rest just like that, mate. Brilliant!" he said, before skipping out of the kitchen.

"Did you see that shit?" Patrick asked. "Instagramming so the boss thinks he's working? Then he just splits like he's going to pop down to the pub!"

I just shook my head and kept on peeling.

"Whatever," he continued. "Guy smelled like a pub already, I'd rather *not* have him around."

Heading into my third hour of peeling eggs, my fingertips were raw and prickling with pain when two of Gallagher's top chefs at the cruise line strode in, wearing immaculate pressed white coats with ornate crests and royal-blue piping. There were four of us on the task, peeling our way toward the sixteen hundred deviled eggs the Miami chef Michael Schwartz would serve the following day.

"My egg team's on point here!" Patrick stated proudly to the two cruise-ship chefs, but they only glanced quizzically in our direction, then back to Patrick.

"Ya didn'a use the product that's already boiled? Already peeled?" the shorter one asked in a rich Scottish brogue. He looked to his colleague, dumbfounded.

"Sixty quid a pail from Dairyland," the other chef said. "Two hundred pieces. Saves you a packet of time."

The cruise-ship chefs didn't realize they were dealing with a man who'd taken few shortcuts in his life and on this, his very last fiesta, with nine kitchens and dozens of chefs on task, he sure as hell wasn't going to make his life any easier.

On-site that evening, the main catering support kitchen—Kitchen Ten—was a well-oiled machine, its K.A.s supplying matériel swiftly to the nine restaurant stations on the floor. Out of a hydra of an assignment, with so many people to answer to on so many details, Patrick had marshaled an orderly, successful party. And since the visiting chefs hadn't had to do much other than show up and man their stations, they were ecstatic. (Save one: Devin Alexander, celebrity chef of the TV show *The Biggest Loser*, was livid that our execution of her "healthy" riff on a McDonald's Big Mac—a "Little Dev"—didn't taste quite like the original: the pickles Pam had purchased were all wrong.)

The sun, which had shone directly in our eyes for most of the event, had finally set, and I noticed Patrick walking among the last guests, looking a little lost as he passed my station. I was ladling out my nine hundredth bowl of clam chowder, but customers were few at that point, so I called out to him and he turned around.

"How you doing, champ?" I asked.

There was a pause, as he looked around to confirm no one was near. "I'm getting emotional," Patrick said, and I wondered for a second if he was going to break down in tears. Back when he'd first told me he'd be giving notice, he feared leaving would be wrenching due to the intense bonds he'd developed with his team members, enduring so many challenges together. "Scar tissue," he'd called it.

But no. As in Hawaii, and in Germany, and in Kansas, and in Richmond, he was already looking forward. "I gave up six years of my life to this," he said. "Now I'm ready for friends. For reading books."

At just that moment, I could see Gallagher approaching Patrick from behind, with a bounce in his step. A bit taller than his protégé, he clamped a hand to each shoulder and looked down into Patrick's eyes. "I owe you," he said. "Big time."

Patrick wasn't having it. "You don't owe me anything. You showed me how to do this stuff."

Gallagher pressed the point: "No. You took this further than I cared to, further than I was able to, and further than I should have taken it."

Aside from that one encounter—for all his years of trials and triumphs, nearly two thousand events—Patrick's departure seemed unceremonious. He was just another morsel of talent consumed by a voracious city. One day, he was everywhere at once in a ten-kitchen slugfest while I ladled chowder as fast as

I could to career cruise-goers and the press (including a magazine publisher I knew well, who looked me square in the face yet didn't recognize me through my service uniform); the next day, both Patrick and I were at our respective apartments, reading books. He'd disappear into Richmond, and the parties would go on.

And what did Patrick's departure mean for me, for us, for "Virginia"? My phone was silent the next day and a couple days after that, too. I didn't have the relationship with Tyler Johnson that I'd had with Patrick, and it seemed awkward to reach out to him. I guessed Tyler knew I wasn't totally worthless—at one wedding, when a service captain was in full meltdown because he couldn't name the four varieties of oyster on the raw bar (the groom was asking), I'd rattled them off like gunfire: Kumamotos, Malpeques, Cotuits, Blue Points. So, during the ensuing month or more of silence, I devoured Rebecca Mead's epic about the bridal industry, *One Perfect Day*. Wedding season was coming on, and if Tyler didn't reach out and bring me on board, I'd call up Robb Garceau at Neuman's Kitchen or John Karangis at Union Square Events, both of whom had in the last year granted us interviews and allowed us to observe events.

In June I got an email from Tyler's new assistant Bethany Morey. Summer season was roaring and I could work any time—prep or fiesta. I stooped to prep to get in his good graces, and I noticed the energy there was markedly sunnier, less edgy. Pam, always quick to smile, seemed almost giddy, and her rapport with Tyler was jovial. She asked if I'd heard any news from our Richmond friends, but that was the only sign Patrick had ever been there. Tyler made some select equipment upgrades—new blades and bowls for the Robot Coupe, new knives, sharpeners, peelers; you no longer had to strap a bag of ice to the motor of the meat slicer to keep it from overheating. When I complimented him on the morale in the room, Tyler let on that until he got his sea legs he'd been gently overstaffing both prep and fiesta, so people weren't being ground to the bone. He compensated by saving time and money ordering in precut vegetables for stocks and soups, and always taking in account context: for a raucous, late-night after-party, where nobody's parsing the quality of pulled-pork barbecue, he'd bring in premade "slider filling"; Patrick would have had K.A.s brining and slow-smoking pork shoulders, saucing them with homemade, long-reduced concoctions.

And Tyler seemed genuinely happy. Sonnier & Castle had rented a carriage house in the Hamptons that had a nice kitchen where he conducted special tastings for VIPs. He, Sonnier's principals, and their event directors would stay there during weekends with parties on consecutive nights, when it didn't make sense to travel back to the city. Tyler's wife had been able to come out a few times, and they'd been to the beach and to tasting rooms at the wineries. The produce at farmers' markets was phenomenal and he loved being on a first-name basis with his suppliers.

Tyler also seemed more confident, less brooding than he'd been as Patrick's sous-chef, which I gather had something to do with the fact that he hadn't simply inherited the position of executive chef, he'd won it. With Patrick's help, the suits upstairs had conducted an exhaustive search, summoning a parade of credentialed New York restaurant chefs into the building to cook-audition for them. Tyler's trial, drawing deeply from his time on the line at Manhattan's Hearth, turning out simple Mediterranean food that was still elegant and refined, had been everyone's favorite and in step with the zeitgeist: all the food magazines that year were featuring *rustico*—plenty of beautiful, vegetable-forward grain salads, served family style.

It wasn't just prep that was transformed under Tyler's leadership: my first fiesta shift that summer had a new vibe that I picked up on soon after I rolled up to Sonnier & Castle to board a van headed to the Hamptons. In front of the building, a few dozen people stood in clusters on the sidewalk, and more loitered up on the loading dock. Vans were parked at the curb, their doors flung open, and I spotted Juan Soto, jet-black hair gelled and swept back along the part, looking more senior than anyone else. He wore an orange knit polo, a Bluetooth headset clipped to his ear, and he gripped a clipboard. He brightened when he saw me. "What's up, man? I saw you on my list!" he said. "We're waiting on two missing, but they coming. Five minutes we're going."

Just then his brother Jorge appeared, backpack slung over both shoulders, a floppy rasta man's knit beret sagging down the back of his neck. "Where you been?" he said, and reached out his fist for a bump.

But Tyler wasn't there, which seemed odd. In these moments before liftoff, Patrick had been ever present, micromanaging pack-out to the last possible moment—bossy, if jocular. The Sotos had a sobriquet—"Chucky" (after the doll in the horror movie franchise that turns into a serial killer when provoked)—for Patrick's alter ego, the person he became in those rare instances when he was truly rip-snorting angry. They loved to rib him at times like these, as the lead chefs scanned the menus he'd handed them. "This menu is looooong," they'd say. "We'll definitely see Chucky today!" The Soto brothers had catered Patrick and Meg's wedding a few years back, were almost like family to him, and Patrick had mostly ignored these jabs.

"Where's Tyler?" I asked, and they looked at each other with tight smiles.

"He's coming later," Juan said.

"What's up?" I asked. "Is everything good between you?"

"It's good now," Jorge said. "It took a while. We had to convince him to trust us, but now we're good."

I didn't press further—it seemed natural to take time for everyone to adapt to the new world order, and I'd find out soon enough whether Tyler's riding in a separate car reflected a deeper conflict or a more conventional, professional managerial style. Patrick had indicated that executive catering chefs didn't typically spend much time on-site at events the way he did—"Gallagher showed up for app serve-out and he'd be gone soon as the first dessert plate dropped." Perhaps Tyler had reached a level of trust with the Sotos where he felt the freedom to step away.

In the near term, not having an executive chef in the van made for a freewheeling and fun ride. La Mega 97.9 FM blasted its mix of bachata, salsa, and merengue. On the Long Island Expressway that day there were no accidents, and though it was by no means a fast trip—the mariachi cover of Bruno Mars's "Just the Way You Are" that was big that summer played no fewer than three times during the journey—it didn't become a slogging standstill until we got off the highway and onto the two-lane coastal route at the de facto entrance to the Hamptons.

The box trucks had already arrived when we got to the estate, and loading into the tents went quickly—despite the huge expanse of green lawn from driveway to tent. Someone had thought to rent twenty or thirty sheets of plywood, over-lapping them end over end across the grass to make a track so smooth the proofers practically rolled themselves. It was a crystal-clear summer Saturday, with a trace of salt air wafting in on the breeze. I'd Googled the venue address on the ride out and learned the couple who'd loaned their lawn for the gala was in the midst of an acrimonious divorce the *New York Post* was following minute by minute. But there was no sign of discord in that field, just industriousness in and around the tent.

I fell in with Jorge, boxing out tables and organizing the coolers. Now that Patrick was gone, Jorge relished showing me the ropes his own way, starting with the basics, and I was grateful for the refresher. In the Hamptons, he said, you had to be extra careful unpacking, checking off every ingredient and quantity, because a re-run here was a different story: you might be able to send a driver to a farm stand or the King Kullen supermarket for an ingredient, but that round-trip could take an hour in traffic, even more the closer you got to dinnertime. He showed me tasks I'd never been assigned before, like cutting a pound of cold butter into perfect triangles and plat-ing them to hold until serve-out; the correct way to wrap bread baskets for warming on top of the proofer.

The load-in and setup was the smoothest I'd seen. Our passed appetizer stations were ready to rock an hour before serve-out. Juan looked out over the gorgeous room-temperature corn soup with its five garnishes, plated and ready for servers to preset, and said, "*Chingón.*"

"What?"

"*Chingón,*" Juan said. "It means 'excellent.'" He dragged the word out slowly for effect.

"But watch," Jorge said. "When Tyler gets here, it's gonna get crazy."

"You said you were all good with Tyler now."

"We're good," he said. "I'm just telling you. He gets nervous. And when he gets here, he'll want changes."

I'd never experienced downtime at a fiesta before. Juan and Jorge conferred over a legal pad, putting together the Monday morning food delivery for their day job. I knew they worked for a drop-off shop in the East Village, delivering breakfasts and lunches to offices and studios downtown, but as Juan dialed vendors, Jorge explained that they manage—but don't own—the shop. They wake up most mornings at 3:30 or 4:00 a.m. in the Bronx and with a small team, just a few guys, they do all the purchasing, cooking, and driving, too. They're the Pam, the Tyler, and the César.

About twenty minutes before hors d'oeuvre serve-out, Tyler arrived wearing wraparound shades, looking tanned and in good spirits. The rapport between him and the Sotos seemed strong until he learned there was no diced white onion for the soup. Jorge had been checking items off the lists and I was frankly shocked, after Jorge's lecture about taking care unpacking, that he'd let this slip.

"How long have you guys been here?" Tyler asked. "If we'd found this out two hours ago, we could've done something about it!"

He also wanted to alter Juan's plan for the plating line—a task complicated by the black-and-white theme of the party, a tribute to the artist Robert Motherwell—which had VIP tables getting white plates and the hoi polloi black ones. There wasn't a single extra plate to spare, white or black, which meant that between that, and the choice of proteins, and the silent vegetarian option, they'd basically be composing every plate to order, and Juan and Tyler had different ideas about whose method would result in quicker service.

Jorge shot me a look that said, "See? What did I tell you?" But the party went off without a hitch. After Tyler had departed, after the chocolate bread pudding had been served, Juan was filling out the party report every lead chef must complete, recording any mishaps and mistakes to send back to Sonnier & Castle, and he wrote down the checklist:

> *Chingón*
> *Chingón*
> *Chingón*

That summer, Juan and Jorge's role in the operation came into focus for me. Sure, they might get reamed for the absence of diced white onion, but they held considerable leverage over the captains of this industry. Within the wildly vacillating, accordion business of catering, they've carved out a stabilized niche that allows them to work more or less on their own terms. Each lowly kitchen assistant's shred of power—as I learned firsthand—lies in being a mercenary, a free agent from one night to the next; you give your availability to the firm, or you withhold it to the extent that you can afford to say "I'm busy" when the chef needs you. The Sotos, through their talents for catering and cultural translation, have amassed an army of mercenaries who show up (or leave) at their command. So they're not only a staffing agency, but one with world-class leadership built in: Juan and Jorge themselves are always on the front lines, sparking the Sternos and sweating through their beanies, inspiring outsize loyalty in their charges. How many

Sotos do you need? With one phone call you can get twelve, twenty-four, thirty-six, sixty-four *chefs completos*. Often the brothers divide and conquer, serving Cloud Catering and Sonnier & Castle on the same night, or another firm, or none at all, if they feel they've been treated poorly.

And if this is your first peek behind the pipe and drape, if it's a mystery to you why these two men are so essential to and powerful in this rarefied, luxury-product delivery system, just consider the leverage they have over their employers: they could, if they wished, shut the proofer doors a half hour before dinner service and stage a kitchen walkout, leaving cabinet upon cabinet of raw lamb and cold parsnips with nobody to move it. Since the Sotos are subcontractors, it's the catering company whose reputation would take the immediate blow and suffer most for the catastrophe. Imagine punting on the main course at a seated dinner for seven hundred that cost guests a couple thousand dollars per ticket! Who breaks that news to the party planner? Who tells the swells: "Please, everybody, stay in your seats—we've ordered in pizza!"

The more I got to know them, the more I saw how adept the Sotos are at playing these power dynamics: it's why they've never accepted a full-time position at any caterer—also why they'll never have to lead that mutiny. Forthright and fair-minded, they tend to get whatever they need or want on any assignment.

Later in the fall, Juan invited me to come work their day job, the place he controls from top to bottom. I spent a couple of shifts with them in the East Village, at Cafiero Lussier Event Design, a business that primarily does "drops" to photo shoots, leaving platters of salmon and bowls of grain salads off for self-service. It sounds fairly routine on the surface, but a typical gig involves prepping breakfast items at the basement kitchen on East Second Street, trucking them to a photo studio; then driving back to the studio a few hours later to collect the breakfast items and drop off lunch; then returning later in the day to collect the remains (three round-trips). Jorge bears the brunt of transportation duties and has cultivated, with gratuities—bottles of red wine, most often—a network of doormen, secretaries, and superintendents in the loft buildings of Manhattan's West Side where the studios cluster, who will do him favors like allowing access to an ice machine or handing over a few rolls of paper towels—thereby saving him a fourth round-trip if something's left behind or missing. "A bottle of red wine here and there is what? Seven dollars?" he said.

When I showed up at the catering kitchen, a few steps down from the sidewalk, several half-hotboxes were stacked on either side of the front door, partially blocking one window. Inside, five chefs clad entirely in black—pants, chef jackets, beanies—worked a commercial range at the back of the room and prepped in the foreground on top of other half-proofers. Larger than a pickup truck but smaller than the typical restaurant kitchen, every inch here was utilized, immaculate, organized.

Juan, with his finely trimmed goatee, wore the same black uniform as his charges, but with shell-top Adidas instead of the usual battered black clogs or working sneaks of a K.A. He put me to work peeling and slicing butternut squashes, parsnips, and turnips into wide tiles, layering them in earthenware ovals for a winter vegetable gratin, and I began to ask him questions at the leisurely pace of prep—except for that first encounter at the Beard House, I'd never been with the Sotos outside of fiesta conditions.

Juan's large Samsung rang, and he took the call on speakerphone. A woman at a small catering firm uptown wanted to hire him to run the proofers for hors d'oeuvres at a cocktail party for sixty people the next day. He expressed gratitude but was curt, asked if he could call her back in a few minutes. He gave it about thirty seconds, then called back to decline.

"I've learned to say no with this place," he said. "We show up and it's never just proofing. We have to fix all the food on-site. They never do what they say before the event."

While I broke down ten heads of celery into steep bias cuts for a roasted vegetable medley, I asked him how he managed to keep this catering firm functioning. Here in the East Village, he was the Pam (purchaser and production manager), the head chef (menu designer and quality control), and quite a few of the people upstairs (human resources, operations manager).

"I don't even need a dishwasher because here we're all dishwashers!" he said over his shoulder from the slop sink.

He explained he makes his life easy by consolidating all his purchasing on just two suppliers, the ones most accommodating—and most expensive. But the cost of ingredients to him is negligible: "The branzino, for example," he said, pointing toward the fish that was cooking at that moment in his new convection oven. "It may cost me three or four dollars per portion, so the dish we serve may cost twelve dollars total for ingredients and labor. But my bosses sell that for a hundred dollars per person. Whether the fish costs two dollars or four dollars doesn't make much of a difference."

By lunchtime, Jhovany, with whom I'd worked numerous Sonnier & Castle fiestas, had put together a lentil soup with smoky ham trimmings and vegetable odds and ends. I reached for quart-size deli containers for the soup, but Juan corrected me, pulling down broad, white ceramic soup bowls from a rack overhead. The soup was soul-warming, clove-scented, and we all ate standing up, as Juan told stories from the trenches. He praised Neal Gallagher for having brought professional rigor and new methods to Sonnier—Gallagher had been the one to introduce to them the concept of portioning food in disposable foil cups, for plating with speed and consistency, but converting him to the brilliance of the hotbox hadn't come without a smackdown. When Gallagher arrived at Sonnier, he had recently won a Michelin star for his cooking at the seafood temple Oceana and he strutted around, telling the Sotos he'd show them "how real chefs cook," mocking them for their proofers and Sternos. At his first large party, a bar mitzvah in Westchester, veal chops for six hundred, Gallagher rented six standing electric ovens for the site at $400 a pop. Fortunately, all the food had been transported in hotboxes, because when the ovens got plugged in—yep, they overloaded the circuitry of the venue's electrical system. Gallagher was desperate.

"He's crying, 'I need you guys to help me! What do we do?'" Juan said, in an exaggerated fake-sobbing voice. "I don't know, Neal, do we call 1-800-Sternos?"

Juan's tone turned serious, and I could tell he'd told this story before. "I said to him, 'Get the fuck out of here and watch me save your ass.'"

And apparently Gallagher never made fun of the proofers, or the Sotos, again.

Juan said every chef was challenging to work for in different ways. With Patrick, it hadn't always been easy. On more than a few occasions, "Chucky" made an appearance, and Juan had had to take him aside, in the heat of the event, and speak to him the way he spoke to his children: "Come here, little man. Look at me. *Tranquilo*. Be cool, take a time-out."

There were more stories: another time electric ovens went down, and he went to a ninety-nine-cent store and bought eight electric hot plates that saved the day. When a burner that showed up on the truck didn't work, and he had a huge pot of pasta sauce to reduce for 150 people, he corralled ten Sternos in the bottom of a milk crate, lined it with foil, lashed plastic wrap into ropes, and formed a hammock strong enough to suspend the sauce pot over the flames.

"Back in Mexico, we were very poor," he said. "And we're very used to making do with little, turning one thing into something else. This invention is effortless for us. As long as I have plastic wrap, foil, sheet pans, Sterno, I can get through any situation."

That afternoon, I spent a couple of hours breaking down seven slippery baked hams into biscuit-appropriate tiles, for a luncheon party the next day. Juan talked about life, his family, and his larger ambitions. He was nearing forty, and he imagined in the next three years he might return to Mexico City or Guanajuato and start a restaurant there. He has a wife and three children, owns two apartments in the Bronx and property in Mexico. Even so, he likes the idea of opening a restaurant here, something like the taco stand he used to run in Guanajuato. He's convinced there's still a culinary gap to fill between Manhattan and the Rio Grande: if only people could taste the authentic flavors and styles of real Mexican tacos . . .

At the end of day, he asked me if I was working for Sonnier & Castle the following night, a wedding in Williamsburg. I'd heard through the K.A. grapevine about this one—the first time Sonnier would be catering the former Williamsburgh

Savings Bank. Somebody had spent $24 million renovating the place into a glittering event venue. I'd seen pictures of the soaring dome and the old tellers' booths in the *Times*, and I wanted to be there.

"Just come, I'll put you on the time sheet," he said. "If anyone asks, just say, 'Juan Soto hired me.'"

I may never become a *chef completo*, but after three years in catering I'd become a "Soto," and it felt great. I could work a party virtually every night for the rest of my life if I needed to.

After a year watching Juan and Jorge Soto and their top proofers* in action, it became abundantly clear that we wouldn't acquire hotbox skills readily in the field. Even at the most organized dinner, the pressure of working against the clock 'til serve-out didn't abide a moment's dalliance with the cabinets. And Matt once committed the classic rookie error, cardinal sin of proofing, of shutting the door tight and snuffing out an entire box at the National Basketball Association's annual brunch at the Javits Center. It could have been years before Juan let us touch a proofer again.

So we rented one, and the next day a white truck pulled up outside the apartment. We rolled it in through the front door and sized it up. Only lightly used, it showed the usual dings at the corners and scratches across its flanks. The back side was painted Pepto-pink, smudged brown-black at shoulder height, where it had been handled most, with a black Party Rental Ltd. hippopotamus stenciled on the center of the panel. The cabinet was five feet nine inches tall, and a few inches from the top was riveted a stamped metallic bar code, with identifying number A000000000007813. Inside, the box looked lightly used and seemed clean.

Our pseudoscientific cooking experiments were all failures. We tried searing steaks (not enough heat, or too much in a spot the size of a half-dollar) and reheated containers of leftovers (by the time the center was warmed, the outsides had crisped). Our tests revealed just how little we knew, but now we at least grasped how much foundational knowledge—what foods should be reheated or cooked in it, and what shouldn't—is required before the cabinet even leaves the prep kitchen. The hotbox was either too hot or too cold for us at any one moment, whether we were dealing with steak, pasta, fish, or a stack of day-old pancakes we were reheating. Home ranges, ovens, and microwaves move food from point A to point B like a motor vehicle; the hotbox is a pogo stick in comparison.

Hundreds, if not thousands, of days of trial and error, over- and under-cooking, and poking and prodding would be required for us to build up a cumulative feel for this device, the kind of fine-tuned knowledge the Sotos carry in their brains and fingertips. Judging heat without a thermometer, using just the eyes, ears, and touch, a quick pat to the flanks of the box, is one thing; but the element of time is yet another slippery factor in the equation. While you're shuffling trays in and out, worrying different blobs of protein, starch, cellulose, and water, time is brutally stretched or compacted. Ten minutes can feel like an hour; then the next ten race by in a few seconds, as you're getting your bearings. (And then the trout is mush.)

---

* The noun "proofer" is used by the Soto brothers to describe the hotbox and also any fiesta K.A.s entrusted with operating one.

WORKING THE HOTBOX

Anita Lo, whose West Village restaurant Annisa charmed diners and critics alike for seventeen years, is one of few restaurant chefs who has also worked extensively in catering and doesn't begrudge the hotbox—though she vastly prefers the controlled, one-plate-at-a-time environment of restaurant kitchens and is decidedly "not comfortable in the zone."

"I still use the hotbox, it's elemental," she said. "It's not unlike a wood-burning oven. In fact, it's kind of the same thing, just not as romantic—it's uglier, and the other one has flavor to it." She added, "Every chef should have these skills, even a non-catering chef."

Lo employs proofers every year when she cooks for the No Kid Hungry benefit (she's a co-chair) and specifies that the nineteen other guest chefs use them as well. A chef who objected one year was supplied with electric ovens; naturally, the circuits blew.

For experienced and confident chefs like Lo, the mystery factor, the imprecision of the hotbox, is actually part of the appeal. "As far as controlling the temperature, it's all about placement of Sterno and food, and how many sheet pans are in between. You can bake, you can burn things—it's fun on some level!"

We weren't having fun, exactly, but we were making some progress in understanding the rudiments.

One detail about the hotbox that surprised us in testing it is that a single can of Sterno is actually quite gentle; to reach searing or baking temperatures, you need five or more canisters on at least two sheet pans. One Sterno generated a plume 260 degrees Fahrenheit (well above boiling) measured an inch above the flame, but after half an hour that single can had raised the temperature of an empty sheet pan placed eight inches above it to only 100 degrees—bath temperature—from 75. Aluminum—the material many sheet pans and the hotbox itself are made of—is extremely conductive, and spreads out that locus of energy far and wide until it dissipates. We knew enough to crack the door to supply oxygen to the flames but wondered why Cres Cor hadn't invented a graduated clasp that allowed the door to be propped open at fixed gaps? In any case, we hacked it the way we'd seen Juan do it, fashioning a stay from a "rope" of aluminum foil.

The most important lessons that this hotbox taught us, however, were when we called Jim McManus at Party Rental Ltd., offered up the bar code, and asked him to run a spreadsheet on every location our proofer had traveled in the prior year. Before he (somewhat reluctantly) sent us the provenance of our cabinet, he challenged himself and guessed fifty total sites, noting that Party Rental owned at that moment 497 hotboxes to serve about fifty thousand events per year from D.C. to Boston. When the spreadsheet came in, the total number of sites this hotbox had logged that year was forty-four, entirely in the New York and New Jersey area. It sounded like a modest number, less than one per week, but that didn't account for times it might have remained in one caterer's custody across multiple events. Still the list was about the most effective overview of a year in high-end catering we'd ever seen.

We did some calculations and figured out that the hotbox we rented had traveled at least 992 miles (again, not counting trips taken if a caterer kept it on board for multiple events) in 2016. The average round-trip for a gig—from Party Rental's warehouse in Teterboro, New Jersey, to the site and back—was 23 miles.

The locations the hotbox had rolled into included most of the larger, grander venues, from the Metropolitan Museum, the Brooklyn Museum, and the New York Public Library, to the IAC (InterActiveCorp, Frank Gehry's dramatic glass-clad building on the West Side Highway) to One World Trade Center. It had been to Lincoln Center more times than anyplace else, to a hospital in New Jersey, and to a Restoration Hardware in Manhattan; to the Lyric Theatre, to Facebook's New York headquarters, and to Ellis Island.

The list of caterers who had taken custody of the hotbox included all of the familiar firms at the upper end: Great Performances, Glorious Food, Pinch Food Design, Sonnier & Castle, Union Square Events, Abigail Kirsch, Restaurant Associates (which accounted for eight gigs), and a couple of caterers with headquarters deep in the suburbs, grabbing some gold by working an event in the big city.

The clients who tasted food from this box before us included many among the S&P 100 corporations—IBM, Morgan Stanley, Bloomberg, Tiffany & Co., American Express—as well as an array of cultural institutions, including the Public Theater, Brooklyn Botanic Garden, Bowdoin College, Mount Sinai Hospital, the New York Philharmonic Orchestra, and the National Kidney Foundation. There were a few not-quite outliers, such as the food magazine *Bon Appetit* and the Dalton School (a private grade school, crucible of S&P 100 CEOs). And our proofer made it to exactly one wedding that year.

9

Can I Even Eat This?

Food Design at the Cutting Edge

SCENE: Cocktail hour, at a party. POV: Guest at the event.

A server walks into the room carrying in an upturned palm a platter of canapés. He proffers them to small clusters of guests, murmuring his script discreetly—"Cheese croustade," or "Mortadella toast?"—enticing the guests to reach for a bite. (Or not.)

Stop the film. Rewind. Now imagine that scene again, but this time the server emerges carrying not a platter, but a parasol, which he's twirling lazily, almost imperceptibly. As he walks toward you, you notice from the tip of each rib of the parasol hangs a length of pink string ending in a small gold S-hook. And from each hook hangs a shard of . . . something. It's reddish brown, faintly transparent, looks a bit like a piece of stained glass.

"Candied bacon?" he asks.

Conversation stops and the people around you gasp. You and a few others reach for the bacon and . . . *wow*. It's perfectly crisp, just enough chew, smoky-sweet. Yum.

"Sorry, I don't eat meat," a member of your circle tells the waiter.

The server says, "Helga will be popping up momentarily with a raw-bar selection," and moves on, in his merry way.

Licking the sticky bacon residue from your fingers, you turn to see Helga, pushing what looks to be the love child of a wheelbarrow and a unicycle. It's a mobile raw bar. In the wheelbarrow's tray, oysters and clams on the half shell are set on a bed of shaved ice, and in between the bivalves are several whole lemons with finger-pump nozzles jutting out their top ends.

"North Fork clams and oysters with lemon mist?" Helga asks.

You reach for a clam and a lemon, and pump atomized juice over the clam, then slurp down this cold, briny, tart bite— the flavor of a perfect day at the beach.

"You'll find further selections on the interactions at the far corners of the room," she says.

"*Interactions?*" you ask.

"Yes, over in the corner, against the wall."

You set off to the corner of the room, but find yourself looking at . . . a blank white wall. But wait. On closer inspection, there are knobs and drawer pulls scattered, apparently at random, throughout that wall. A waiter appears at your elbow. "Go ahead," he says. "Pull on any of them." You pull one, and out rolls a cabinet of sorts, only six inches wide, but four feet tall, and open at the sides. Suspended from horizontal rods that stretch all the way back into the wall and out of sight are square-shaped mini-flatbreads the size of a pack of cigarettes, and by the coloring on each piece of flatbread, each rod appears to hold a different flavor. A friend next to you pulls another knob on the wall, and out comes a broad horizontal tray, like a desk drawer, that's full of spiced mixed nuts. And so it goes. In another corner of the room is a narrow shelving system holding ranks and ranks of clipboards suspended at a 30-degree angle. Pick up the clipboard and it becomes the tray for the flat array of charcuterie and cheese it holds, the print on the paper underneath detailing what you're about to put in our mouth. By the time dessert emerges—white platters of mini chocolate-ganache-filled meringues floating through the room suspended by white balloons—you may feel you've gone wholly through the looking glass.

But in fact you're simply at a party catered by Pinch Food Design, the brainchild of Bob Spiegel, a forty-year catering veteran who cut his teeth in the early eighties at Glorious Food, and T. J. Girard, a production designer, who eight years ago teamed up with Spiegel to take what passed for novelties in catering circa 2010—the oyster "shooters," the smoked salmon "lollipops," the mini lobster rolls—and blast them into the twilight zone. Almost overnight, Pinch became the undisputed industry leader in "wow-factor," design-driven catering. (Pure coincidence? Instagram was launched the same year they opened their doors.)

Pinch headquarters is a lofty, fishbowl-like storefront appropriately situated in the art gallery district at the northern edge of Chelsea. Look at a Pinch canapé—a charred square of steak pierced onto the tapering point of a custom-fabricated stainless-steel spoon skewer, a puddle of electric green in the spoon's narrow bowl—and it wouldn't seem out of place mounted on a pedestal in any of the neighborhood's galleries. Spiegel paints beautiful, drippy abstractions—his medium? scallop seviche—on tables the size of a bedsheet that make you think: *Can I even eat this?*

Spiegel and Girard have created their own catering language. The surfaces they create for presenting food, whether a sleek, freestanding shelving unit with slender birch-tree columns or the spike-covered Bakelite tray for serving doughnuts are "food furniture." An "interaction" is Pinch's term for what most people would call a buffet station, which at first seems a little silly. But when you think about it, even a stationary presentation of a piece of food at a Pinch party—the charcuterie clipboards, say—insists that the guest engage with it in a manner more conscious and knowing than absentmindedly picking up that second sodden tomato bruschetta. You have to be present with the food at a Pinch party; you must meet it halfway. It's self-conscious, it announces itself: *Look at me!* In their parlance, a "pop-up" is a mobile interaction—the raw bar, the parasol—that comes to you where you are and practically compels you to contend with it.

Spiegel and Girard draw as equally from the design and fashion worlds as they do from art. They refer to their "collections," themed around an idea (drawers and rolling cabinets, pulled from a wall, say) and they present new collections every season at an event they call "The Peep Show," attended by party planners, their best corporate and social clients, and the food media. When prospective clients come in for a tasting, meeting around the conference table in a room that displays their latest food furniture, they're presented not only with food but with "lookbooks," like you'd see at a fashion house.

Detractors call Pinch's work gimmicky. "I might use them for a wacky bar mitzvah," one event designer told us, "but I can't think of anything else." For their part, Spiegel and Girard understand that they're not for everyone, or for every party. Their brand is innovative food (and beverages, of course; their bar division, with an assortment of odd machines that make booze luges and funnelators seem staid, is called Twist), and they get that not everyone is looking for Alice in Wonderland.

"If a client comes to us and wants their own specific, custom thing, we're probably not the caterer for them," Spiegel told us.

"You can go to a tailor and have a custom suit made, or you can go buy an Armani suit—that's how I describe what we do," Girard added. "Are we capable of making you a custom station? Yes, but the time and energy we spent making our Pinch collection is a far greater amount of attention."

187

Spiegel put it slightly differently: "When you go to Per Se, do you ask them to make your grandmother's kugel? Or do you order off the menu?"

Fortunately for Pinch, enough brands and brides *do* want photo-ready food. They're the go-to caterer for any business looking to have their event blow up on social media, and that happens to include a lot of companies in fashion, tech, and entertainment, and charities who want to sex up their mission.

"A lot of our clients are corporate, they're using marketing dollars for their parties, and they want to know what's the return on their investment?" Girard said. "Food isn't just: let's make sure to keep them from being hungry, and drinks aren't just: these people need a cocktail. It's: how do we make that cocktail a part of that party."

"You want that guest to wake up the next day, like . . . pinch me, did I dream that?" Spiegel added. "And because of the creativity we showed, those guests donate money to the charity, or invest in that company."

Pinch is the rare breed, almost one of a kind among the top tier of caterers in New York, because it has prioritized design. Everything else comes next. For the vast majority of catering chefs, however, the design of a food item is tertiary at best, determined after flavor, texture, budget, and logistics are figured out. What's the cost of the branzino fillet and how much labor's required to prepare it? Do I have enough space for tables and hotboxes to cook this entrée for the number of guests? Will this hors d'oeuvre be crisp or soggy?

Since prep-kitchen labor is less than half as expensive as fiesta labor, dishes that can be fully cooked in the prep kitchen and simply reheated and garnished on-site will always be winners on the balance sheet compared to items that require more labor and assembly to build at the party. So canapés like pigs in blankets, the little triangular phyllo-dough pies called beggars' purses, and Chinese-style spring rolls, that a single chef running a hotbox can fire up all at once, will always be the executive catering chef's heroes. By contrast, Sunny-side Quail Egg with Tomato and Asparagus on Brioche (from chapter 1), which requires at least two if not three on-site wage earners to serve out, will give your chief financial officer palpitations (even if its brilliance helped impress the client at the tasting). Balancing more economical options with ambitious ones and avoiding the impression of being all over the map—*Pig in a blanket? Meet tuna-tartare taco bite!*—is key for a conscientious chef. By the same token, main courses like short ribs and lamb shanks, slow-cooked meats that become more tender and unctuous the longer they hold, which can be cooked through in the prep kitchen, then simply reheated, will be perennial. *Garnish it with something green and let it go!*

Catered food often comes with such indifferent design and low expectations because of the economic and logistical pressure, which leads chefs to congregate around the same safe dishes. If you've been to a lot of seated dinners, you almost know the textures and flavors you're about to eat before you arrive at the venue. But it's also why it's relatively easy for a caterer to make a splash by doing something remarkably different.

A revealing case study in the competing demands of food design, labor, and cost was a first course witnessed across two years of the same benefit gala. Same catering firm, two different chefs. The first year was Patrick Phelan's first time doing this particular event. At the tasting, the board had chosen a new salad he was quite proud of and, in classic Patrick style, was so complicated to assemble that it required fourteen K.A.s (the cheapest of whom were costing Sonnier & Castle $25 an hour) nearly two on-site hours to accomplish at the event venue. After the course was cleared, it was faintly demoralizing to see how many came back to the kitchen nearly full, only picked over. We had tasted it and thought it was delicious—even if the frisée was a tad twiggy and it could have used a shade more dressing.

The following year, Patrick had moved to Richmond and it was Tyler Johnson's turn to perform at this gala. Perhaps the party planner didn't trust Tyler yet, but for some reason he insisted upon a first course of his own devising, a custom recipe that required virtually no on-site execution: a "pumpkin hash" served in a hollowed-out ghost pumpkin. Tyler howled privately at how retro—and not *cool* retro—it seemed, adding, "It's way too rich, and the portion is way too big!"

189

But his bosses knew it was on the party planner if it flopped, that the fallout wouldn't affect him. And from a cost-labor perspective, it couldn't be better. Sergio had whipped up a few tilt skillets' worth of the hash—precut pumpkin, onions, butter, and seasonings—in an afternoon. The ghost pumpkin vessels had come in from the produce supplier pre-scooped, with the tops off. Tyler had a couple of K.A.s fill the 750 pumpkins with hash and arrange them on speed racks. They were served at room temperature, so the only finish labor performed on-site was one K.A. in each kitchen sprinkling chives and parsley over the top and another who put the lids on. And they went out to the floor.

Tyler watched the first-course plates come back to sanitation and said quietly, "Holy . . . shit." Seven out of ten of these pumpkins were scraped clean! People *loved* the giant pumpkin. Whatever you might think of a hash in a hollowed-out pumpkin, you can't argue with inexpensive-to-prepare, crowd-pleasing food. The proof was in the empty plates.

A skillfully built salad is just a salad. A ghost pumpkin hash makes more of an impression, so much the better if it actually is delicious. And this is where complicated design in food can get a chef into shaky territory—and it's why there's so much pressure on the food at a Pinch party to *taste* great. Because the more attention a chef brings to design and gesture, the presentation and form, the more he or she raises expectations about the performance in the mouth. Eye candy *has* to taste good. There's a lot of conceptual distance between a hollowed-out pumpkin and beignets that pop out of holes in a wall, and there are plenty of places for chefs to get tripped up in between.

Imagine you're at a seated dinner, for example, and a small jewel-like piece of sashimi is placed before you, beneath a glass cloche. You may ask yourself: *what's under there?* It looks like a piece of sashimi in a terrarium, but because of its presentation—under glass!—you prepare for some sort of sensual payoff when the bell jar gets lifted. You're looking for that *ta-da!* moment, so when the waiters arrive in teams, removing the cloches simultaneously, you lean in close to discern—was there an aroma trapped underneath? What's going on? And when what's beneath that cloche turns out to be simply a bland piece of raw fish, as it did at the Whitney Gala in 2016, the course is a total dud. It was an empty gesture (and not an inexpensive one, when you consider there were six hundred guests and those cloches are an item that—whether rented or owned—had to be carefully packed and shipped to the site).

That same night, the main course also had a similar ante-raising appearance: a log-like loin of lamb enrobed in a dusting of powder the color of an army jacket. Its daunting appearance was an implicit challenge, making you think: this *better* taste good. So, when that powder, a "pea crust" made of ground, dehydrated English peas, actually tasted *bad*—earthy-musty, with a faintly algal aroma like the smell of an unclean fish tank—guests up and down the table scraped it off with their knives. Purely from a food standpoint, the dinner was a double fail and the speeches hadn't even started.

Some event planners actually believe that, despite the current mainstream food mania, in the context of everything else that happens at a special event, especially a charity fund-raiser, the food is not so important. And that might be true, to an extent, if the food is simply unremarkable; when food is bad, it can really have a profound effect on the room and the people in it. As the Whitney event progressed to the speeches and performances, the guests decided—perhaps unconsciously—

191

that they were likely to be burned by dessert. The moment Seal's riveting acoustic performance had wrapped, three-fifths of the room got up and left, either for home or for the after-party. By the time the servers came out with dessert, just fifty of the original six hundred guests were left in the room. And 550 plates of a build-your-own sundae—as it happened, the most technically challenging and by far the most successful course of the night—went in the trash.

Another hazard of food design in catering can happen when a concept is really too brilliant: it may attract imitators. When social media are able to broadcast a cool canapé instantly to millions of people around the world, the chef's original design is likely to be knocked off by somebody, somewhere, in a matter of hours. For an outfit like Pinch, it happens regularly, even though the bright idea may take years to trickle down to the more conservative firms. Eight years after Pinch created the parasol pop-up, Brooklyn-based caterer Abigail Kirsch, one of the largest mid-tier catering firms in the city, tweeted out a photo of her new "pretzel umbrella." To be sure, the imitation went only so far: this was a rather more ungainly take on the parasol—a clear plastic umbrella with New York–style pretzels hanging from it. And the notion required two servers: one to hold the umbrella, a second to follow behind with a squirt bottle of mustard.

We emailed the Pinch folks the image and followed up with a phone call asking if they'd seen it.

"We don't actively pay attention to other caterers," Spiegel said.

"I don't investigate or do reconnaissance," Girard said. "In fact, I don't want to know."

"We wouldn't have seen that photo if you hadn't sent it."

There was dejection in both their voices, but Girard brightened a bit. "It's a little disheartening, but we're not dwellers. We've inspired this industry and that's flattering. And at the same time, it forces us to dream up something new."

Spiegel was still downbeat. "It's sad for me to bury something, but the 'brelly will have to go. We love the idea and we know the effect it has on people. And to say good-bye to it just because somebody else is doing it is hard."

He confessed to having reached out once or twice on social media in the past—much to Girard's chagrin—to call out former chefs who'd worked in his kitchen and posted knockoffs of Pinch designs without giving credit.

Girard was optimistic, noting with enthusiasm that she'd heard from a wedding planner that there's a shorthand in the industry for demanding that the caterer make the food look better, be more attention-grabbing, perform a little bit: "Can you *Pinch* that up?"

"Look, we jump-started something new," Spiegel said. "The definition of catering was always 'give people what they want.' We've gone beyond that by creating food you never even imagined."

As many events as we'd worked by that time, we'd never served out food that sought to do anything beyond looking beautiful and being delicious. High-concept design seemed to add only more dangers to the risk calculus of the traveling circus. But perhaps this trendy, fun-factor food brought so much happiness and joy to guests that it actually eased the tensions and pressures of the event in ways that weren't calculable. For example, when the balloon wafts past, holding aloft its tray of mini brownies filled with a milk panna cotta, does anyone say, "Sorry, I'm allergic to dairy. Can you make me something else?"

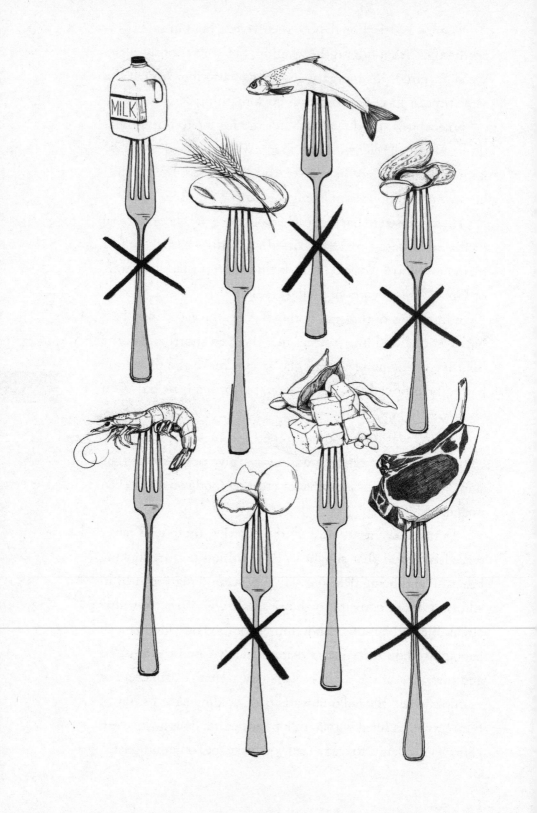

10

No Milk!
(Butter and Cream Okay)

How Allergies and Preferences Have Transformed
Special Events

Ask anyone who's worked in catering a generation or more, and witnessed the trends and changes, the cataclysms of 9/11 and the financial crash of September 29, 2008, and they'll all tell you: no body blow to the economy or to the national psyche has changed the way people party in the last twenty years like the new sovereignty of allergies, intolerances, and preferences. The very nature of catering—fulfilling people's desires—means that firms have met this new demand, devising an array of strategies to respond to special requests in advance and à la minute. In doing so, they may have accelerated the shift in the balance of power, away from the creativity of the catering chef—away from the host, even—and toward the diner, even if that person is a guest with no financial stake in the event.

The shift has impacted everything from the way party invitations are composed, to how menus are designed, to how service staff is trained. Most critically, it has deeply complicated life in the fiesta kitchen.

Working the plating assembly line is, for those laboring behind the black curtain, the climax of any seated dinner event. Kitchen assistants bellied up to the work table wait for the signal, rocking back and forth like sprinters before the gun, leaning in occasionally to reinspect the sample plate the executive chef composed—the fillet placed off center, potatoes at three o'clock, sweep of sauce just so. When the chef in charge shouts, "Go-Go-Go!" the conveyor belt lurches into motion and each K.A. lays down in series a single piece of the puzzle: a scoop of puree, a fistful of fingerlings, two scallops, a squirt of sauce, a scattering of herbs. And always pushing plates sideways, left to right (or right to left), each plate building toward the archetype as it slides down the table. At the line's end, someone stands with a stack of wipes to swab at splatters and smudges. Servers swoop in to pick up the perfected plates, one in each hand, peeling away from the kitchen toward the floor in brisk succession.

That plating line has an early twentieth-century cast—it's fully analog, an ungainly, human-powered food-delivery system, complete with spills and curses, which is why it's hidden behind the pipe and drape, out of the sight of guests. But once the lines find their rhythm, there's something like beauty to the synchronicity of those first few minutes. As with any engine, this one functions best with some warmth and grease and momentum.

Seasoned K.A.s on the line know that these days this plateau of proficiency rarely lasts long. Usually, within a few minutes of the first plates entering the room, a doom force of service captains in suits will enter the kitchen with a salvo of interruptions.

Chef, I need two vegetarian! Now three! Three vegetarian all day!

Is there any soy on this plate, chef? SOY, chef? SOY?

I need four gluten-free! No farro on quatro por favor!

Chef, is there mayonnaise in this sauce?

When K.A.s in a plating line are halting the train every few minutes to make one without the polenta—or one with the polenta but without the sauce; or one with the polenta and sauce but minus the lamb shank—at what point does catering to each guest call into question the very premise of sharing a meal? The expectation that everyone at a dinner event be served simultaneously—a logistical challenge whose solutions (e.g., the hotbox, the plating line) took decades to perfect—crashes headlong into this idea that almost every plate must also be personalized for each individual. It appears that success at producing near-restaurant-quality food at catered events may have also created, over time, the expectation of restaurant-level accommodations—even if the wedding banquet is taking place under a tent in the middle of a park.

In an earlier catering era, guests took their seats in front of empty plates and were attended to by waiters trained in the art of transferring portions of the roast beef or shad roe and its accompanying starches and vegetables from a large platter to the guest's plate. Customization by opting out, on the order of "no potatoes, thank you," was easy to implement; sending the waiter back to the kitchen for something entirely different was unthinkable. At today's parties, the very invisibility of the catering function may create a false impression among guests that the plates marching out from behind the pipe and drape were created in something resembling a fixed restaurant kitchen, rather than on a card table propped up in an elevator vestibule: *can't you just whip up something else for me?*

To be sure, caterers have never been strangers to special meals. The sheer diversity of the population in U.S. urban centers acquainted caterers there with the dietary restrictions of their religious communities. Even when meal options for a party are not explicitly solicited on a reply card included with an invitation, observant guests know: if they give the host advance notice, they can request and should receive a special meal. Providing kosher meals for large catered events, especially in the New York area, is routine. Almost all New York caterers purchase kosher meals from Le Marais, a steakhouse and butcher in Manhattan's theater district. The restaurant delivers these boxed dinners directly to the event venue in transparent, plastic disposable clamshell containers sealed shut with a dated, signed sticker. They're kept in a separate proofer until serve-out, at which time a service captain will deliver the boxes, their seals intact, to guests. Diners keeping kosher can be confident that no hands have touched the meal between the *kashrut* kitchen and the table.

But at some point in the last decade it became common for a diner to express to a server his hope (and, depending on his temerity, his expectation) to be served a customized plate according to his vegetarianism, veganism, or his allergy to any number of comestibles, from wheat to dairy to soy to nightshade vegetables. Food allergy and food-intolerance products are currently the fastest-growing category in the food industry, a $24-billion-a-year market that reflects a heightened sensitivity nationwide to the body's responses to food. The industry loosely defines a food intolerance as discomfort an individual may feel when ingesting a certain ingredient—especially a surfeit of it. An allergy is a more serious condition whereby exposure to a particular food, even in trace amounts, induces an immune response called *anaphylaxis*. The body floods itself with enzymes that can cause throats to close, heart rates to drop, lungs to collapse. Anaphylaxis can be fatal.

Food allergies are no joking matter. We have a friend who left a Paris restaurant on a gurney because a waiter took it upon himself to interpret her stated *Capsicum annuum* (bell peppers) allergy as merely an intolerance. Another friend is fatally allergic to *Arachis hypogaea* (peanuts). Serious allergy sufferers carry epinephrine pens that can inhibit some allergic reactions. They never take risks, because the appearance of EMTs—emergency medical technicians—and a stretcher kills the vibe of any celebration. And any veteran chef who's seen a severe allergy attack unfold at a party will work in good faith to make damn sure it never happens again.

But more and more Americans dress up mild intolerances and preferences for food in allergy drag, perhaps to absolve themselves of the rudeness of expecting to be served a customized plate. Chefs and waiters share stories of such behavior constantly: guests who are "allergic" to dairy until the chocolate pudding comes out for dessert. The "celiac" who needs his first course and second course gluten-free and then asks for a second slice of cake.

"It's every party now," Robb Garceau, now executive chef at Neuman's Kitchen, told us. "Guest says: 'I need a vegan first course!' So we build a special salad just for her. And then we send her a vegan main. But she's seen somebody else's salmon.

Captain tells me: 'She wants the fish course.' And I'm like: 'What?! You were vegan half an hour ago!'"

Given the explosion of requests for special meals, it's a miracle that event hosts haven't abandoned the plated dinner wholesale in favor of a buffet, with numerous stations fine-tuned to check off all allergy and diet buttons. Nightshade-free? Check. Soy-free? Check. Raw options? Check. But many large occasions still demand the streamlined formality of a plated dinner, so over the years catering chefs and party planners have refined their strategies to alleviate the strain of exceptions and preferences on the kitchen. Offering a vegetarian option has become industry standard at large events in New York, and RSVP cards often supply options to be checked off. An executive chef can then develop a separate vegetarian plating line, if needed, that operates in tandem with the meat or the fish main course. But counting your chickens is never enough in catering; the moment is the thing, and people often evolve in the time between RSVPs and the big event.

A smart catering chef will design a vegetarian option that is also vegan, gluten-free, and soy-free (or at the very least can be made vegan or gluten-free by the simple subtraction of a single element in the line—which may bog down plating but won't cripple it). She may even engineer the meaty main course in the same way, such that any elements involving wheat, soy, dairy, or nightshades can be easily withheld. Even with the vegetarian line planned out, every clever caterer nowadays packs a pile of washed salad greens, a soy-free dressing, and a sheet pan of dry-grilled vegetables for occasions when it's just impossible to make that one person happy.

Perhaps the cleverest adaptation strategy that caterers and party planners employ is the so-called silent vegetarian option, or SVO, whereby the vegetarian option is unannounced. The sweet potato lasagna comes out only on request, when the guest pipes up as the waiter moves in to place a plate of halibut. It's catering's equivalent of negative-option marketing: most guests—unless they're strict vegetarians—will still simply accept the meat or the fish because it's the one that's delivered. Because the silent option reduces the number of guests who order the vegetarian entrée, the caterer makes fewer of those meals, and can shave some cost and complexity from the event. (As a general catering principle, if there's a choice on the menu between two items in a course, the beef filet or the halibut, for example, a caterer will typically prepare 70 percent of each option, of the total diners expected at the event; caterers typically bring only 30 percent of an SVO.) Offering a silent vegetarian option has its risks, because word of it can spread readily—particularly if it happens to look more appealing than the main offering. A kitchen can be caught short, without enough pumpkin agnolotti, and with the service captain facing some unhappy vegetarians.

At a recent Robin Hood Gala, the northwest kitchen—one of four placed strategically at the corners of the airplane-hangar-like Javits Center, each serving eleven hundred guests—ran out of the silent vegetarian option with thirty tables of ten people still waiting to be served. The Heirloom Bean Stew with Smoked Onions and Thyme was coffee-brown in color, downright wintry for early May, and Union Square Events executive chef John Karangis had no reason to anticipate it being a smash hit. But something about it—maybe it was the terra-cotta bowl, warm and rustic, in that warehousey monstrosity of a room—made everyone in the northwest quadrant request it. Because of the event's size, each kitchen was separated one from another by 150 yards of polished concrete. The sight of two kitchen assistants flat-out sprinting two hotboxes, packed with heirloom-bean stew, through the north wing of the Javits Center was made only more surreal by the sight of the pop star Sting, the evening's talent, and his entourage sauntering on a direct collision course toward them, until a chorus of captains and servers awaiting the delivery shouted: *Watch out! Cuidado! Look out!*

The SVO going viral among guests represents the best of kitchen-stress scenarios because it ultimately reflects the chef's talent in creating a dish so special that everyone craves it. At the other end of the spectrum are occasions when people's need to be served specially divides the guests into factions, undermining the sense of unity at the core of the celebration. Case in point was the Drury engagement, a fête for four hundred in the Celeste Bartos Forum, the soaring Beaux Arts ballroom at the New York Public Library crowned with a glass and steel dome. Entering the massive stone portal at the back entrance of the New York Public Library on Fortieth Street is always thrilling. The guts of the place are the grimy, majestic gray of a nineteenth-century tintype. Sonnier & Castle's truck was parked at the indoor loading area, and most of the proofers had been rolled into their respective kitchens. We hopped up onto the dock where Bethany conferred with Juan Soto about kitchen staff assignments. The K.A.s were listed on her sheet under headings: Hors D'oeuvres, Main Buffet, Pasta Station, and Small Plates. Our names weren't among them. Then Ted spotted them, in the margin, under the heading: NO ONION.

"No Onion?" we asked.

"You're in charge of Allergies," Bethany said. "Allergy proofer's in the main kitchen, with Juan." She shuffled some papers on her clipboard and handed us a party grid. Across the top was written: ALLERGIES: NO PEPPERS/NO ONION/ NO GARLIC/NO MILK.

The engagement party was a cocktail buffet, running from 7:30 to 10:30 p.m. There would be eleven different hors d'oeuvres passed from 7:30 to 9:00 p.m. At 8:15 p.m., four steakhouse stations and four pasta stations and four passed small plates would begin serving and run until 10:30 p.m. After every item in the menu was a note in bright red lettering:

Shrimp Seviche, Pineapple, Diced Celery, Chili Lime Sauce [NOTE! LESS Lime, LESS Spice]

Baby Artichoke, Foie Gras, Croissant and Black Trumpet Stuffing [NOTE! Use Gluten-Free Bread Crumbs].

Salmon Tartare, Dill Crème Fraiche, American Caviar, Fresh Dill [NOTE! NO Crème Fraiche, SUB Dill Aioli NO Garlic]

This was confusing. Were we serving *everyone* who professed an allergy? Were these substitutions and modifications to make all these dishes edible? How was it even possible to know how many guests had allergies?

"Oh, here's another sheet for you," Bethany said. She rifled through her papers again. "The bride can't eat anything at the pasta station."

"I don't get it!" Matt said. "Are we making the food for everyone who has allergies?"

She threw back her head and laughed. "No! This is all for the host family and the engaged couple—ten VIPs. Check the half-proofer that says 'Allergy,' it has a skull and crossbones on it. I think there's some roasted veg medley, gluten-free bread, maybe a few other veg substitutions in there."

She found the sheet she was looking for and handed it to us. It was an email, forwarded from the Sales Department to the kitchen team the day before, subject line: VIP Allergies.

"Hot off the press," it read. "New allergies . . . please print this out for our VIP Servers to carry around."

The groom was a pescatarian; the bride was gluten-free and allergic to corn, cucumber, kiwi, pork, and cow's milk, though sheep and goat milk were A-OK. As for the Drury family, there was a list.

NO ALLIUMS (including chives, garlic, leeks, onion)
NO PEPPERS (including hot peppers, paprika, chipotle, etc.)
NO MILK (Cream & Butter OK/Lactaid OK)
NO CUMIN or PAPRIKA
NO PICKLES
NO BANANAS
NO CABBAGES (Brussels Sprouts OK)

Cross-referencing the grid, which had been marked up with some dishes crossed out entirely, others with check marks, things began to come into focus. Although the event was a large self-service buffet, the ten hosts would have four VIP waiters and a service captain devoted exclusively to them, a party within a party. We'd be their allergy kitchen, in constant contact with the VIP servers, assembling plates upon request, coordinating pickups and drops of the foods they could eat.

And then one of the VIP servers that night was at my

elbow. "Michael says it's really important that you make the VIP food look like it's not special."

"What?"

"It can't be special: the Drurys don't want their guests to know they're getting anything different from their guests. *Do you understand?*"

"Sure. We're just taking some garnishes away, subbing in some extra veg sides for their steak. There's gluten-free bread back here for them."

"But you really need to take special care to make the allergy plates not, you know, *obvious.*"

"Don't you think having four dedicated servers hustling them plates at a self-serve buffet is a little . . . I don't know . . . more *obvious* than anything I'm going to do?" Ted asked.

"You know what I mean!" she said, and stomped off toward the floor.

The entire experience made us long for what may be the next wave, a catering patron possessed with enough self-confidence to specify for his party the all-vegetarian menu (no legumes, no alliums!) of his dreams, what he truly prefers and loves to eat, but with an SMO—a silent meat option. Such a sensibility is sure to arrive soon, if it hasn't already.

11

Great Expectations

Catering Comes of Age, Raises the Bar, and Evolves

Examining the effects of the latest wave to hit catering made us curious again about its recent past. Our last dive into history left off in the early Reagan era, when modern techniques were being perfected and anything seemed possible— parties had been liberated from square banquet-hall settings, theatricality was embraced, and the business was evolving into something greater than a service industry. Martha Stewart, perhaps the most famous caterer in American history (and is there really *any* caterer besides Martha who became a true celebrity?), had established her business in 1976 in Westport, Connecticut, about forty miles from Manhattan but well inside the penumbra of New York money and influence. Stewart was among the first people we wanted to interview about the history of catering—we'd met on a few occasions, written for her magazine for almost a decade, and had even seared salmon with her on her network television show. Her assistant politely got back to us saying she'd find a time, but after we followed up twice we moved on. Stewart's moment in catering—a decade, give or take—was relatively brief compared to that of Liz Neumark. If Stewart is the best-known person from the catering world, Neumark is widely considered one of the most influential and innovative figures in the industry today; she was among the independents who crashed the scene in the early eighties, challenging the hegemony of the Glorious Food boys' club. Today she leads Great Performances, the largest off-premise catering firm in New York and one of the top three revenue earners among the nation's independent caterers.

Neumark invited us to meet her for lunch at Mae Mae, the café her company runs out of a corner of the twenty-three thousand square feet of leased space in an industrial building on Vandam Street, in Soho. In 1982, the same year the cookbook *Glorious Food* appeared in bookstores, Neumark hatched an idea for a small business. She was a native New Yorker, recently graduated from Barnard with a BA in political science, but she aspired to be a fine-art photographer and needed money for film and darkroom supplies, so she signed up with Lend A Hand, a temporary employment agency, and waitressed at fancy parties (including a few at Leonard Bernstein's house). Neumark's idea was to create a party-staffing agency by and for women artists and performers, so they could make money between casting calls, rehearsals, and performances. She asked her father for a loan of $250 to set up the phone line for Great Performances/

Artists As Waitresses, Inc.,* and set up the office in her bed-room.

Her first hire was a friend, a flamenco dancer from Min-neapolis. Strictly by word of mouth, and within a matter of weeks, Neumark amassed a quorum of staffers and a stellar reputation among the city's newer, younger caterers—ones without the deep bench of waitstaff that Glorious Foods main-tained. Great Performances grew rapidly by responding to cli-ents' demands, first by bringing men aboard[†] and later by bringing the hors d'oeuvres and canapés themselves. In those early days, Neumark purchased pigs in blankets, chicken satay skewers, and cucumber sandwiches (crusts off) from the very caterers who used her staffing services, and her crew simply transported the food to parties. One day, an employee told Neumark she had a nice kitchen in Queens and could make better food at a cheaper price, and very soon after that they realized they'd need a larger kitchen, one more centrally located. Neumark had been in business less than a year, but she secured a loan from the First Women's Bank for $25,000 and signed a lease on fifteen hundred square feet of ground-floor space on Crosby Street, between Prince and Houston Streets, in Soho. The neighborhood was still largely a manufacturing district, and the new premises allowed Neumark to move Great Performances' office out of her bedroom, gave every-one plenty of room to cook, and created a space to throw parties once in a while. The new kitchen seemed palatial to

---

* Neumark's father, committing a Freudian slip par excellence, wrote the check out to "Great Expectations."

† Neumark learned, much to her chagrin, that New York hostesses in the early eighties stubbornly preferred male bartenders.

her then; little did she know that in ten years she would sign a lease for a space with five times that footprint.

Among the first calls Neumark made to clients announcing the move into catering was to a guy she'd been buying hors d'oeuvres from—Ronnie Davis, chef and owner of Washington Street Café and Caterers. Davis was none too pleased about having a new competitor, but he wasn't in a position to protest, as he'd already booked Great Performances staff to serve food and pour drinks for his entire roster of parties that year. (Immediately after our lunch with Neumark, she introduced us to Davis, who now works for her, running the division of the company that produces its most elaborate and far-flung events.) Davis's own business had grown exponentially in the two years since his first New York catering gig, a brunch for six thousand—three thousand per day across two days—on the lawn of Gracie Mansion during the 1980 Democratic National Convention. Like Neumark, Davis had an undergraduate degree (sociology, Villanova), but catering ran in his blood. He was third generation in the business, born in Philadelphia to Harry and Lydia Davis, the top kosher caterers in the city, who, like Harry's own father before him, produced lavish bar mitzvahs and weddings at all the fanciest banquet rooms on North Broad Street. Davis had grown up apprenticing to his father and, after college in Pennsylvania, worked in Annapolis, assisting the private chef to financier Barron Hilton—Paris and Nicky's grandfather. He followed a girlfriend working in the fashion industry to New York City in 1976 and eventually got hired as chef at the Wine Bar in Soho, one of the first spots in Manhattan to offer wines by the glass, served with small plates of cheeses and pâtés purchased from the spanking-new gourmet food purveyor around the corner,

Dean & DeLuca. During Davis's tenure at the Wine Bar, he was invited to bid on the contract to cater New York City mayor Ed Koch's 1980 Democratic Convention brunch, and he won. To be sure, that event had had its hairy moments—for those numbers, he had to mix pasta salad in the bathtub of a walk-up apartment (see Bathtub Pasta Salad recipe, pages 231–33) but there was a eureka moment as well. Standing next to Koch and Senator Ted Kennedy on the sun-splashed lawn of Gracie Mansion, he watched as two New York Fire Department boats motored up the East River and idled in front of the lawn of the mayor's house. One boat shot its water cannon, a geyser of water dyed blue, and the second boat shot out red, high arcs that crossed one another in midair. And it was then that Davis thought: I want to produce events like this.

He gave notice at the Wine Bar and started to build out his own restaurant in a small warehouse with a loading dock on windswept, industrial Washington Street in Tribeca. He installed warm lighting, painted the exposed-brick walls a shade of creamy peach,* and built one of New York's first open restaurant kitchens, from which he turned out a small menu of French bistro classics: veal marsala, tarragon chicken, filet au poivre, tortellini with Roquefort cream sauce. Washington Street Café, as he called it, was a casual joint, more ragtag than the sleek brasserie the Odeon that opened that same fall a few blocks east, but with a similar bohemian clientele of neighborhood pioneers. And in off-hours, Davis used the café's kitchen to prepare for the catering jobs he'd begun to book the very day of the Gracie Mansion gig. In addition to Mayor Koch and Senator Kennedy, he'd met the commercial

---

* This *was* the eighties, after all.

cinematographer Bob Gaffney, who hired Davis to cater his birthday celebration. At Gaffney's party, Davis met executives from several top New York advertising agencies and a smattering of TV networks. And those contacts led to more catering jobs—some of which required production chops in addition to food preparation: he chartered a barge and parked it under the Brooklyn Bridge for a family reunion of descendants of the landmark's designer, John A. Roebling, on the centennial of its completion. That same night he met Hollywood TV legend and producer Norman Lear, who hired Davis to cater and produce the first People for the American Way gala dinner at the Puck Building. In Lear, Davis had discovered not only a client but a mentor, who taught him the stakes—and rewards—of event production at its most ambitious level. The morning of that first PFAW gala, Davis invited Lear in to inspect the room—the tables had been set down to the last dessert fork, the chairs were in place, the sound system had been installed, and all the decor and lighting were positioned. Lear clapped three times and listened to the echo. "Terrible acoustics, Ronnie," he said. "Carpet the place."

"Norman," Davis shot back. "No."

"Carpet it," Lear said, and walked out of the building.

So Davis ordered ten thousand square feet of a tan-colored carpet and instructed his crew to move every piece of furniture, the table settings, all the glasses off the floor. They carpeted the room and had it reset in less than six hours, well before the bars opened and first hors d'oeuvres went out.

"I didn't think you were going to do it," Lear said when he arrived at the venue for the party.

"I did it," Davis told him and sheepishly presented him the bill, in the low five figures, for the carpet and extra labor.

Lear took the bill, smiling, and said, "Fine!" And for the next decade, until the organization moved its headquarters to Washington, D.C., Lear made sure that Washington Street Caterers always produced the organization's annual dinner.

The progressive politics and downtown location of the People For the American Way gala were seemingly a world away from the Upper East Side precincts in which Donald Bruce White and Glorious Food had found their prosperity. But the younger caterers were finding plenty of money to be made outside of the *Social Register*, and their very kitchen locations reflected a cultural shift taking place in Manhattan, as heavy-manufacturing companies departed the nineteenth-century cast-iron loft buildings of the downtown commercial districts for outer boroughs, New Jersey, or counties upstate. Where the previous generation of off-premise catering pioneers had started out of their apartment kitchens uptown, this new wave was building businesses that from the beginning were more professionalized (the bathtub pasta salad notwithstanding), but housed in comparatively inexpensive—and infinitely more serviceable—commercial lofts and warehouses of downtown Manhattan.

Liz Neumark had settled in Soho and Ronnie Davis in Tribeca; the Flatiron District was home to Susan Holland, who, like Neumark, had grown up on the Upper West Side of Manhattan. Holland attended the High School of Music and Art and Pratt Institute, and after graduating she began to achieve some success as a painter, showing in galleries in New York and Los Angeles. In the late sixties, she married and moved with her husband to Washington, D.C., and soon learned that if she was going to eat a decent loaf of bread there, she'd better bake it herself. With unsold canvases piling up in her studio,

Holland found that baking bread—consumed and enjoyed the same day—gave her the immediate gratification she'd been missing in her art career. She threw herself into food and cooking with a passion. Holland began hosting dinners for friends that generated excitement in her social circles, so much so that in 1972 the wine club her husband belonged to, the founding chapter of Les Amis du Vin, asked Holland to be the chef for a tasting dinner in a rented corporate apartment. The club* had initially conceived the event for thirty guests, but on the strength of Holland's reputation the count swelled to sixty. She recruited a food writer friend from New York, Carole Lalli,[†] to come down and help her cook, and the evening was a smash success. Les Amis du Vin invited Holland to teach at its cooking school, where *Washington Post* food editor William Rice and Carol Mason, a caterer, were also instructors. With Mason, Holland formed her first small catering company, We Cook, in 1973, doing small dinners in private homes in Georgetown, Bethesda, and Silver Spring.

By the late seventies, Holland had divorced and moved back to New York City, where she opened a firm, Susan Holland & Company, in a loft on the fourth floor of a building at the corner of Nineteenth Street and Fifth Avenue. Upon settling in New York, she began to see the way her art training in color, pattern, and abstraction meshed with her enthusiasm for cooking and interest in ephemerality, how all of that came together in the course of an event. Dinner wasn't just delicious

---

* Among its members was a college student named Robert M. Parker Jr., who would later find fame as the most polarizing wine critic in the world.

[†] Lalli would become editor in chief of *Food & Wine* magazine, an editor at the book publisher Simon & Schuster, and caterer Liz Neumark's collaborator on the cookbook *Sylvia's Table*.

ginger-chicken skewers and boeuf à la mode served at the right temperature—it was also candles, flowers, conversations, everything converging in a site-specific "installation" of escalating, transcendent moments for guests.

In marked contrast to that grand vision, Holland's New York career began with the same routine at-home dinners and dreary cocktail receptions that she'd booked in D.C. But Holland soon learned that in New York there was a demand for excellence in catering—and she could charge handsomely for it. This was the dawn of the eighties: entertaining—the way food was served, the style in which one celebrated—was increasingly becoming a part of newly wealthy New Yorkers' public personae. Holland's first big break came in 1985, when the young, upstart producer Scott Sanders, who'd been hired by Radio City Music Hall to turn around the fortunes of the moribund theater, tapped Holland to cater the food for a series of celebrity-filled soirées at the venue. And although she'd never before cooked parties at this scale, she had an inkling these would be the dinners that provided the opportunity to realize her holistic artistic vision. She threw herself into the culinary challenge with gusto and, before long, Sanders made her event producer of all opening nights, with complete and total design control over the party. From the eighties through the mid-nineties, Holland trained on her feet, learning lighting and florals and furniture and props, indulging her artistic whims at the same time she rolled the pastry for the pigs in blankets. These nights at Radio City were the early foundation for Holland becoming, twenty years later, "the go-to designer," according to the *New York Times*, for the city's most extravagant gay weddings, and, eventually, for her triumphant return engagements in D.C., the city where her food passion had been sparked, in the role of designer of White House state dinners for President Barack Obama and First Lady Michelle Obama.

Glorious Food reigned supreme in New York in the early 1980s, when this younger generation—Davis, Holland, and Neumark—was just getting on its feet. But as the eighties folded into the nineties and the art and music of downtown came to define New York culture—with its own wealth, its own style, its own parties—Glorious Food's standing in the firmament began to show the limitations of dwelling in the air up there. Glorious couldn't cater every party in New York on any given night—it might not have even wanted to—but Sean Driscoll didn't like losing out on business to anybody. When, in 1992, Madonna launched her book *Sex* at the meatpacking-district photo studio Industria—one of the decade's most lavish and most photographed parties—were her reps going to give Driscoll a call? Not a chance. (They called Davis.)

And Glorious Food's dominance began to show weaknesses in other ways. In 1986, Glorious folded its catering operation in Washington, D.C., after only three years. The *Washington Post* covered its closing in an unusually in-depth story that barely disguised the writer's schadenfreude. "In the end," trumpeted the lede, "there weren't enough people in Washington with expensive tastes for glorious foods."

But back in New York, the catering business was beginning a wild ride—even as it was ravaged by the AIDS crisis.* More and more independents were getting into the game,

---

* "Catering and events was a magnet for young gay men in the arts, because it was the perfect freelance work, and the community was devastated in the way that all arts-heavy communities were. I had twenty friends; sixteen of them died," said party planner Susan Holland.

inspiring the food writer Nancy Jenkins to write a story spanning the front page of the *New York Times* Living Section on November 28, 1984, headlined: CATERED PARTIES: NOW IN ALL SIZES. Her interviews made plain the breadth of new caterers in the firmament and also noted that the establishment was feeling the presence of competitors (if maybe not yet the pinch). "Catering is the cottage industry of New York," Donald Bruce White told Jenkins. "All a caterer needs is a Cuisinart, some pots and pans and a couple of food magazines to start out." And if his dismissiveness hadn't been obvious enough, he added: "They get jobs, though they don't necessarily get repeats."

Jenkins credited the explosion in catering to a number of factors, among them the emergence of the "obsessive interest in food that seems to have gripped New Yorkers," and also the rise of two-career couples eager to entertain business associates, friends, and family, but with scant spare time. She reported that the new breed of caterer was open to creativity and to global influences, and less likely to hew to White's tenet that the customer was always right. One Brooklyn-based caterer she interviewed had created a feast of Japanese dishes for one client, but rejected the request of another for a Jell-O mold.

As the clientele for catering grew, the choice of places where people might party also expanded. By the late seventies, both the Metropolitan Museum of Art and the New York Public Library had opened their doors to "externals"—one-off events hosted by non-Met-affiliated people, but their kind and number changed dramatically by the mid-eighties. Hosting an event at the Met in 1979 required completing an application proving your event's artistic mission (a colloquium, say); if approved, you made a donation to the museum of $5,000.

Broadening that policy became quite controversial among the Met's board of trustees, but financial imperatives won out. By 1985, the doors were fully open, so to speak: anyone could rent one of its grand spaces for the night (the glass-ceilinged modern hall housing the Egyptian Temple of Dendur was among the first and most popular) as long as they ponied up the then $30,000 fee.

The success the New York Public Library and the Met had in monetizing their spaces for product launches and weddings got other cultural institutions, such as Lincoln Center and the Frick, hip to the earning potential of their majestic lobbies and ballrooms—all the more essential in the wake of the financial crash of 1987. Amid this constellation of emergent party palaces in the late eighties and early nineties, Liz Neumark made waves again, pioneering a new sector of the catering industry most firms had never considered: venue management. Great Performances became the first of the independent event caterers to contract with the city's cultural institutions for exclusive- or preferred-status relationships. An "exclusive" at a museum meant that GP (as the firm came to be known as it grew) ran the museum's café and was the only option for a bride and groom wanting to throw a reception there; "preferred" status meant the happy couple was incentivized to use GP as their caterer but could choose from a list of independent, preapproved firms if they paid a premium on their rental fee. And since GP retained the contract to run the café regardless of how many weddings or corporate holiday parties went down at the museum, the relationship served to stabilize operations at the prep kitchen during down cycles in the economy.

Another lasting development in the hotbox landscape was that caterers began emulating restaurant food and culture more directly. "Nouvelle Cuisine" had crossed the Atlantic in the early eighties, and chefs were no longer just laborers, they were now artists. The late eighties saw the dawn of the celebrity chef, with *Food & Wine* publishing its first "Best New Chefs" issue in 1988, and the James Beard Foundation holding its inaugural awards ceremony in 1990, to dole out to American chefs what became the restaurant industry's top achievement awards. The nineties were a veritable boom time for dining out in New York City. Ruth Reichl assumed the role of restaurant critic at the *New York Times* in 1993 and was on her way to becoming America's first celebrity restaurant critic, reviewing (and adoring) places like Gramercy Tavern, Union Pacific, Jean-Georges, and Vong, where the outlook was international, the flavors zingy and bold, and the presentations playful. Francophile cuisine was on the way out.

When Bob Spiegel and Carla Ruben opened their firm in 1990, calling it Creative Edge, they were staking a claim for a forward-thinking, artistic approach to catering, in line with the restaurants of the time. And when Russ Sonnier and David Castle opened Sonnier & Castle in the latter part of the decade, they knew they needed to bypass the Glorious old guard to capture a younger clientele, customers who would compare the food at S&C events to the city's exciting new fine-dining spots.

Sonnier & Castle plucked its talent off the line of important or promising restaurants, finding chefs in their late twenties who had grown weary of the *Order! Fire!* routine, and were curious about the pay raise that came with a move to catering. With restaurant-trained chefs, there was a learning curve, however, and Sonnier & Castle had to invest time with someone like Robb Garceau, who came from Vong, or Scott Forzaglia, hired away from Daniel, teaching them the catering-specific tricks of event-kitchen management, proofing, plate-up, planning, and flow. But the firm valued the culinary acumen and attention to detail these chefs brought when it came to sourcing, freshness, technique, and presentation; hiring artistic-leaning chefs (the kind who would struggle creatively against the compromises of off-premise catering) differentiated S&C from its competition.

Just as caterers in the nineties began to align themselves with restaurant culture, restaurant chefs with name brands got into catering—partly due to demand from their customers, but also because their kitchens represented a huge fixed cost as rents increased; if a kitchen isn't maxed out twenty-four hours a day, that's earning potential squandered.

"For a very long time," Neumark told us, "caterers were the bottom feeders of the industry, and no reputable chef would do catering." All that changed in 1994, the year Daniel Boulud, one of *Food & Wine*'s first class of Best New Chefs, debuted Feast and Fêtes, the off-premise catering arm of his eponymous restaurant, which had opened just one year before (1994 was also the year Boulud won the James Beard Award for Outstanding Chef). Helmed by Jean-Christophe Le Picart, a catering veteran who'd sold his own firm, Tentation, to a French conglomerate just a couple years before, Feast and Fêtes was an instant hit, and Le Picart remains president and partner in the operation twenty-five years later. Leagues of restaurant chefs would look to Boulud's success when they attempted to cater, but few could pull off this bipolar challenge. As Neumark explained, "Putting out four hundred, six hundred, a thousand perfectly uniform plates in fifteen minutes is alien to most [restaurant] chefs, and the really smart ones know their limitations."

Many restaurant chefs we talked to in the course of writing this book told us they'd foundered on the shoals of event catering, whether it was a chef who did a one-off experience and ran screaming back to the comfort of her gas ranges, or Bobby Flay, who took the full plunge, opening a catering division of Mesa Grill in the early 2000s. "That was the worst year of my life," he told us. "I had to torch that business, I got rid of it." Beyond the operations and logistical challenges he faced, he was incensed whenever a wedding planner, post-tasting, would circle back, angling for a better deal. "When have I *ever* had a customer at my restaurants say, 'I know the hanger steak is seventeen dollars, can I get it for fourteen?' *Never!*"

Eric Ripert, who has won multiple James Beard Awards and whose modern French seafood temple Le Bernardin consistently garners the highest accolades from the *New York Times*, witnessed enough horrors in his youth to vow never to cater outside the comfort zone of a restaurant kitchen. "We never put ourselves in those positions. The quality dictates everything around it, and we will never compromise," he told us in a recent interview.

The one exception to his rule was a wedding for eight hundred outside Boston, for a client with especially deep pockets. But true to his credo, there was to be no compromising on the food or the equipment: "To be able to do that, we asked the gentleman to build four kitchens for us. Same thing as Le Bernardin: cooking fish à la minute." His entire staff traveled to Massachusetts two days before the wedding to make sure everything was in place with the four new Le Bernardins. "The gentleman also paid for Le Bernardin in New York to be closed for three days," he added.

But an even more expensive and more telling object lesson in the gulf between the restaurant and catering businesses may be seen in the rocky path hospitality guru Danny Meyer, New York's most famous restaurateur, took into catering. We were eager to learn how, in 2005, he had added the traveling circus hustle to a portfolio of bricks-and-mortar restaurants that thrive on the serenity of their fixed locations, their *houses*. Patrick Phelan—who'd interviewed unsuccessfully for the chef position at Meyer's new firm, Hudson Yards Catering, when Robb Garceau left it in 2011—had tipped us off that building a catering business hadn't been all wine and roses for Meyer.

We met Meyer and his catering manager at the time, Mark Maynard-Parisi, in a suite of offices in a cast-iron building on the east side of Union Square. They were friendly, but circumspect at first. Meyer wanted to know: were we writing a hit piece? *Catering Confidential*?

We explained how we'd been impressed by an off-premise team we'd observed at the James Beard House, and were wondering why nobody had written anything about the world of grand-scale food events. We were hoping to educate ourselves, and the general public, about the subculture of catering.

He seemed reassured, because once he got started, it was difficult to get a word in edgewise. He had stories to tell, and they were mostly lamentations. "Every night in catering is ephemeral, it's one-and-done. Nobody on the team knows where they are. Every movement is labored and contrived and self-conscious."

As skilled as Meyer and his team had become in pulling off large events by the time we met—they'd recently prized the Robin Hood Gala, that biggest, baddest charity fund-raiser in America, a forty-four-hundred-person, $3,000-a-plate dinner, from the clutches of Glorious Food—Meyer expressed more than a little regret for ever having entered the catering game. He confessed his group would never have done it if they hadn't been so desperate in 2005 to open a new fine-dining flagship (the one that became the award-winning restaurant the Modern) inside the Museum of Modern Art. When the museum (MOMA) put out the request-for-proposal to operators, Meyer's team learned the operating contract had stipulations: if you wanted to run the restaurant, you also had to run MOMA's 350-seat staff cafeteria, its 300-seat café for museum visitors on the fifth floor, and the 65-seat café on the first floor. Lastly, you got "preferred" status as caterer to the museum's event-venue business (which has no dedicated kitchen at all, just the same loading dock where the crated Warhols and Matisses get shipped in and out during the day). So Meyer's group had raised a ton of money from investors, built the O'Hare Airport of commissary kitchens in the Terminal Warehouse building in far West Chelsea to support the catering operation, and soon discovered some very painful lessons about the new industry they had entered.

Meyer's team hadn't realized that being "preferred" caterer for MOMA's event-venue business by no means meant that Hudson Yards was the museum's exclusive caterer; it meant only their name was at the top of a list of two dozen such preferred caterers. And the fact that Meyer ran some of the best restaurants in New York City didn't matter a whit to risk-averse party planners; as a new firm, it'd be a pariah in the industry until it garnered a reputation for doing large events well.

So Hudson Yards was in a classic chicken-egg situation, and Meyer soon found out how different the staffing challenges were from restaurants to catering. Because events is an "accordion" business—one night you're cooking for eight people, the next night eight hundred, and the next night zero—most of your staff are freelancers; you can't afford to buy them uniforms, so they're wearing the same basic black pants and dress shirts they wear to every event, regardless of what caterer they're working for. Since your staff is constantly in flux, people are being trained on the fly, and they're taking whatever skills you do manage to impart to them to one of your competitors the following night. The ills of the restaurant business that he had spent decades taming returned by the dozens in catering.

But the most demoralizing point of difference in Meyer's mind was the lack of collegiality among caterers; he had no mentors to hash out his problems with because it's a cutthroat, market-share business, especially so at the upper end. Sure, the thousands of restaurants in New York compete with one another, but Meyer still had a vast community of restaurateur friends he could meet from time to time to chew over problems. Not in catering. Shortly after they'd won the bid for the museum businesses, he spotted the owner of a competitor firm dining at the Modern with some friends, and he approached their table to introduce himself.

"I hear you're getting into off-premise," the other guy said. "Well, good luck to you."

"Any time you want to get together," Meyer said, "I'd be happy to meet for lunch."

"Are you *crazy*?" the man retorted. "That's not how it works in catering! Every event we get, you don't get; and every event you get, we don't get. You and I are never going to be friends!"

Although Meyer's O'Hare of kitchens was doing only a

Midway Airfield's worth of parties, they gradually, fitfully, built Hudson Yards from mostly small and medium-size functions, inching up toward larger ones, gaining some confidence and momentum. Then the crash of 2008 hit, and quite a few catering firms didn't survive that year. What saved Hudson Yards were two things: the New York Mets called, wanting Meyer to bring Blue Smoke and Shake Shack (the burger joint in Madison Square Park he'd begun as a side hustle partly to maximize the off-hours potential of the Hudson Yards prep kitchen) to the team's new Citi Field. Second, they rebranded the firm, changing the name Hudson Yards to Union Square Events, laundering its checkered early reputation by allying the firm with its stellar sister restaurants. It was also a more overt method of pushing their catering clients toward the menus those restaurants offered, and away from the labor-intensive, free-form customization of menus common among most boutique firms in New York.

Alas, now that his catering business has found its footing, Meyer confessed he brought a wistfulness to even the most wondrous parties they pull off that arises from the doubt that a special event could ever aspire to the warm embrace of hospitality found at his restaurants. "If I go to an event," he said, "I usually don't know the guests very well and I don't know every person on staff. To be honest, it all feels a little . . . *hollow*."

Perhaps wanting to brighten the picture, Maynard-Parisi spoke of the thrill he gets from a beautiful, glittering wedding in full swing.

"I always love walking around the head table after the main course drops," he said. "Seeing the bride and groom and their parents enjoying the reception, then walking back to the chaos of the loading dock. I often think: I wish the bride could see just how insane it is, where all this magic is coming from . . ."

"*No!*" Meyer said, laughing. "No we don't! We hope she never does! The best catering is like good special effects—you don't even realize they're special effects."

As true as the statement seemed—the mechanics of catering need to be hidden behind curtains and doors so the pageant appears effortless—it also made us wonder: do caterers only ever enter a guest's consciousness when someone's messed something up? Is the invisibility somehow beneficial, like an averted glance—a way to escape notoriety if things go awry?

And that nagging question returned, What kind of person chooses to throw himself into the breach, night after night after night?

Since Meyer and Maynard-Parisi had so much experience around both restaurant chefs and catering chefs, we asked them whether they'd found common characteristics among the men and women who choose the catering world over restaurants.

"Perfectionism," Meyer said. "They seek perfection in the planning, but they won't be demoralized by what happens. You can't be demoralized in catering."

Maynard-Parisi offered, "They'll say 'I'll climb a higher mountain.' 'I'll jump out of the airplane.' When you see them in the kitchen tent, it's like a war room. They love it."

HOTBOX

In the past decade, restaurant and catering cultures have become especially cozy, with celebrity chefs appearing at large catered parties to lend sizzle and a lauded restaurant's imprimatur to dinner—a trend that shows no signs of abatement. Liz Neumark, again, was at the forefront of this, creating events she now calls "hybrids." They arose out of Great Performances' success providing operational support in the early 2010s for out-of-town restaurant chefs who descended on New York to cook for the James Beard Awards Gala. A hybrid is a larger-scale version of the dinner where we first met Juan, Jorge, and Patrick, an event where a crew of hotbox heroes supports a restaurant chef working in unfamiliar environs. The marquee chef arrives in the GP kitchen a day or two before the event and collaborates with chefs and K.A.s there on the best way to translate her dishes at volume. GP is by no means the only firm doing such events; it's a format that's become popular with party planners and especially corporations, who have the big bucks and who see the marketing value in having a name-brand chef in the house. Mimi Van Wyck, who runs the tony event firm Van Wyck & Van Wyck with her brother Bronson, recently hired a handful of such chefs for a dinner, each assigned to a different course. At events like these, Van Wyck always brings in a well-versed catering team to support the celebrities, and she typically insists on a day or two of dress rehearsals for the kitchen, adding considerably to the expense of the evening but greatly increasing the odds of success. "It has to be like clockwork," she said. "There are no second chances."

When Bronwyn Keenan, the event director of the Metropolitan Museum of Art, produced her first hybrid party for the Met's Chairman's Council Dinner, she tapped Daniel Rose, executive chef of Coucou, the French restaurant in New York that in 2017 won the James Beard Award for Best New Restaurant. The evening required massive coordination, a level of production Keenan had never attempted for an event that small. There were only one hundred diners but, as with the

Frick dinner Matt worked, just down Fifth Avenue, these were the most important ones . . . trustees/billionaires. It entailed a total of four catering teams: Rose and his chefs from Coucou added a second crew from Starr Events, an off-premise caterer owned by the restaurant group that owns Coucou. There was also staff from Restaurant Associates, the on-site caterer who has the venue management contract with the museum and could best translate the quirks and limitations of the facility; a fourth caterer, Olivier Cheng, known for superior staffing, provided the waiters and waitresses.

"It was the *pinnacle*," Keenan said. "Absolutely the closest we've ever got to a restaurant experience." The members of the Chairman's Council were ecstatic, she said. "Now they want it to be like this all the time!"

And therein lies the problem. When you succeed in making catered food the equal of restaurant cuisine, you dispel the protective fog of low expectations, the rubber chicken factor, that can surround such events. Every Chairman's Council Dinner sets the bar higher than the one before—and it must, or the job of the person responsible is in jeopardy. To a party planner charged with producing an annual event, the future looks like an ever-steepening slope; the creative pressures of a one-off event like a wedding seem tame in comparison. Planning for next year's even-more-perfect dinner must begin the following morning.

We're confident the catering industry will deal with the escalating pressures it faces in the ways it always has, slashing operating costs wherever possible, investing in labor-saving technology, and by raising prices—in short, by adapting. In the relatively brief time we worked in catering, we witnessed more and more caterers adopting the industry-standard software CaterExpert, which integrates a kitchen's recipe book with purchasing and billing, to allow a chef to calculate the food cost of a party down to the last penny and pinch of salt. Digitizing the torrent of information that Pam Naraine holds in her brain allows everyone throughout the organization to see in real time the bottom-line benefits of menu standardization (and by contrast the high cost of customization).

In this latter regard, too, we sense a swing of the pendulum in catering culture, away from the client and back to a more focused, holistic approach to food that acknowledges, especially at the higher end, the wisdom of the catering chef. As long as there are billionaires willing to pay handsomely to get their dreams brought to life in food, there will always be a market for hyper-personalization, but large caterers at the upper end are beginning to look again at the long-disdained practice of driving clients toward set menus, A, B, C, D, and E, tailored to certain seasons and types of events, that best showcase the firm's talents and keep the food production on terra firma.

Another change under way: just as downtown Manhattan precincts became the place to set up shop in the eighties and nineties, Long Island City, Queens, has become ground zero for catering firms changing with the times; in our two-plus years working in the field, at least three firms moved to larger, less expensive leased premises in the neighborhood—allowing them to grow their production capacity while remaining within striking distance of all Manhattan's glittering venues and new ones in Brooklyn.

Tricolor Rotini with Black Olives, Feta, and Sun-dried Tomatoes for Six Hundred

Ronnie Davis is the tough-talking, silver-maned Eric Clapton look-alike who runs Ronnie Davis Productions, a niche business within Liz Neumark's company Great Performances—the largest independent caterer in New York City, with about $50 million in annual revenue. If you can imagine a special-events catering operation crossed with a luxury-travel agency, that's Davis's domain. He's the guy you tap when you're the CEO of a Fortune 500 company and it's been a good year and you've got a few million dollars in the budget to take your executive team and their spouses on a celebratory trip to Rome (or Panama, Sydney, Kyoto, Beijing).

Davis orchestrates it all: the Michelin-starred meals, of course, but also the hotel suites, theater and concert tickets, museum admissions, spa treatments, transportation, security. It helps that he's the kind of person who loves nothing more than some city functionary standing in his way, telling him he can't launch fireworks over the Tiber River at midnight, the finale to an opera-themed dinner in the Knights of Malta Room at Piazza Colonna for those Fortune 500 executives.

Davis *will* find a way around any obstacle, a talent he honed in far less grand circumstances. Forty years ago, he was a journeyman chef trying to get his fledgling Washington Street Café and Caterers off the ground in the emerging (and then-desolate) neighborhood of Tribeca and bid on a job making brunch for six thousand people. At the time, he had little more than a rented apartment in Soho and a borrowed kitchen in the friendly wine bar downstairs. Against all odds, he won the bid and arranged for the corner bodega to loan him its walk-in refrigerator for a few days. He cleaned his apartment bathtub, which became the bowl for tossing the six thousand portions of pasta salad.

One gets the sense that Davis's stories get taller the longer he tells them, but in this case, one of his former employees, Sara Foster, confirmed the story without prompting. Sara is the celebrated cookbook author and chef-owner of Foster's Market, in Durham, North Carolina, and we knew that in the eighties, she'd been a lead chef at Martha Stewart's catering operation in Westport, Connecticut. So we called up Foster to see what kind of war stories she had, and when we asked where she first learned to cook professionally, she dropped Ronnie's name. She'd been a chef at Washington Street Caterers for a couple of years and learned everything she knew about how to cater large parties from him.

"We had so much fun back then," she said. "It was wild. Would you believe we used his bathtub to toss pasta salad?"

It turns out you can use your bathtub as a pasta salad bowl. We don't necessarily condone it, but if you ever have to make pasta salad for several busloads of people,

ve a choice. And should you choose to accept the chal-
his recipe, whose Italianate flavors pay tribute to the quin-
e catering in 1982.

pending on how porous the enamel in your bathtub, the
ve it a light shade of pink, as it did in Davis's case. Although
d himself to replacing the tub once his lease was up, his
ed he'd done it on purpose: she loved the color and found

Yield: 30 gallons (600 four-ounce servings)
TIME: 12 HOURS

Equipment:

One 5-foot-long (measured end to end at the rim) enameled cast-iron
bathtub, with drain plug and drain catch

Two or more 32-quart stockpots

Six 22-quart Cambro containers

A chest refrigerator or walk-in

Large food processor

One 36-inch wood stirring paddle

For the pasta salad:

Kosher salt

Olive oil or vegetable oil

22½ pounds dried tricolor rotini

45 pounds ripe tomatoes, cored and cut into medium dice (about 30 quarts
diced)

4½ pounds sun-dried tomatoes, drained of their liquid and chopped (about
15 cups)

11¼ pounds pitted and chopped kalamata olives (about 37½ cups)

30 pounds feta cheese, cut into medium dice (about 26 quarts plus 1 cup)

For the dressing:

1 gallon plus 3 cups mild-tasting olive oil

1½ quarts red wine vinegar

3½ pounds sun-dried tomatoes (about 11 cups)

60 cloves garlic (about 5 whole heads), peeled

¾ cup kosher salt, plus more to taste

½ cup freshly ground black pepper, plus more to taste

1. Stopper the bathtub drain and fill two-thirds full with cold water. Cook the pasta: bring as many stockpots of salted water as will fit on your stovetop to a boil. Once the water boils, add ¼ cup oil to each pot, followed by the rotini, about 5 pounds per pot. Cook until just tender, about a minute less than the time indicated on the package.

2. Drain each pot of pasta (reserve the cooking water for the next batch) and, working as quickly as you can, use the Cambros to transfer the rotini to the bath water to cool, stirring with the paddle until the temperature of the water and the pasta are equivalent. Replace the stopper of the drain with the drain catch and strain. Transfer the rotini back to the Cambros and place in the refrigerator to cool completely.

3. Repeat steps 1 and 2 until all of the pasta has been cooked and cooled. In a large food processor, make the dressing in six batches: pour about 3 cups of the olive oil, 1 cup of the red wine vinegar, about 2 cups of the sun-dried tomatoes, 12 cloves of the garlic, 1 tablespoon of the salt, and ¾ tablespoon of the black pepper into the bowl of the food processor. Process until the dressing is smooth.

4. Plug the tub drain with the stopper and transfer the chilled pasta to the tub. Scatter the tomatoes, the sun-dried tomatoes, the olives, and the feta cheese evenly over the rotini and paddle the salad around the tub to evenly distribute the ingredients throughout. Pour three-quarters of the dressing evenly over the salad and continue to paddle until the dressing is evenly distributed. Season to taste with more dressing, salt, and pepper.

5. Transfer the pasta salad back to the Cambro containers and return to the refrigerator until time to transport to the venue, not more than 12 hours. The salad should be served at room temperature.

12

The Happy Couple Fancied Themselves Food Curators

Matt Examines the Role of Food in Weddings

Whoever said "Food is love" never worked for a caterer—and certainly never worked that quintessential catered event, the wedding. Two people joining together in holy matrimony of some kind is the oldest story in human history; gathering friends and family around a meal to celebrate this bond is just as natural: invite people you love. Serve foods you love. If you want to load the deck further, play music you love. And yet weddings are never this simple.

What makes it all so complicated?

The British journalist Rebecca Mead, who in 2008 published *One Perfect Day: The Selling of the American Wedding*, heaps a good deal of blame for the consumerist spectacle and attendant stresses of the American wedding upon the bridal industry. For Mead, wedding planners, dress designers, cake bakers, and caterers have tarted up newfangled, fabricated rituals in the drag of "tradition" in order to sell more bejeweled cake knives, scented bridal candles, and wedding-night lingerie ensembles. *This is what was done in the past*, the marketing goes; *now you must do this, too.* Although Mead's book is enormously entertaining—the scene of wedding planners at their annual convention taking swings at a "Bridezilla" piñata is priceless— it was pilloried by some critics for the bah humbug it rained on all the joyful silliness of "the big day."

Today, Mead's account of the excesses of the great white wedding seems downright quaint. She published her book two years before Pinterest and Instagram went live, enabling every- one with an iPhone and a WordPress account to be a reporter, a wedding planner, a bridal-lifestyle brand, an "influencer." In Mead's world, the thick, heavy magazines—*Modern Bride, Martha Stewart Weddings, Brides*—still held sway, with their copious advertisements, lavish fashion spreads, and hyperventilating editorial (SEVENTY-FIVE YEARS OF FABULOUS GOWNS, *Brides*, December 2008). But today's bridal tastemakers are constel- lated across the digital landscape in tens of thousands of blogs, social media accounts, and "verticals." Their fashion, decor, and food ideas are published the moment they click Send, then broadcast again once those ideas get adopted (or *adapted*) IRL (in real life). Then, if all goes well, they're viralized by wedding guests in Snapchats and tweets, Facebook Lives and Insta- gram Stories, around the world, ad infinitum. This system is likely to blame for the "flash-mob" processional, among other fun/cute wedding innovations.

Over the last ten years, the stream of bridal culture across the collective conscious grew into a social media Niagara Falls, and while that's taken some pressure off weddings to be "traditional," it seems to have been replaced by the pressure to be "original," with all the anxiety that entails. (As with "tradition" in 2008, "originality" in 2020 need not be factually demonstrable; the appearance of originality is what matters.) Today's couples are less after the "fairy-tale wedding" than the Tale That's Never Been Told, that's unique to them, the story of *us*, the one that catering salesman Collin Barnard is ever soliciting. As a bride recently told *Vogue*, "It was important that all of the events [at our wedding] felt authentic to each of us individually and to our relationship." That meant in addition to Giambattista Valli heels for her and patent-leather Yves Saint Laurent sneakers for him, the bride and groom commissioned Brooklyn-based artists Leimay to craft a work of performance art for their reception—a dance inspired by an episode of the bride and groom's favorite radio program and performed both on land, among the circulating guests, and in a synchronized pool routine, by three women wearing bespoke dresses and headgear composed of hundreds of toy butterflies. (And you may have thought a specialty cocktail on the bar was a gratuitous personal touch!)

I learned firsthand the way "authentic to us" plays out in the field of food ethics on the very first wedding I worked, at Locusts on Hudson. Despite the grim portents of the name, this riverside acreage just ninety miles north of New York City was one of the nation's most coveted farm-idyll wedding venues. (The guy who named the estate, just a decade after the signing of the United States Constitution, surely never imagined the place renting out for $4,000 a weekend in 1797 dollars—$60,000 in 2016 ones.) Patrick Phelan was still Sonnier & Castle's chef on that wedding, a Sunday before Labor Day. The temperature was in the high nineties with

237

100 percent humidity, and there was no trace of a breeze. Through the haze, the Hudson River was a thick brown soup.

It was exactly the kind of wedding Patrick loved. The happy couple fancied themselves food curators and had worked with him over months, making each course of their dinner a tribute to a trip they'd taken, a chef they'd met, or a particular food passion of theirs. For the cocktail-hour passed hors d'oeuvres, they'd chosen the cutting-edge bites from Patrick's playbook: sepia (cuttlefish) with compressed watermelon; sous-vide shrimp with squid-ink aioli; chicken liver with chocolate; a raw bar. We were nine kitchen assistants plus Juan and Jorge Soto, Patrick, and Tyler; the ceremony and reception were happening on the terrace of a manor house overlooking the river. The dinner would go down further into the woods, at a complex of Victorian barns—massive cathedrals in weathered wood, with ornamental quatrefoil windows. Stunning, and stifling, as the barns were entirely without air-conditioning. The box truck with the food got lost and arrived an hour late, so when it finally pulled in, we were rushed. I was assigned to hors d'oeuvres serve-out with Tyler and a few others, and after we'd unloaded our proofers, coolers, and dry packs into the tent by the river, Patrick and the rest struck out for the barns to set up dinner.

Tyler delegated to me what seemed to be the easiest hors d'oeuvre—Chicken Liver Mousse with Chocolate-Madeira Cookie. I'd seen this canapé, downright bizarre, on Patrick's Instagram feed: you took a gossamer-thin chocolate wafer the size of a Scrabble tile, dabbed a dot of chicken liver mousse at one edge, then stuck another chocolate tile over the liver, edge to edge, to form a tentlike thing that stood up on the platter. Twelve little pup tents to a platter, they looked like Donald Judd sculptures in miniature. When Tyler handed me the first sheet pan of chocolate cookies, I noticed there were nearly as many desiccant packets packed beneath the plastic wrap as cookies.

"Don't unwrap these yet," Tyler said. "With the humidity, we'll need that silica gel 'til the last possible moment."

The latte-colored chicken liver mousse in the cooler was hard as a rock, so I took the top off to temper it and pulled the sheet pan of chocolate wafers close, getting my station orderly for the first-platters call. As soon as the pâté had warmed, I tore a small hole in the plastic and tried making a sample. The first tile I picked up cracked immediately under the pressure of my fingers, so I tried again, more gently, but that one crunched, too. With the point of a sharp petty knife, I released the entire sheet of cookies from the parchment, piece by piece, without breakage. Ever so carefully, I swabbed a tiny dab of chicken liver gently against the edge. I laid another wafer gently on the chicken liver and tapped it. Voilà! My weird little chocolate-liver tent looked exactly like Patrick's photo and I set it carefully on my platter.

But when the call came in for first passes, I discovered that my sample had been a fluke. For every three I attempted, one broke, and the longer the cookies sat out in the heat, my failure rate increased. After the first half hour, I was down to one completed pup tent for every three or four tries.

The server picking up my hors d'oeuvres came back from the floor with her empty platter, and she'd wait patiently for five or fifteen minutes—however long it took—for me to get twelve pieces to send out to guests.

"Chocolate and chicken liver sounds so gross," she said, brightly. "But people seem to like it!"

Tyler passed by, saw me struggling, and all the wasted

cookies I was generating, and said, "Just do the best you can." So I muddled on, mashing shards and crumbs into liver. When the reception was over and we were packing everything away, I learned I wasn't the only one agonizing about wasted effort. I overheard servers from the oyster bars grousing that they hadn't had much interest, with the ice melting so fast, dribbling into the oysters. Who wants to eat a warm oyster in August?

We all were transported to the dinner kitchen and immediately folded into the plating of the smoked trout salad on the main floor of the barn. "Take a look at the sample and get moving," Patrick said. "We need to push these to the floor before they wilt." It was only the second of six courses.

At the end of the night, waiting for the van to come pick us up, I was still smarting from my disastrous hors d'oeuvres service. I told Patrick I didn't think it was my fault. "Why would you set us up to fail like that?"

"You think *I* put that one on the menu?" he said. "Fuck no, that's on Sales."

"Who eats oysters on a hundred-degree day?" I asked.

He blamed the sales team for that, too. "Look, I can talk to Sales 'til I'm blue in the face—seasonality, weather, all of it," he said. "But their job isn't to make our lives easier, it's to sell parties."

We were checking our phones when he told me the planner, a twenty-year veteran in the industry, had just texted him that the food was "best-ever." The bride and groom were over the moon. I wondered how any guest could process the story that the oxtail-and-lobster surf and turf was supposed to be telling in the heat of that barn. Why hadn't they spent the oyster-bar budget on air-conditioning?

"Just watch," Patrick said. "Stick with us, and you're going to look back and see. Tonight is just a blip on the map. Like, *ping!*" He flicked his finger. "Gone."

And yet I kept that memory throughout my time in catering, along with other nights that seemed to corroborate two lessons: a) the most stressful moments for workers in off-premise kitchens arose from bad decisions made months earlier, in places very far removed from the reality of the kitchen, and b) the larger the party budget, the more likely it was that unwise and risky decisions would be enabled.

Weddings add another layer of complication. A company throwing its holiday party or a charity hosting its annual gala is pure business—an event-as-marketing device or fund-raiser (sometimes both); two human beings joining 'til-death-do-us-part has mortal and spiritual stakes: families merge, fates are sealed, souls are laid bare (and God, presumably, is watching). The human-drama quotient is off the charts, and yet I'll bet you my best chef's knife that no one preparing the food knows so much as the bride's name. That profound disconnect—"hollowness," to use Danny Meyer's term—amid all the purple sentiment on the other side of the pipe and drape was almost unbearable.

So when the Soto brothers asked me to join their team on a wedding at the former Williamsburgh Savings Bank, I was tempted to decline. But there was something about a wedding in a bank—setup to a thousand father-of-the-bride punch lines—that piqued my interest beyond knowing about the lavish restoration. I'd seen the outside of the building's Beaux Arts dome countless times from the elevated M train, but I was itching to get inside; artist friends who'd deposited their meager earnings in the place back when it

241

was an HSBC branch in the nineties said it was Met Museum majestic.

On a chilly Saturday in November, I rolled up on my bicycle to the corner of Driggs Street and Broadway to find Juan and Tyler in puffy parkas, smoking and shuffling their feet to keep warm. The truck hadn't arrived with our proofers yet, and Tyler was eager to show us around. We walked through the service entrance into a long gallery with masonry barrel-vaults rippling across the ceiling. Servers were already building bars in the room, stacking rocks glasses on linen-set tables. Juan passed me the party grid—it was a cocktail reception and seated dinner for three hundred, with a migratory run of show: the wedding began with the ceremony on the second floor; guests would then descend to this gallery space for an hour-long reception, then head back upstairs once the second floor had been reset for dinner and dancing.

Through a small door off the gallery was a corridor that would be our hors d'oeuvres kitchen, and we shucked back-packs and coats against a pillar—one of two huge columns in the room that, along with stacks of rental crates and prep tables, made the space a labyrinth. It was already claustrophobic and none of the food had been loaded in yet.

"All the proofers'll fit in here?" I asked Tyler.

He laughed. "They better. You have no idea, there's so much food on this party."

I glanced at the grid again. Dinner was only two courses—a salad, then a short rib and sides—but the cocktail hour that preceded it featured two bar snacks, eight passed hors d'oeuvres, and a full Asian-themed buffet station with fifteen items: five kinds of sushi, sesame and udon noodles, three flavors of steamed dumplings, and an array of yakitori (Japanese-style grilled skewers). We'd need to cram at least a dozen separate stations into that room.

Tyler ushered Juan and me through the gallery and up a narrow staircase of filigreed ironwork, into a Gilded Age–meets–Hogwarts scene of marble, polished wood, and brass door fittings. Arriving in the main rotunda, we gazed up at the dome a hundred feet above. The wedding's designer had parried all the dizzying, baroque grandeur with a minimalist-rustic chuppah (the canopy where a traditional Jewish wedding ceremony is performed), a sculpture of intertwining birch branches hung with fresh white orchids, smack in the center of the hall. We stood there just taking it all in, until the production crew setting chairs for the ceremony hustled us along.

Adjacent to the main rotunda was another massive hall where long dinner tables were set with mirrored tops that reflected the round, stained-glass oculus some sixty feet above us—the apex of a domed ceiling only slightly less ornate than the first. Tyler led us past the original bank vault with its crazy-thick door propped open, past an iron birdcage elevator—the oldest in operation in New York City—and back down the stairs, ticking off the challenges we'd face over the next six hours. We'd have only a few minutes to transform the reception venue into the main-course plating line, then each plate would require its own steel cover to keep the food warm traveling up that narrow staircase. Teams of runners would hoist plates six at a time on trays to hand off to the waiters; as for salad plate-up, we'd need to juggle jack stands and double-decker the prep tables since the room allotted for first course had the square footage for only a hundred plates. In short, we'd need to have our sharpest wits about us.

But our most immediate challenge, one that became all too

apparent when the gallery became clogged with K.A.s and servers moving coolers and proofers into the corridor, was finding space to work. Tyler and Juan doled out assignments, and I was paired with Saori, on bar snacks and *grissini*, Italian breadsticks in three different flavors that were stuffed into highball glasses to accompany the main course. Everyone clambered around the room, reaching into proofers, coolers, and dry packs, spinning speed racks, trying as fast as they could to locate ingredients and claim stations. Saori found our bar bites—sticks of carrot, celery, and cucumber and green goddess dressing for a crudité, and tubs of Parmigiano-Reggiano crumbles for piling artfully on a wood plank alongside the veg and dip. I found our planks and the cylindrical glass bowls specified for the veg and the dip, but we'd been shorted a few pieces of each. We didn't have a table to work on, so we fashioned one from cutting boards placed atop stacks of glass-rental crates. The room had settled down, except for a forlorn kitchen assistant who couldn't find space to work and had collared a service captain, to inquire if he could move a very large cardboard box that was taking up room on a table.

The service captain was peeved. This wasn't his kitchen, after all. "What even is this?" he shouted.

"I'd look inside," he said. "But there's no seam on top." He knocked on the box and it made a hollow sound. He shouted out to the entire room, "Does *anyone* know what's in this box? Who put this here?"

One of the K.A.s waiting for the table to clear began banging on top of the box like a drum. Soon his buddy joined in, and they were drumming from the top and the sides now. I squinted to read what looked to be a logo discreetly rubber-stamped in the top corner of the box, but I could barely make it out from my station across the room. Then it hit me—it was a mark I'd seen on a delivery van on Metropolitan Avenue, outside Milk Bar, a popular bakery.

"STOP!" I shouted. "THAT'S THE FUCKING WEDDING CAKE!"

The two guys who'd been drumming on it went silent. The service captain rolled his eyes and stomped off to find Tyler, who, when he arrived, asked me to write "FRAGILE" in Sharpie on all sides. Once they stopped molesting the wedding cake (a six-tiered number that cost $6,000, I'd later learn), there it sat—unrefrigerated, in a space so liminal and chaotic it would have been safer resting on the sidewalk. In only a few hours it would be shuttled from this corner of the makeshift hors d'oeuvres kitchen to take its central role in the pageantry of the wedding.

The rest of the night spooled out pretty much as Tyler had warned—the compression of the venue came with risks. A jack stand of 110 burrata and roasted carrot salads nearly went down when one of its casters sank into a soft piece of floorboard. A server bit the dust on the stairs carrying a tray of main courses, but we replaced those six and recovered. When Tyler cut me and a couple of others loose for the night just before the wedding cake was served, I was grateful.

As I headed home, I wondered if the couple had hired an independent cake mover—yes, that job exists in New York, yet another line item on the budget (about $1,000 or more). Probably not, or it wouldn't have ended up as a musical instrument. I thought about my teammates, working to put out the best food they possibly could, but with minimal resources and knowledge. The cake incident seemed to prove that if you take away enough information from the workers, you're undoubtedly setting them up to fail. Who would stack the odds against the kitchen any more than they already were?

A couple of weeks passed and I went online to see what images of the team's handiwork I might find from that wedding. I discovered a slide show of almost two hundred photos, not only beyond the pipe and drape, but from hours before the event had even been set up. The bride's $1,200 studded Louboutin pumps, poised heel to toe, against a polished concrete floor. Now the bride in lingerie in the duplex loft of a Brooklyn hotel with the Manhattan skyline in the background, gazing up at her gown hanging in the window, the dress alongside the Empire State Building. Now she's trying on the gown, in front of the bridesmaids, fresh from the hotel's spa in their matching black robes. Now it's the groom's turn to get dressed, throwing a series of male-model pouts ("who me?") and set pieces for the photographer. I clicked forward wondering what, if any, food might be pictured. Surely an alluring cocktail? The gleaming architecture of the tuna tartare? My tricolor grissini spiking artfully out of their highball? In almost two hundred photos were just two, both of the wedding cake from Milk Bar Bakery. The food, the segment of this wedding that held perhaps the greatest creative potential, was also the most intimate, since everyone ingests it. Yet for all that centrality to the experience, the meal we prepared was apparently a throwaway element. Contributing to that may be the evanescent nature of food itself, quick to disappear and decompose down three hundred gullets; the Louboutins will live on, so inspire greater tribute. But was that okay? Was it okay to put so much premeditation, work, and care into a once in a lifetime banquet, only to see it disappear with little notice? Is it enough to make the food safe, in a literal sense, and little more? It didn't quite sit right with me, and yet my coworkers seemed copasetic. A blip on the radar, *ping!*, there are two more fiestas tomorrow!

As it happened, the most successful wedding I worked from a culinary perspective was a simple buffet of comfort food. I was nearing the end of my time in catering and wanted to go out on a high note, and this wedding held the promise of high-wattage celebrities.

I showed up at Sonnier to board the van on a Saturday in midsummer, and Tyler was in good spirits. He had some new ringers on the kitchen team, gave me the clipboard with the K.A. roster, and told me to make sure everyone got on the van. He was driving to the venue in a separate car, picking up Juan Soto and Jhovany León Salazar in the Bronx. Since he figured he'd arrive on-site after the kitchen van, he asked me to lead the troops, getting the kitchen boxed out, linens on tables, until he landed. I found my people and checked them off.

In an hour's time, our team met up with the service van in a parking lot in Greenwich, and we all boarded a larger shuttle that drove us through a leafy neighborhood with mighty mansions and manicured lawns. The bus dropped us off at a driveway with a sprawling neo-Gothic stone estate at the end surrounded by parklike grounds. Midway down the drive was a tented table manned by two giant security guards, remarkably friendly despite appearing to have settled quite a few bar brawls. We exchanged our cell phones for claim tags. A paparazzi helicopter did a lazy circle overhead.

The day was hot (welcome to wedding season!) with storm clouds brewing. A guard led us in groups along a brick path to a broad expanse of lawn where an enormous white party tent had been erected and, beyond it, the service tent for both kitchen and sanitation. I did my best to rally the team, even though there were quite a few new faces, and we conferred over the grid and the kitchen plan. An hors d'oeuvres kitchen on the far side of the estate wouldn't be staffed and stocked until the box truck arrived. A refrigerator rented to chill the wedding cake had already been delivered, so I matched it up on the kitchen plan and dispatched some K.A.s to set tables in place to receive the cake. I couldn't locate the table linens, so I collared the service captain in charge. He was out on the floor, amid a swirl of fabric (not mine), and he suggested my linens may have ended up on the far side of the property, in the cocktail kitchen.

I took off across the lawn just as the rain began. The house was to my right on the top of a slight rise. I was halfway past the house, couldn't yet see where the cocktail kitchen was—and I began to realize that the ground beneath my feet was supersaturated from the previous day's rain. I noticed my clogs were getting wet just as I heard behind me someone shout: "HEY! CHEF!"

I froze. A female security guard in a black suit was sprinting as best she could across the pudding-soft lawn from the dinner tent toward me, with a walkie-talkie in her hand. "STOP!"

I instinctively looked up toward the house, and silhouetted in a French door set into the side of the house facing the lawn was an impossibly tall figure in a gown, likely the doyenne of this family of stars.

"She does not want *anyone* stepping on this wet lawn!" the security guard said. "Do you understand?"

I apologized profusely, asked her how to get to the cocktail-reception kitchen. She pointed out the right way to go, back by the driveway near the phone check. "You're already on the lawn," she said. "It's too late. You might as well cross now. But *don't* do it again!"

By the time I got to the reception kitchen, my clogs were soaked, my pride shot. But I found those damn linens, bundled some over crossed arms, recruited a sanit guy to carry the rest. On the way back to the kitchen tent—the correct way—I looked across the green and saw, in the distance, three or four of my kitchen team, whom I'd commanded to stay put, ambling across the wet grass in front of the house, looking like they were out for a Sunday stroll. In seconds, the security guard materialized, chasing after them, shouting—full meltdown. I couldn't bear to look, and felt grateful my name wasn't higher on the leaderboard for this event.

The linens were in place and taut by the time Tyler arrived, and he seemed pleased, but I had to inform him of the lawn faux pas—last thing I wanted was for him to hear it from the party planner. He laughed it off—he had bigger problems on his mind. Rain was coming down in buckets now, just as we were unloading the truck, and Juan and I spotted a waterfall pouring down from the tent flaps onto the electrical transformer for the kitchen tent. I reached for a sheet pan to fashion a shield for the box. Juan said, "No!" and handed me a plastic bus pan that fit perfectly over it. "Don't take any chances," he said. "That's metal." I was grateful those guys were on-site now—what *other* instincts of mine were going to trip me up that day?

As it turned out, none. Despite the scolding, that event was one of the happiest ones I worked. The thunderstorm passed just after the ceremony, and the sun shone through, bright and hot. Leave it to the truly famous to order up perfect party food—three buffet stations of pure comfort, foods people love: fried chicken and mac and cheese, Bolognese and wild-mushroom ravioli with Parmesan cream, a roast beef carving station. And by now I knew: you can tell a great celebration because the servers become like mirrors, reflecting the energy of the room. When they return to the kitchen with empty platters, sashaying to the music, and saying, "They're *demolishing* this mac and cheese!" you know guests are having fun, and you feel compelled to work faster to keep pace with the energy and consumption level. As the hours advanced, things loosened up. There was plenty of dancing, and celebrities started chatting with servers.

I was on a mixed bus back to the city—service and kitchen. Most of the K.A.s crashed out, sleeping, but the waiters and waitresses were ebullient from their proximity to stardom. One waiter—a struggling actor—who'd been delivering drinks to the groomsmen before the ceremony, called his mother on speakerphone to run down the names of everyone he'd met. She went nuts. He'd endured a scolding, too, from the matriarch—for over-serving the guys. As the van tacked off Interstate 95 and swayed down the Henry Hudson Parkway, I tipped my head back and thought through the dozen or so weddings and engagement parties I'd worked in the last two years, and about the food at Ted's wedding (barbecue, catered by Blue Smoke, served family style; ten years on, everyone still remembers the ribs). What had I learned? By the time the van pulled up in front of Sonnier & Castle, I'd come up with a few Food Rules for Successful Weddings, which I shared with Ted when I got home (my own wedding was family-only, a table for twelve at the late, much missed New York restaurant Chanterelle). We polished them up and offer them here.

- Serve what you like to eat. If you're the bride or the groom, and you're requesting a special meal, maybe everyone should be eating the special meal. (If it's a chicken cutlet, make sure it's *damn* good. Remember the rubber chicken joke.)

- The more items you put on your buffet, and the more courses there are in a seated dinner, the less likely anyone will remember any of it the following morning. $1 + 1 + 1 + 1 = 2$ when it comes to wedding banquets.

- Let deliciousness be the most memorable thing about the food. The more you force what you serve to tell a complicated story about you (anything more than the fact that you chose it, which is implicit), the more likely your guests will put down the fork and disengage from the tale.

- When selecting the food for your wedding, think first about seasonality in the context of the venue you've chosen. Is there any likelihood of it being infernally hot and humid? Or, alternately, frigid? Make certain the food you choose envisions the most extreme conditions for the time and place.

- Either the bride or the groom should take a quick moment if at all possible to step behind the pipe and drape, to offer a smile and a thumbs-up to the kitchen staff. Connecting on some level with the people making your wedding happen will make it memorable for everyone.

251

- Number of weddings in the U.S. in 2017: 2,180,000

- Average cost of a wedding in the U.S. in 2017: $33,391

- Average cost of a wedding in the most expensive place to get married in the U.S., Manhattan, in 2017: $76,944

- Average cost of a wedding in the U.S. in 1979: $2,200 (7,845.65 in 2017 dollars)

- Number of weddings annually at Weylin, a venue in Brooklyn: 24

- Percentage of those that happen on a Saturday: 95%

- Percentage that happen on Fridays: 2%. On Sundays: 2%

- Most popular months for weddings at Weylin: October and November (tie)

- Average guest count for weddings at Weylin: 200

- Percentage of weddings at Weylin cooked on hotboxes/proofers: 60%

- Percentage of weddings at Weylin that use preferred caterer Abigail Kirsch: 75%

- Average number of vegan weddings annually at Weylin: 1

- Number of wedding cakes that have fallen on the floor at Weylin since the venue opened its doors in 2013: 1

- Party features prohibited at Weylin: fire, confetti, and helium-filled balloons

- Strangest item to show up in Weylin's lost-and-found after a wedding: an adult male's tooth

Sources: TheWeddingReport.com; TheKnot.com; *Wall Street Journal*; Weylin, Brooklyn, NY

NUPTIALS BY THE NUMBERS

13

Piercing the Veil

The Lee Brothers Work Their Final Fiesta

Absurdities and grotesque entitlements become routine when you immerse yourself in high-end catering. There is a young, ambitious caterer in New York whose food-obsessed, billionaire client regularly charters a Gulfstream G-Five jet to smuggle into the United States a half-dozen *poulet de Bresse* chickens from Rungis Market in Paris. The cost? Roughly $200,000, inclusive of French ground support. There's an event planner with clients who demand custom, artisan-made plates and bowls for their dinners, used for one night only, because rentals simply won't do—they're too common. As Bronwyn Keenan, events director at the Metropolitan Museum, who presides over hundreds of events annually, said, "We're way, way beyond the Gilded Age. Budgets for parties are multiple times what I paid for my own house. Every week I'm building a house over forty-eight hours, and then tearing it down in twelve."

Spend time in this world, and it's easy to lose sight of the fact that at the root of the $12 billion catering industry is a universal impulse: the same emotional spark that drives the backyard cookout with your neighbors, or your niece's sweet sixteen at the church parish hall, or your grandparents' sixtieth anniversary in the assisted-living community—*let's celebrate!* In the latter part of the twentieth century, when events became fully transportable, loosed from the fixed landmarks of the parish hall, the club and hotel banquet room, hosts were free to seek out new environments, built or natural, to gather their friends and family and live it up. And the impact that liberation had in the marketplace was to encourage people with money to create new reasons to party as well: how might this party perform for my company? Or for my arts institution? Or for my charity?

A group of people coming together over a meal soon became a marketing tool for corporations and nonprofits. And in boom cycles especially, what passes for a celebration in the culture became increasingly spectacular, year upon year, with the quest for novelty and one-upmanship perpetually driving new ideas and dimensions in events. While it's true that economic catastrophes of the past thirty years—like Black Monday in 1987, or 9/11, or the crash of 2008—served to slow the growth in catering for short spells, the hyper-customization in catering we encounter today may have actually planted deepest roots during those worst of times. Since it was only ultrarich families and businesses who still had discretionary money to entertain, event caterers desperate to keep revenues flowing were compelled to say yes to every outlandish whim. When the bar is lowered in a downturn, it can be difficult to raise it again once the economy comes roaring back.

But it's clear to us now that the more features and menu line items you add to a party, the more vendors you bring to bear upon it, the easier it is for everyone involved to detach and lose sight of that elemental desire for human connection that spawned all that labor. Keenan said that when she first came to the Met in 2012, from a similar position at the Guggenheim Museum, she had to fight the notion within the institution that an event was "a bunch of boxes that had to be checked. What is an event? It's a party, it's supposed to be *fun*," she said. "Every museum I've worked in, it's: how can we just get back to the fun, and stop taking ourselves so seriously."

Our *Hotbox* journey began by being amazed at the specialized skills of food mercenaries who run the kitchens that feed the most ambitious American celebrations. We were curious to learn the particulars of their specialized food crafting in food-inappropriate spaces, but also why their labor seemed unjustly underappreciated, mostly invisible to the outside world. And the more we learned, the more questions we had. At first it seemed the dissociation between prep kitchen and event kitchen, and between the event kitchen and the "floor," was at cross-purposes to the very goals of a party. It was inconceivable that an executive chef might not know the host's name! In any kitchen, there's typically a "lineup" before service when the chef tells servers what's on the menu; why not institute a lineup with party planner and host, introducing themselves to the kitchen and sharing their ideals for the fiesta? Wouldn't it at least make a modicum of sense to play the same two-minute mission video they're playing for the moneybags in the room that night for the catering crew? So that there's some context for that beet-tartare canape that's going to stain my fingers red for the next three days?

What we were surprised to discover was a culture that in some ways craved its own invisibility, the ease of gliding from one night to the next, one emergency yielding to the next catastrophe with total concentration, unflappability, and detachment. Not caring *too much* is a defensive mechanism that can prolong your career in the industry, increasing the odds of survival. The Hotbox Nation is populated by people who instinctively, in Danny Meyer's words, "climb that higher mountain, jump out of the airplane." But there's a rootless, restless element to the psychology of the catering mind that becomes apparent only once you've spent time inhabiting it. According to Meyer, "nomadism is in their wiring, and they don't seem to crave the family-unit a restaurant foundation affords." Which feels true generally—and certainly when you understand the common itinerant-theatrical and military threads connecting the Patrick Phelans, Sean Driscolls, Donald Bruce Whites, and Jean-Claude Nédélecs—but falls apart on the example of the Soto brothers, Juan and Jorge, who have studiously crafted a measure of success and a semblance of family within all the shape-shifting meals on wheels, night after night. In fact the Mexican and Central American diaspora, which has indelibly marked modern catering's language and resourcefulness, seems largely responsible for preserving what humanity remains in the business.

One of the last catering jobs we worked was an annual Labor Day party in the Hamptons, an event we'd signed up for the previous two years running. By the numbers—225 people—this was hands-down the highest-dollar-per-person production of any event we ever touched (the first-year guest count had been 160, and everyone called it a "cookout"; in year two they dispensed with that euphemism). The site was the private home of a cable television CEO perched above the golden-white sand of East Hampton Beach. For days in advance, various crews worked to prepare the property, covering the swimming pool with flooring, erecting the kitchen tent on the far side of the driveway, building a stage and overhead lighting truss for the band (no local acts here; think Rod Stewart or Diana Ross), trailering in air-conditioned "comfort stations," and trellising them with a small forest's worth of live Virginia alder so they blended with the hedgerow along the property line.

The lane that dead-ended at the party location was bucolic and residential, so a parking lot had been secured four miles away for the various vendors' trucks and trailers, and a transport firm shuttled the personnel back to the site: the landscapers, the A/V producers, the security team, the tent crew, the caterers, and the sand sculptors. A life-size shark-attack tableau down below the bluff, on the beach, in the lee of the dunes, took the sculpting team several days to complete and served as focal point for the kids' dining area (which had its own small kitchen, on the sand behind a bamboo windbreak). After the musical star's last number, a fireworks show by the Gruccis would light up the sky with strobes and willows, comets and chrysanthemums, detonated from a launchpad a couple of miles downfield, so nobody on the terrace had to crane their necks to see. Like the Macy's Fourth of July show, but just for you.

The first year of that party, we had been so green and clue-less, we spent the entire time trying to stay out of the way of the other kitchen assistants, whose movements seemed so intu-itive and lightning-quick. Patrick sensed our disorientation and managed to assign tasks a safe distance from the kitchen tent. Ted grilled three hundred hot dogs on the host's gas grill up on the terrace and, from that vantage point, served Martha Stewart (who didn't recognize him out of context) and witnessed some big-picture triumphs firsthand, like Patrick convincing the party planner that running an electric fryer in the sand dunes (so the children's french fries wouldn't lose their crisp-ness traveling from the kitchen tent to the beach kitchen) was a recipe for disaster.

We were eager to witness what had changed year after year at that party—if it might say something about where the cater-ing business was headed. But we also wanted to see how far we'd come in our own understanding of what mattered and what happened in the field. The first year, the sheer quantity of food being shoveled out was astonishing—once dessert had been served to the guests and we were closing down the kitchen, we were able to feed all the vendors that night from the leftovers, almost a hundred more people: the entire cater-ing team, the security guards, the valets, the babysitting crew, the A/V folks, and the members of the band's entourage. The second year the menu had virtually doubled, even though the guest count had risen by only fifty. Where there'd been one buf-fet station in year one, now there were three, each with a dif-ferent themed menu. And outside vendors had been brought in around the periphery of Sonnier & Castle's bill of fare. There was a Del's frozen-lemonade cart for the kids. A food truck had driven out from Manhattan and parked at the valet station, giving away enormous Belgian waffles heaped with fruit, chocolate, and whipped cream in paper boats to take away—just in case the banana split buffet with six flavors of ice cream and sixteen toppings, the four pies on the pie bar, the s'mores station, the cake in the shape of a shark baked by television's "Cake Boss" Buddy Valastro, the brown-sugar-glazed pineapple kebabs, the sliced watermelon, and the fresh-fruit skewers had been insufficient or unappealing.

This Labor Day—our third time doing this party—the ride out on the Long Island Expressway was slow going, traffic rubber-banding from the Queens border all the way out to the East End. And once we exited the highway, the coastal route 27A was backed up to a standstill. Juan Soto knew this geography well and gamed the traffic, tacking the van north of the two-lane blacktop, shuttling past cornfields and vineyards, and then crossing south of it. The streets became leafier, the hedges higher, and the houses larger the closer we got to our destination. We turned onto Lily Pond Lane, the road Bob Dylan recalls going "when the weather was warm" in his 1975 confessional "Sara," and Juan halted the van at the security checkpoint at the top of the dead-end street. A beefy older guy in a black polo and wraparound Oakleys was interrogating the driver of a golf cart in front of us. Between a break in the hedge outside my window, there was a rambling, Grey Gardens–esque home with barnlike gambrel roofs and gothic windows. Mature, overgrown rosebushes climbed up its cedar-shake walls, weather-beaten to the lustrous silver-gray of moth's wings. It seemed entirely possible that the Bard himself, in a rumpled blazer, bolo tie, and guitar slung over his shoulder, might walk through the hedge any second.

The security guard waved the golf cart down the street, and

Juan pulled the van forward to the invisible line where he stood. He stepped to the window and Juan uttered a single word, "Cater." The man lowered his shades on their tether, took a cursory look inside the van, chef coats hung over the windows shading the dozers, and waved us on through. A service captain waited at the end of the lane to escort us to the kitchen tent, and we gathered our belongings and piled out.

The box truck with the food had already backed up to the kitchen tent, and everyone crunched across the gravel driveway toward it, slowing to ogle the spanking-new red Ferrari, low-slung and wide-bodied, and, parked next to it, a showroom-condition sixties vintage Porsche convertible, also red. The team whistled and gawked at the vehicles before the service captain reined it in with a curt, "Hustle, people." On the opposite side of the kitchen tent, for ours and the other vendors' use, were two weathered porta potties, familiar from previous years. We had hoped staff facilities might be improved upon with each passing year, with each doubling of the menu options, but apparently not.

Once we loaded in the proofers, coolers, and dry packs, Tyler gathered everyone in for assignments, and we got a look at the party grid in his folder. It was a full three pages long, forty menu items per page. Guest count had increased by only ten over year two, but the quantity and variety of food seemed to double again. There were four bar snacks and thirteen passed hors d'oeuvres, five buffet stations, all with a boilerplate New Orleans twist. A raw bar set up in an ice-filled rowboat offered East and West Coast oysters (none from the Gulf), clams, jumbo shrimp, crab claws, and five seviches: scallop, red snapper, shrimp, tuna, and hamachi. The slider station had three BBQ options and a vegetarian lentil burger. There was a jambalaya station and a manned po' boy action station, stuffing sandwiches to order with shrimp, chicken, or blackened grouper. Finally, there was a "main" buffet with cedar-planked salmon, barbecued chicken, meat loaf, tofu steaks, and six vegetable side dishes. The s'mores station was back for dessert, but new this year were a cake, pie à la mode, and cobbler bar with five varieties of pies, four-layer cakes, and ice creams shipped in from the Cincinnati scoop shop Graeter's. Also: passed desserts, five kinds of ice-cream sandwiches along with Big Easy–style pralines, served with shots of Baileys Irish Cream. *Burp.*

There were more lead chefs in the kitchen tent this year, and Tyler assigned us to work seviches with one of them, Christian, who'd recently become one of Tyler's main deputies. He was a sullen guy, who seemed to relish the opportunity to reprimand or school K.A.s, with attendant eye rolling and head shaking. It didn't matter so much, as we were feeling comfortable compared to the two prior years, when we had mostly doused fires. Find the missing skewers! Wash these enamel pails! At those events, it was difficult to tune out whatever was happening in the peripheral vision, so the work seemed doubly chaotic. Even though there was so much more food this year than last, more K.A.s and traffic in the tent, the structure and the flow of it all made a kind of sense now.

We were tasked with marinating the various seafood items in lime juice to "cook" them. The event planner had made a last-minute decision to have the server at the station spoon the seviches to order from large bowls into shot glasses, rather than having us preportion the shot glasses in the kitchen tent, which made things easier. We had all our seviches mixed and in their bowls by go-time, so Ted helped Jorge Soto's hors d'oeuvres team, wiping clean the platters when they came back and passing them to their stations to refill, while Matt organized the backup seviches, making sure we had enough to replenish on the fly.

The party was in full swing and the buffets had been open an hour or more when Tyler transferred us off seviches and up to the terrace, to the po' boy station. The stage backed up against the house, and Harry Connick Jr. had just begun performing his first set on the piano as we threaded our way through the crowd and into position. Among the faces watching the show were Martha again, Oprah and Gayle, Dr. Oz., and we recalled Patrick's admonishment the first time working this party, about the style of service Sonnier called "Always Correct": a K.A. or server on the floor only ever acknowledged a guest with a nod and smile, and never spoke unless spoken to.

The po' boy station was farthest across the terrace from the stage, next to the platform where a team of guys in headsets controlled the sound and light boards. Our area had a little stage of its own, a level surface at the rim of the bluff overlooking the driveway. The topography of the bluff meant the fryers were set up at the edge of the floor, not far from the feet of the guy serving out the food. Our fryer chef stood in the grass and smiled with relief when we arrived. He passed mixing bowls, quarts of buttermilk, and deli containers of a breading mix, and we knew what to do. There was really nowhere to set up, but the sound guy moved a couple of crates from the end of his platform, at the perfect height for us to fashion a dredging station. We dunked the shrimp, chicken, and grouper into the buttermilk in series, taking care not to cross-pollinate the fishy buttermilk with the meaty buttermilk, then tossed them in bowls of breading mix. The dripping, battered protein chunks we handed off in fits and starts to the fry guy, and we soon hit a rhythm. The demand was strong, and after an hour or so, our buddy passed a deli of fried shrimp to offer to the dude on the sound stage who'd provided us with the clutch space.

Before long, we'd caught up to the line at our station and were able to relax somewhat, to appreciate simply being outdoors on a beautiful night and working with a team. It seemed a reflection of how far we'd come that we could almost wordlessly migrate into a station, barter for resources, improvise, swim with the stream. When demand for po' boys slowed further and we had plenty of backup protein, Tyler transferred us again, off the terrace and down to the driveway. The Ferrari and the Porsche had disappeared, but a bright red stagecoach wagon branded CAFÉ DU MONDE, the legendary New Orleans coffee shop, had been set up precisely where the waffle truck had been parked the prior year. Tyler explained: guests would receive bags of hot, freshly fried beignets and chicory coffee on their way out. Two waiters would proffer and serve up the coffee and beignets, but he wanted us frying just a few yards behind the wagon.

We organized our station with mountains of chilled dough that had been shipped in from New Orleans and with aluminum pans of cinnamon sugar and powdered sugar to toss the doughnuts in once they came out of the fryer. The last glimmers of light were disappearing to the west, and just as Harry Connick Jr. finished his encore the fireworks show lit up the sky. A party planner emerged on the scene with Café du Monde–branded aprons and giant T-shirts we awkwardly pulled on over our chefs' coats. Paper hats, too. We must have looked ridiculous. And by the time the oil was bubbling and our first batch of beignets went out to the stagecoach, people started to leave the party.

We were incredulous that any of these guests had room for a doughnut at this point, but the beignets were popular. And most of these people were savvy enough to spurn the ones the servers had sandbagged on the station for the rush; they wanted piping-hot beignets, fresh from the fryer. So there was plenty of attention on our frying area, and scrutiny eventually on us. And we enjoyed it. Ted took over the fryer while Matt tonged the beignets into their waxed paper envelopes and dusted them with powdered sugar.

In the backup of people waiting for the hot ones were Alec and Hilaria Baldwin, Ron Howard, Chuck Schumer, and Nancy Pelosi. And then House minority leader Pelosi jumped the line and started toward us.

"Hello, there!" she said, and Matt smiled, a bit confused. "*Yoo-hoo!*" she said. Ted looked around, caught the eye of the party planner in the shadows.

Then it hit us. She thought we were members of the Fernandez family, owners of the legendary café, flown in from New Orleans to serve her a beignet—a notion entirely consistent with the concept of this party.

"I was *just* in New Orleans!" she said. "For the Katrina tenth anniversary!"

We knew the "Always Correct" service rules. Matt had been spoken to, so had license to reply. But what could he say? *I'm sorry, you're mistaken—I'm not from New Orleans, I'm just the kitchen assistant manning the fryer in a Café du Monde T-shirt I put on a half hour ago?*

Matt just smiled and nodded. "Beignets, Congresswoman

Pelosi? Fresh from the fryer?" And then, as if matters couldn't get more awkward, a man a few paces behind us shrieked, "Oh. My. GOD!"

She braced herself for an introduction with a broad smile, and for a second we were relieved she'd been collared by a fan—we could get back to frying, flipping, tonging, and sugar dusting. This was the excruciating life these people live: forever in the spotlight, surrounded by total strangers who claim a kind of intimacy in private moments.

Then the same voice said: "What the *fuck* are the Lee brothers doing here?"

Our cover was blown. It was a friend from grade school we hadn't seen in at least a decade. There was the House minority leader, with a look of bemusement, maybe a tinge of disappointment. There was the party planner, thoroughly confused, bordering on annoyed. And there was Peter Robbins.

"Want some beignets?" Matt asked him, loath to break character. A bear hug was out of the question. "What are *you* doing here?"

"We're the scrappy neighbors they're obliged to invite," he said, sotto voce, waving over his wife, Page. "Our house is the falling-down one at the end of the street. Where the security checkpoint is? We're right there."

We'd embedded in catering to study how the food gets made and who makes it. And we'd come to a deeper appreciation of how the business works, and of the people who labor in its ranks, from the pot scrubbers to the ace proofers and executive chefs. We'd learned how these insane contemporary food productions came to be, how they function in today's culture, and the ways in which the invisibility of these kitchens can, paradoxically, grant the people who work them the authority and confidence they need at a challenging fiesta. We remembered the days nearly three years ago that we'd first put on our beanies, chef's coats, black pants. Giving ourselves up so completely to the starchy, plain K.A. uniform was empowering on a number of levels, but mostly because it rendered us invisible to most of society. Now a guest—Peter—was addressing us for our selves rather than as the K.A.s at the fryer. He'd pierced the veil. We felt bared in that awkward moment but also strangely liberated. The more seconds that ticked past with our small talk, the more it held up our process, and we itched to get back to catering. We had guests awaiting hot beignets, people who needed our services. And we were eager for this gig to be over, so we could begin telling the story.

It was nearing midnight by the time Juan Soto circled back from the off-site parking lot with the van. The coastal route was empty, and we made good time getting back to the highway. The van was silent for a while and when we looped around the on ramp to the expressway, Jorge called over from the passenger seat, "*Policía*, Juan."

"*Si, si*," Juan said, and let off the gas a bit.

Juan cranked the A/C high to keep himself awake, so the K.A.s wore their chef coats like blankets and stuffed the vents overhead with dishrags. In time, we passed a similar white passenger van, whose driver turned on its interior light as an acknowledgment and greeting: *are you our crew?* We saw the bright white shirts of a catering team inside the other van and Juan turned on our van's interior lights, causing a few protests from K.A.s in the back who had nodded off.

"Not our guys," Juan said. And then both vans' interiors went dark again.

In a few minutes, the same semaphore exchange with a different white van happened. And then again, another. All along the expressway, the people who don't speak unless spoken to, and who cook, and serve, and make the ugly stuff disappear after the meal, were headed back to their catering kitchens, and, after that, to their homes, for a few hours of rest before the next fiesta.

Acknowledgments

We offer our deepest thanks to those who set this book in motion and propelled us forward, including Peter Milewicz, the first caterer we ever met, whose cheese *croustades* are still our favorite canapé; Amanda Hesser, who hired us to report the column The Industry for the *New York Times Magazine*; Patrick Phelan, Jorge Soto, and Juan Soto, who graciously welcomed us into their lives and who framed our entire experience in catering. And to Biz Mitchell, Vance Muse, Jaime Wolf, Andy McNicol, our agent, and Gillian Blake, our editor, who encouraged our detour from cookbooks to write about the traveling food world. Their insights and patient guidance were invaluable.

We are eternally grateful to the professionals who labored alongside us in the prep kitchen and at fiestas, generously sharing expertise while enduring our slow pace and unsure hands, including Michael Alge, Lucy Astudillo, Matt Bishop, Marilu

Cantor, Manuel Cruz, Isabelle Donovan, Matt Greene, Brian "Patches" Holbach, Danita Holt, Steve Jackson, Saori Kurioka, Bethany Morey, Pam Naraine, Ryan Ostrander, Roxana Paredes, Wilmer Rodriguez, Ian Rynecki, Jhovany León Salazar, Christian Sibucao, Casey Wilson, Gustavo Zepeda, and many others.

Our heartfelt gratitude goes to the catering-industry veterans whose stories and knowledge put our field experiences into context, including Collin Barnard, Ronnie Davis, Sean Driscoll (R.I.P.), Megan Fitzroy-Phelan, Bobby Flay, Sara Foster, Robb Garceau, T. J. Girard, Meg Gleason, John Harenda, Susan Holland, Tyler Johnson, John Karangis, Bronwyn Keenan, Anita Lo, Mark Maynard-Parisi, Jim McManus, Danny Meyer, David Monn, Jean-Claude Nédélec, Paul Neuman, Liz Neumark, Yann Nury, Eric Ripert, Gina Rogak, Bob Spiegel, Mimi Van Wyck, and Steve Wenger.

Endless thanks also to Elliott Holt, Sarah Gray Miller, Ryan Smernoff, and Caroline Wray, whose readings helped keep us on track and strengthened the manuscript. We thank Lauren Nassef for her chapter illustrations of the world behind the pipe and drape, and Pat Eisemann, Carolyn O'Keefe, and all the staff at Henry Holt who have helped nudge this book into being.

Last, but not least, we acknowledge our stalwart cheering section, Liza and Will Lee, Caroline Lee and Mike Nees, and the home team, E. V. Day, Gia Papini Lee, and the littler Lee brothers, Arthur, Lorenzo, and George, who endured our many absences over the years.

About the Authors

MATT LEE and TED LEE are the authors of several bestselling cookbooks: *The Lee Bros. Southern Cookbook, The Lee Bros. Simple Fresh Southern*, and *The Lee Bros. Charleston Kitchen*. They have written for the *New York Times, Food & Wine, Travel + Leisure*, the *New York Times Magazine*, and *Saveur* and have appeared on many TV shows, including Anthony Bourdain's *No Reservations* and the Cooking Channel's *Unique Eats*. Their cookbooks have won two James Beard and four IACP awards.